REAL

LANCASHIRE

Frontispiece: a map of the historic county of Lancashire by Robert Morden, early eighteenth century. Before 1974 Lancashire was a far grander affair, stretching from Wrynose Pass in the north to Warrington in the south, and from the sands of Formby to the moors of Littleborough.

REAL LANCASHIRE

A journey through the history of the old county

by Phil Smith

Of related interest:

Dr Alan Crosby, *Lancashire: A history* (forthcoming, 2009);

Dr Derek Beattie, *Blackburn: A history*

Dr David Hunt, *A History of Preston* (forthcoming, 2009);

Peter Aughton: *Liverpool: A people's history*;

Professor Alan Kidd, *Manchester: A history*;

Stephen Bull, *The Civil Wars in Lancashire, 1640–60* (forthcoming, 2009);

Malcolm Greenhalgh, *The River Ribble: A local and natural history*;

Peter Shakeshaft; *St Anne's on the Sea: A history*;

Professor Michael Bush, *The Casualties of Peterloo*;

Mike Williams with D.A. Farnie, *Cotton Mills of Greater Manchester*;

Professor John K. Walton, *Blackpool*;

David Brazendale, *Lancashire's Historic Halls*;

Geoffrey Mather, *Tacklers' Tales: a humorous look at Lancashire*;

J. Lumby, *The Lancashire Witch Craze: Jennet Preston and the Lancashire Witches, 1612*;

Thomas Potts, *The Wonderfull Discoverie of Witches in the Countie of Lancaster*;

Johnnie Woods, *Growin' Up: One Scouser's social history*;

Mike Clarke, *The Leeds and Liverpool Canal: A history and guide*.

Full up-to-date details and secure online ordering at
www.carnegiepublishing.com

The Real Lancashire: A journey through the history of the old county

Copyright © Phil Smith, 2008

First edition

Published by Palatine Books,
an imprint of Carnegie Publishing Ltd
Carnegie House,
Chatsworth Road,
Lancaster, LA1 4SL
www.carnegiepublishing.com

ISBN 978-1-874181-26-2

Typeset by Carnegie Book Production
Printed and bound in the UK by Alden Press, Oxford

CONTENTS

To Maggie, my wife and fellow explorer

The drawings at chapter openings are by Lucy Day and Ivan Frontani.

INTRODUCTION

DOES IT MATTER WHERE WE LIVE? Today, with the nearest supermarket often within an easy car drive, with more and more people having access to the internet, with television and radio beaming the world in to our living rooms, everything we seem to need comes to us irrespective of where we are. Life is in danger of turning into one of those futuristic films where the cities and landscape in which people live are a dystopian nightmare of crumbling buildings and barren wastelands, yet people go on happily existing within a domestic cocoon of scientific wonders and electronic marvels. From Hemel Hempstead to Cumbernauld, as the same massive chain stores and monopolistic financial institutions dominate our lives, our towns and regions are blighted by the same box-like houses and windy parking lots which pass for what architects call modern retail parks. What we eat and wear, our leisure activities and favourite holiday destinations, have all become standardised. Even what we think and feel is pretty much the same thanks to the influence of the mass media. We may raise our hands in horror at the prospect of human cloning, but modern life is doing its best to reduce us all to human clones. Real individualism is as rare as fish with feathers. So I repeat the question. Does it matter where we live?

When I step out of my house in the Cliviger Valley near Burnley and climb up the nearest hillside I can look out across the valley and witness the tidemark of time and the imprint of the men and women who have lived here down the ages. The escarpments have been sculpted by the ice of glaciers, leaving raw buttresses of rock that still manage to look prehistoric. But lower down, etched into relief by the shadows of the winter sun are earthworks where in the past men have grubbed coal, iron, even lead from the hillside. Plough-lines show up where crops have been planted and fields harvested. All these activities seem a world away from today where the valley hums with

Sculpted escarpments.
PHOTOGRAPH: AUTHOR

the roar of articulated lorries speeding towards the motorway network and the sky is laced with vapour trails from jets taking people abroad on package holidays. And if I look towards the town I can see a handful of black mill chimneys pointing skywards, the mills they once served, their stain of soot sandblasted away, now housing furniture warehouses or keep-fit gyms. There's a handsome railway viaduct that was once busy with goods and passenger trains, carrying wakes weeks holidaymakers in their thousands to Blackpool or bringing daily fish from Fleetwood. Now you'll be lucky if you see a rickety railcar rattling along a single weed-strewn track to a station made of bus shelters. The very configuration of the housing speaks of a different age and different priorities: regimented terraces built for the cheap convenience of mill-owners who wanted a workforce close at hand to weave their wealth, while they themselves lived in a fine mansion up on the hillside well above the smog line. Churches and chapels with splendid neo-classical frontages can suddenly surprise amongst rows of dingy terraces, lasting monuments to a fine spirit of non-conformist thinking and a poignant belief that, whatever the miseries of this world, the bliss of an afterlife was assured by a lifetime of honest decency and toil. Everywhere, despite the efforts of our planners to knock it all down and bury it away like a dirty secret, is evidence of a distinctive past that made us different, that made Lancashire unique.

I was born and brought up further down the Calder Valley and both my father and mother spent years of their working lives in the mills. In fact, in my childhood it was difficult to find people I knew who were *not* touched by the mills: awakened every morning to the clatter of clogs on cobbles, deafened by the roar of the looms when the weaving shed doors were thrown open to let in a bit of welcome fresh air and sunlight, delighted by the surrounding countryside as an escape from the narrow, smoky little valleys, embraced by the warm sense of community and revived by the dark and anarchic sense of humour that was an insurance against us all being ground down by the mills. Historically speaking we were all united by the fact that we were mostly relative newcomers to Lancashire. My great-grandparents came from Westmorland and Norfolk, driven by rural poverty into the new industrial towns by the promise of better wages. (When people these days moan about economic migrants, they need to remember that many of our ancestors right here in Lancashire were just that themselves.) So we are a fairly mongrel lot, which, as any Darwinist will tell you, is no bad thing if you're looking for health and vitality, to say nothing of a good survival instinct in your offspring. But it also makes us a bit tricky to define, to pin down by saying exactly what a Lancastrian is and what makes us different from all the others tribes of Britain. But I think a good point at which to start to find out is by exploring these common experiences which make up our past. In a word, our roots. And if you're a gardener like me, and you've ever tried to dig up a dandelion root, you'll know what a difficult job that is; how they fork and twist this way and that, and can run to extraordinary depths. In fact, just like history.

A sense of history – of who we are in terms of where we came from – is vital to our wellbeing. Without it we are vagrants, mere wanderers, ships without anchors. Rootless. Each day, I believe, we need things about us that remind us of our history, our roots. It helps us to make sense of the sometimes apparently random, meaningless nature of life by placing us within a process we share with the rest of humanity, those who have gone before and those who will follow us. And that helps to put our life and times into some sort of perspective and remind us of the debt we owe to history. When people today scoff at the idea of 'the old days', and dismiss our industrial past as irrelevant to the sophisticated world of today, writing off those who harp on about them as sentimental nostalgists, they are ignoring an important truth. We would not be where we are today, enjoying the lives we enjoy, without the men and women who went before. The humble Lancashire weaver threaded her shuttle and helped to build the nation that we have today. Her efforts created the wealth that built the civic buildings which still stand and the public amenities we still enjoy, whether they be public parks, or reservoirs for our drinking water. Her militancy helped the suffragists obtain the vote. The blood of our forebears shed in wars, as well as their sweat in our factories, helped create the stability of peace and prosperity which is the foundation of our lives today.

Today, we stand upon their shoulders. And we need reminding of this, and what better reminders than the physical fabric of our towns and countryside that still survive. As a Lancastrian I probably deserve banishment for it, but I freely admit that one of my favourite places is York. For the people who live their lives in York, their past is laid out before them. From Romans through Vikings to the Middle Ages, even the wonderful railway heritage of the Victorians. It's all there. You bump into your own history at every turn, and it's exhilarating. Here in my part of Lancashire we are not so lucky. I live next to a building which dates from the early 1600s which has been systematically destroyed, pillaged and vandalised, not least by official vacillation and indifference. Our mills have been too readily knocked down and tarmacked

'We stand on their shoulders.'
PHOTOGRAPH: HARRIS MUSEUM AND ART GALLERY

Sunset over Burnley.
PHOTOGRAPH: AUTHOR

over as car parks. Our town centres have lost their traditional, distinctive appeal and been replaced by shoddily built modernisation schemes which pay lip-service to the past by including a few bogus cobblestones and lamp standards. In that self-deprecating way which is one of the endearing qualities of the Lancastrian, we have often underplayed our past achievements and allowed our heritage to be steam-rollered away, the genuine article often being replaced by the tacky merchandising of the modern heritage and tourism business. Our past too often lies discarded, concealed or neglected amongst the concrete and plate glass of the modern world.

This is a journey in an increasingly homogenised nation to discover what differences we in Lancashire have managed to retain. I shall travel from the remote moorlands of the Pennine hills to the crowded seashores of our coast. It will be a journey in time, too, from the mysterious hilltop settlements of our early ancestors to the busy modern developments of our cities. I shall stop off at churches and abbeys, stately mansions, derelict mills, Victorian terraces and modern office developments … and whatever else takes my fancy. And in the process I hope to uncover some of the history behind the places and the people who make up the rich fabric of our county. Now whether or not I emerge with a portrait of a Lancashire which is as unique as the reader might like it to be will depend upon how well we have resisted the modern forces of conformity. The outcome will be a measure of the spirit of the people of

Lancashire to preserve their individuality against the upheavals of the modern age. I truly hope I shall not have to report the death of Lancashire as we older people know it, of what I regard as the 'real' Lancashire. As far as any omissions of your favourite places in the county are concerned, I apologise in advance. But then this is by no means to be regarded as an extensive travelogue or gazetteer but merely a journey taking me as far as my curiosity and travel pass will get me. And I hope that in these pages I don't become too opinionated, but if I do you must remember that this book is neither specifically a history nor a travel guide but the personal observations of a somewhat old-fashioned and habitually critical Lancastrian taking a journey through his native county.

CHAPTER ONE

OUR EARLIEST ANCESTORS

IT MUST BE ALMOST FIFTY YEARS AGO that I last visited Bleasdale Circle. I was little more than a kid and that early shine had still not worn off things. We thought nothing of going off on expeditions to hunt a ghost that someone had read about or search for buried treasure. And history wasn't some dull and dusty thing from the schoolroom, but something that came clanking out of ruined castles in suits of armour or flying through the greenwood on an arrow with some thrilling message attached to it. And our notions of Bleasdale Circle came with that same sense of magic. Perhaps there would be druids' circles of cowled celebrants raising offerings to some unspeakably terrifying deity? Maybe even a human sacrifice! We even went at night on Midsummer's eve to encourage every expectation of something wonderful happening. But it was raining and the mist was down over the fells, and we stumbled around muddy fields among disgruntled sheep without ever finding the circle. I recall journeying home aware that yet another dull shutter had come down upon the romantic dreams of youth.

Nearly half a century on and it begins to look as though nothing has really changed. I still can't find Bleasdale Circle. This time it's broad daylight, a Saturday afternoon in the summer of 2004. The mist is still hanging around the fells, but in thin wispy curtains. The fells themselves form a protective semi-circle around the site to the north-east. Beyond is the rugged heart of Bowland fell country. West and south are the flatlands of the Fylde and the Lancashire plain, all sky and the brightness that proximity to the coast brings. But today I'm drawn in the other direction, to the hills and the shadows of distant history, our buried ancestry. I wander from the path which has taken me past the church at Admarsh into a scrubby field that is full of hares, or so it seems. For as I wander about on my quest and put one up, he lollops off only to hide in the reeds further ahead, leaving me to disturb him again later, a wonderful tawny creature with an age-old reputation for disguise and magical transformation. Perhaps he's deliberately drawing me away from his sacred site? But he doesn't need to. I'm quite capable of misleading myself. I'm expecting the prehistoric circles to be out in the open, like Stonehenge, or in a prominent position in the hills like Castlerigg above Keswick. What I hadn't bargained for was that after its discovery in 1898, to protect the site they planted trees around it, so that now the circle is hidden inside a coppice of birches, beeches and Scots pine. You can't help thinking that what with the shortage of signposts or official footpaths to the site as well as the secretive shelter of trees, some people would just rather we spent Saturday afternoon at the supermarket instead of poking around searching for clues to Lancashire's first settlers.

But step through the outer curtain of trees and you're soon glad to have made the journey. The trees lend a strangely hallowed atmosphere to the place. They blunt the force of the wind which sweeps down from the fells, leaving only a whisper of leaves. The undersides of the birches tremble with pale alarm. And there are rowan trees, too, revered for their magical properties by the ancient Britons. Underfoot the fallen pine needles and brash deaden your tread. You can't help but feel that you have entered some sacred place, some natural place of reverence.

Bleasdale Bronze Age Circle.
PHOTOGRAPH: AUTHOR

And almost at once you stumble over a shallow ditch and into the burial circle. Here stood a henge of eleven oak posts, three feet thick and forming a circle 34 feet wide. Within were buried funeral urns containing the burnt remains of human bones. You are standing inside a Bronze Age burial site, a 'habitation of the dead' or 'ghost henge'.

But there's more. Further excavations uncovered the remains of a larger outer enclosure, again consisting of huge oak logs with palisades between, this time forming a circle of 150 feet in diameter. The whole structure represents a mighty effort: a henge in wood to rival Stonehenge.

The posts of the burial circle have been removed and replaced with concrete blocks. There's something grotesquely mundane about this, akin to a recent suggestion to replace the stones of Stonehenge with polystyrene to protect them from damage. But don't let the presence of the concrete drag your mind back across the chasm that separates us from our early ancestors. Instead, sit on one of the blocks like I did. Try to ignore the blarting of the local sheep and listen to the liquid cadences of the curlew as he glides off the flanks of the surrounding hills and imagine yourself as some silent witness at whatever mysterious ritual took place here 4,000 years ago when the first farmers buried their dead. Or look to the east through the four stones which mark a ceremonial entrance and observe in the distance the notch in Fair Snape Fell and wonder if that's where the sun first appeared as it rose on the midsummer solstice or spring equinox. And if that sounds too fanciful let me tell you that as I left to retrace my steps to the church, I chanced upon a man who told me that he was visiting the circle because his mother was a Glover, still a local Bowland family, and her mother used to visit the circle on certain 'auspicious days', which he thought might be something to do with hoping for a good harvest. Encounters such as this help to bridge the gulf of history and bring our Lancashire ancestors much closer.

But even after I'd left Bleasdale I hadn't finished with its prehistoric circle. Or perhaps I should say, the circle hadn't finished with me. For such is the power that its dark mystery exerts over the imagination that the next day I found myself in the basement of Colne's public library rummaging through the *Proceedings* of the Lancashire and Cheshire Antiquarian Society. If anyone could be guaranteed to have immersed their scholarly noses into the origins of Bleasdale, or any other of our county's historical conundrums, it would be this splendidly august and archaic body.

We don't have many antiquarians these days, more's the pity. Today is the age of specialisation, so narrow as to become baffling to all but the initiated. But look at the record of the inaugural meeting of the Lancashire and Cheshire Antiquarian Society in 1883 and you can't help but be impressed by the refreshing and confident breadth of their approach. The society has been set up, they boldly proclaim, 'for the study of history, architecture, manners, customs, arts and traditions relating to Lancashire and Cheshire'. Among the founder members are plenty of FRSs, a professor, lots of MAs, MDs, FSAs and MRCSs, a sprinkling of reverends and even the odd bishop.

They sound rather a patrician lot and I looked in vain down the list of names and addresses for a humble artisan, self-taught perhaps, or a product of one of the many self-improving societies of the time. Apart from one unadorned name, one John Robinson of 56 Church Street, Eccles, they all came from rather splendid-sounding homes and seem to have been largely drawn from the business elite and intellectual glitterati of Victorian Manchester. Could it have something to do with the half-a-guinea annual membership fee when a weaver's wage in 1883 was only a pound a week? I have a mental picture of them strolling around the sites of their occasional archaeological excavations in their tweeds and brogues, legs well spatted against the Lancashire mud, mumbling learnedly to one another but at heart as thrilled as kids at a conker championship. The maps and diagrams drawn to illustrate their lectures show all the meticulous attention to detail of earnest schoolboys in the grip of an obsession. And there's nothing they like more than a good controversy to get their teeth in to as you can tell by the way that particular articles will inspire others championing an alternative theory.

At the risk of sounding like a grumpy old-fashioned elitist, I think it's a great pity that there's no room on our library shelves any more for such publications. Today our public libraries seem to feel obliged to turn themselves into video stores and branches of the Citizen's Advice Bureau as much as repositories of good books. It was for this reason that I found myself, as I say, in the library's basement storeroom, manipulating a set of rather frighteningly heavy mobile shelves between which you have to squeeze in order to peruse the volumes, fearful that at any moment someone eager to consult the shelves next door will creep up and push them together again, leaving you pinned between several hundred ancient tomes like a choice specimen of bookworm.

But sure enough, two years after the discovery of the Bleasdale circle, the Lancashire and Cheshire Antiquarian Society has an account of the excavations conducted by one Shadrach Jackson. (How our Victorian forebears knew how to enliven a dull surname!) Written by Professor Boyd Dawkins, who seems to have been the leading luminary of the society for many years, it sets out his view that Bleasdale is unique not only to Britain but to Europe and is a habitation of the dead built on the plan of the homesteads of the living. Such are the slow but passionate rumblings of academic debate amongst these learned gentlemen, however, that we have to wait eleven more years and I have to undertake many more thumbings of the society's volumes, before the arrival of a paper by the Reverend S. E. Collinson, vicar of Broughton, Preston, throws hefty quantities of cold water on the Bronze Age burial henge theory. The Rev. Collinson insists that Bleasdale is nothing more than a stockaded Celtic village, the stockade being for the rather mundane purposes of keeping their cattle in and enemies out rather than the boundaries of a taboo area containing the sacred house of the spirits of the dead. And the circle containing the funeral urns? Well that was a large roundhouse with a circle of pillars supporting a heavy thatched roof which was a communal living space or 'alehouse'.

Now, having retained more of those romantic dreams of youth from that first visit to Bleasdale than may be good for someone who lives in an age of telesales and reality TV, I just don't want to believe the Reverend Collinson's theory. I want to believe that here in Lancashire we possess Europe's only house of the dead surrounded by a ghost henge for containing the spirits of the departed. It suits a mind nurtured by the misty moorland of the Pennines and reared in the superstitious shadows of Pendle Hill. And on as severely practical a level as I can muster: Why on earth would our ancestors want to sit carousing among the bones of dead people? And what sort of a thatched roof requires eleven supporting posts, each two-and-a-half feet thick? That's the thickness of a natural beech tree. No, Reverend Collinson, I'm sorry. And I should be moved myself to deliver a paper saying so, should you and your venerable colleagues have not gone the way of all things and turned to dust.

Only if ashes could speak would we get to know the truth about Bleasdale. But the small dish of charred remains resting in a display cabinet at the Harris Museum in Preston is saying nothing. These are the contents of the Bleasdale burial urns, and I went to pay them my respects and bid a fond farewell to Lancashire's first settlers. The two funeral urns are there, too, restored to their terracotta glory, intricately decorated with combed lines and punch marks.

A notch in the fells above Bleasdale.

Alongside is a smaller vessel, a cup for which no one knows the purpose. There are birch poles from the ditch which surrounded the inner circle which have been carbon dated to 1700 BC. There's also an account of the origin of the wretched concrete blocks – or 'stumps' as they prefer to call them, as if they could conceivably have had some natural origin. After the first excavation in 1898 the buried wooden posts were raised to ground level for visitors to see. Not surprisingly they soon rotted and were replaced by the concrete in 1935 (the era of those horrid pre-war bungalows you see around). But perhaps the most eloquent part of the display is the photograph which has been enlarged to cover the whole of the back of the cabinet. It shows the circle before the trees were planted. If you can ignore the flagpole they raised to celebrate their discovery, at last you get an impression of the brooding mystery of the site. Lonely moorland stretches to either side, and filling the skyline are the hills, a cirque of dark fells hunched protectively around as though conspiring to keep the secret of Bleasdale from us for ever.

A fascination with our county's history, whether it be what Bronze Age man got up to in Bleasdale Circle or what granny did in the mill, is really part of the same preoccupation with our roots. And here in Lancashire we value strong roots. This may be because for many of us our roots are muddled. We don't really know where we came from. The Industrial Revolution was a great magnet which drew our great and great great grandparents from the countryside all over Britain to work in the mills and mines and shipyards. And unless you are very persistent or lucky, or famous enough for someone to want to find out about you, tracing your ancestry back to before the great industrial upheaval of the nineteenth century to some village where your family name is chiselled on some mossy gravestones in a churchyard is impossible. But I think that when we did settle, especially in the narrow valley mill towns of the Pennine hills, we did our best to make up for our fractured past by binding ourselves together in a quite remarkable way.

These bonds are still surviving into the twenty-first century in places such as Bacup. And I went to Bacup because I was still preoccupied by our prehistory and I knew I would find plenty of examples of flints and arrowheads unearthed from the surrounding moors, and I'd also find an organisation similar to the Lancashire and Cheshire Antiquarian Society that had survived from Victorian times to become a real focus for the community's roots.

The Bacup Natural History Society – the Nat to everyone in the town – meets every Thursday night at 7.30 in a building that was once a pub, then a doss house, and now contains the most fascinating and sometimes bizarre collection of antiquities, specimens of natural history, weapons of war and general domestic paraphernalia which will keep a magpie mind like mine happily occupied for hours.

I described the Lancashire and Cheshire Antiquarian Society as being patrician. The Nat is just the opposite. Step inside the short corridor where the hatch of the bar used to be and turn right into the lecture room, and the

All about curiosity. The Bacup Nat.

welcome is warm and hearty. You'll soon be in a chair in front of a roaring gas fire – it was July when I went and I guess fires are a year-round feature of life in Bacup, altitude 800 feet above sea level – with a mug of tea and a choice of biscuits and invited to reveal your life history. Now this might be construed by the sniffy, the more constrained net-curtain brigade, as nosiness. But I prefer to see it as curiosity. And the Nat is all about curiosity. Intellectual curiosity. It is intellectual curiosity which has amassed its unique collection of material from Bacup's past and its surroundings. And it's intellectual curiosity which unites its members and fills the lecture room every Saturday night in winter for their slide shows. It is curiosity about birds which has made Geoff, to whom I'm introduced, into the society's expert on ornithology. Or John its expert on heraldry and Catholic history. Or given Marion a passionate interest in the Scottish wars of independence and the history of the Vikings. And the list goes on. The Nat is a wonderful example of enthusiastic, self-taught amateurs joining together to preserve their historical heritage, expand their minds and push back the turgid tide of inanities with which the modern media threatens to overwhelm our culture.

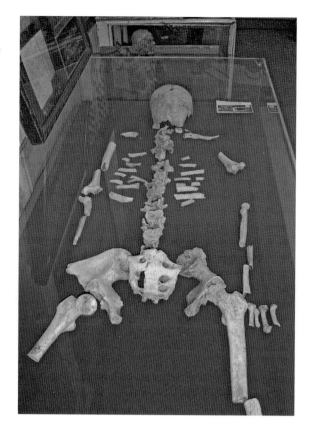

So on the Thursday night I visited them, instead of sitting at home watching the latest dismal chronicle of human unpleasantness we call TV soaps, Betty is trawling through a collection of local newspapers which go back to 1863 and has just discovered an account of the suicide of one of her relatives. John Crawshaw is reciting an eye-witness account of the wildness of the Lancashire countryside in the late Middle Ages. Marion Connolly is attempting to persuade me that the Battle of Brunanburgh in AD 937 did not take place near the banks of the River Brun in Burnley but probably somewhere in Northumbria. And Harry O'Neill is trying to steer me in the direction of the society's huge collection of over 5,000 local photographs he's in charge of. And on Saturdays, once the winter season begins and the heating had been ratcheted up even further, local people can sit and enjoy slide lectures on subjects as diverse as 'Explosions of Steam Boilers' and the 'Circumnavigation of Antarctica'.

And if that isn't stimulating enough you can always go upstairs like I did to spend an absorbing hour or two in the museum. You climb the steps under the watchful eyes of the portrait of the society's founder, Joseph Hardman Worrell, sporting a beard like a hedgehog but gazing contentedly out of history at the way his brainchild has retained its hold over the imagination of his fellow townsfolk for the past 125 years. The museum is an archive of Bacup life with plenty of exotic additions. You pass into the room through the old cell door from the police station. But believe me, it's a liberating experience. There are collections of birds' eggs culled from the mantelpiece of rich textile manufacturers to make a modern conservationist weep. There are whales' fins, sharks' jaws and saw fishes' saws. In all, there are 65 display cases of stuffed birds and animals. And there are 60 cases containing souvenirs from royal occasions, local industries and memorabilia from local church and institutions that exist no more. And Bacup people must be great travellers. One adventurer has staggered home bearing a rock from Lake Baikal in Siberia, while another has filled a whisky bottle with the most exquisitely intricate weed from the Sargasso Sea. So heavy are some of the specimen cabinets with minerals, fossils, coins and historic manuscripts that they've had to be placed over the roof beams for fear that one day they might plunge through the floorboards and flatten the slide show audience beneath.

My guide, Ken Simpson, the curator, shows me the cap of a Bacup man who went out to fight in the American Civil War. 'I've tried it on,' he tells me. 'And he had a very little head.' Ken's a most genial fellow, and I think he'd like me to have a go, but I pretend to be very interested in a rather revolting puffer fish caught forever in mid puff. The Nat encourages local schools to send parties to the museum and they get thankyou letters from the children. Despite the abundance of guns, knives and swords to appeal to small boys, Ken recalls one letter they got which said, '… the thing I liked most was the dehydrated rat and the hair ball from a cow's stomach.' Another, when asked at the end of the conducted tour whether there were any questions, pointed out of the window to the street below and asked, 'Whose is that red car out there?' I gather that visitors from local schools are not so frequent these days. An incident which occurred during my visit seemed to symbolise the struggle that an organisation like the Nat has in trying to preserve the history and culture of the past in the face of modern indifference. As I browsed among the display cabinets the cry went up, 'We're under attack!' Across the street the society has set up a crushing stone, a three-ton millstone grit wheel used to crush stone to sand for sprinkling on floors in the days when people couldn't afford anything else (known as 'Irish Lino'). Some local youths are in the process of removing the long wooden axle from the centre of the stone and making off with it. A posse of irate members rushes out to retrieve it and stagger back to put it in safe keeping in the lecture room. 'It'd have ended up on t' fire if we 'adn't rescued it,' observed one elderly member stoutly.

The curator, Ken Simpson, and secretary, Ken Bowden, often remove items and take them to lecture at women's institutes. One of the most popular exhibits is a blue and white hand-stitched dress worn by the wife of a town official who was invited to the opening of the Manchester Ship Canal in 1894. Ken Simpson is justly proud of the dress but worries about its condition. 'It was getting a bit grubby so I decided it needed a wash. I got some advice and put it in a bath of warm water with some washing powder, very mild. It's turned out all right although it's a bit puckered now.' His latest worry is a tear in the full-length dress which has been patched with a piece of sellotape. Ken's next plan is to find an expert seamstress to repair it. The society gets no public money or fancy grants but survives off the sheer dedication of its members, determined not to see their heritage die. And people in the town are still sending their family heirlooms. Ancient washing machines are a favourite, but there's no more room for such heavy things. The one they've got is from the late 1800s. It resembles nothing so much as a lethal weapon of war, and is aptly named the Torpedo.

The museum's most renowned bequest is Blodwen. She was found by a member in the late 1880s in a cave on Little Ormes Head in Llandudno. She turned out to be a Neolithic Welsh lady who died in 3510 BC. Since her death she had become the most well-travelled person in Bacup. Her bones have been all over the world for measuring and testing. It is now known that she was in her late fifties, suffered from osteoporosis and died of breast cancer. There are not quite as many bits of Blodwen on display as there once were. This is again due to certain members' passion for cleanliness. Thinking she looked a bit dusty after 5½ thousand years, one zealous member took her home and popped her in the washing machine. Fortunately the member didn't seem to be in possession of a spin dryer, and Blodwen has been carefully reassembled by experts and she now lies resting in a specially made glass case, content perhaps in the knowledge that her life in the Stone Age living among bears and hyenas, whose bones were found beside hers, was not half as eventful as her life thereafter, but that at least she's finally ended up among friends.

That we had our own Neolithic ancestors around Bacup at the time Blodwen was alive is clear from all the Stone Age weapons and tools that have found their way into the museum. After the most satisfying diversion, I'd finally met up with what I came here to see: evidence that Neolithic hunters had ranged the moors of the Pennines. Axe heads and arrow heads, all found locally, are on display. A glimpse of that grey-green polish of flint and the cunningly knapped arrow heads complete with barbs and tiny necks for fitting to a shaft, soon had me dreaming again about our earliest ancestors. These flints belonged to people from an age further back than Bleasdale man, but were they settlers? Or were they simply hunters passing through who had taken advantage of the retreating of the last Ice Age and the arrival by around 5,000 BC of a climate here a lot like that of southern Europe today? (No need for gas fires in Bacup then.) With forests of oak, elm and alder covering our moors, they would have taken advantage of the rich wildlife to fill their cooking pots. But about this time, instead of hunting and then moving on, our ancestors would have begun to use their stone axes, like the one in the Nat found on Ramsden Clough, to clear the forests for grazing cattle. From being wandering food-gatherers they had become settled farmers. The very first Lancastrians?

CHAPTER TWO

THE ROMAN WAY

IF YOU DRIVE NORTH UP THE M6, I reckon that twelve miles from Garstang to Lancaster will take you about ten minutes. But try shifting twelve miles east and making the same northward journey, from Cow Ark in Bowland up Croasdale to Salter Fell just east of Ward's Stone, Lancashire's highest hill. It's a journey of a comparable distance, and on the route I have in mind you'll have to walk most of the way. And it will take you all day. The route is the old Roman road from Ribchester to Hadrian's Wall, and it was the first-century equivalent of the M6. Twelve or thirteen miles is the distance which the poet and military historian, Hilaire Belloc, believed the Roman armies could march in a day. Of course, they wore heavy armour, but the roads they made were the high technology of the day, raised and flagged and in this case seven yards or more wide.

But the point I want to make is one of perspective. Ten minutes up the M6 and what do you see apart from the tailgate of the pantechnicon in front of you? Or, if you dare to take your eyes off the road for a second, where the road and the railway meet for a few miles you might see an inter-city express train roaring past. But for the motorist and the train passenger all sense of distance has been annihilated, shrunk to the time between the last exit and the next or the distance between stations. You can drive through Lancashire in less than an hour, and all the richness and uniqueness will have been lost, compressed into a narrow conveyor belt of monotonous tarmac, shorn of all visual and mental stimulation for the sake of our modern fixation with speed and getting there on time. But pull on your boots and take to the Roman road through Bowland, and you at once realise what a vast, wild and exhilarating place our hill country is. Fell after fell reaching to the sky's edge, expanding as far as the eye can see, concealing lonely passes where it seems that the ice has only just retreated, or sudden welcoming valleys with hidden

Roman road near Cow Ark.

villages you've passed your life never knowing about. And all the richness of wildlife, of weather and changing light, as you inch forward along paths your ancestors took as far back as the Roman road makers. And you may be going slowly, and the distance between one hilltop and the next may seem to take for ever, but each footstep you take is a step away from the narrow, clamorous preoccupations with the modern world into the old perspective. And you can feel your mind and spirit being enlarged.

To put me in the Roman way of things I went to Ribchester. This was the Roman fort of Bremetennacum, established during the reign of the Emperor Vespasian, and the garrison fort for the Roman cavalry. The rather excellent museum is full of Roman finds. One of its most spectacular exhibits is the tombstone of an Asturian cavalryman. The Asturians were a fierce tribal people from north-west Spain, renowned for their horsemanship. The tombstone shows the horseman riding down a Celtic warrior. 'The cavalryman is showing no mercy as he impales the barbarian with his spear,' crows the caption, aptly capturing the triumphalist mood of the whole relief. In fact, the hoof of the horse is shown grinding into the head of the poor, fallen warrior. Poor? Yes, looking at it I at once felt I ought to identify with the oppressed, a short figure with a rather big nose. After all, barbarian or not, he was probably one of our Lancastrian forebears, a Brigante, quietly minding his own business grazing his stock and feeding his family in the forest clearings, when this mighty military machine, with soldiers co-opted from every corner of the known world and enlisted for their war-like capabilities, suddenly arrived and took over.

I'm sure there was nothing the Romans wanted from Lancashire: no corn or spelt wheat fields in the forest; no gold, tin or copper in the hills. They were just eager to impress their military might on us as has been the way of all overblown colonialist powers throughout history. Why couldn't they have just driven their road through, moved their troops as far north as they needed to build their walls and define the limits of their empire and leave us alone with the smoke from our alehouse fires quietly curling up from the roofs of our thatched roundhouses into the forest air? Well, who knows? Perhaps we were a tiny bit troublesome, rather resentful of their intrusion, painting our naked bodies with frightful blue woad and beating our chests from the nearest hilltop. But isn't that what any gutsy northern tribesman would have done faced with an invasion? Anyhow, we were soon conquered, and it was undoubtedly the Roman roads that helped to do it.

An Asturian horseman
crushes our ancestor.

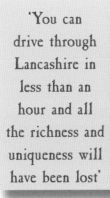

'You can
drive through
Lancashire in
less than an
hour and all
the richness and
uniqueness will
have been lost'

In the museum at Ribchester I was struck by another carved tablet. This time it was an altar stone to Marcus Aurelius. There's something splendid about the Latin inscription which can't fail to impress. The lettering is bold, confident and exquisite in its simplicity, and it occurred to me that these were just the qualities which the Romans brought to their road-building. I determined to spend some time exploring a Roman road.

We probably have the best record in England of Roman roads on our OS maps here in the North West. This is entirely due to the efforts of a Bury schoolmaster, John Just, who, when the OS was in progress around the 1840s, being a keen amateur archaeologist, he offered them his services. He proved so useful that he was given an official position on the survey. So the route of the Roman road northwards from Ribchester to the Roman wall at Thirlwall, known as the Maiden Way, is plain enough to see to any map owner. But, as I soon discovered, you don't always need a map to spot it. As every schoolboy knows, Roman roads are straight. It enabled troops to get about with alarming swiftness. It also removed the dangers of surprise from hairy Celtic warriors hiding in ambush round the corner. But a straight line also offers an uninterrupted view of cardinal points for the road-building. This is dramatically illustrated if you follow the road out of Ribchester on its journey over Jeffrey Hill, three-and-a-half miles north.

Jeffrey Hill was for me one of the undiscovered gems of Bowland. At almost 1,000 feet, it offers all the pleasures of a fell-top vista without any of the arduous efforts to reach it of its more remote relatives. Indeed, there's a car park on the top from which you can set out and be at the top in the time it takes to cry 'Julius Caesar'. There must be lots of visitors because the sheep are quite the tamest I've ever come across. I went with my wife and

The idyllic view from Jeffrey Hill.
PHOTOGRAPH: AUTHOR

she had read that sheep appreciate being smiled at and it stops them running away. We didn't have to bare our teeth once at the sheep on Jeffrey Hill. You can walk right past them and they refuse to panic. And what a view from the top! Southwards you can look across the Lancashire plain and see the Menai Straits and Anglesey. To the north, where the escarpment of bracken and heather drops sharply, there's a marvellous view over Chipping Vale and east into Ribblesdale, as idyllic a scene of woody knolls, ambling lanes and snug pastures as you're ever likely to meet this side of the hobbits' Shire. But round the dome of Parlick Pike a sense of darker things, of mystery in the knowledge that Bleasdale Circle lies hidden in the cirque of fells to the north-west. But it was just to the east of north to where my eye was ultimately drawn. The unmistakable line of the Roman road arrowing northwards towards Browsholme Height and Marl Hill, etched by the course of the country lanes and their hedgerows. And it becomes immediately and excitingly apparent how they got it so straight. On the horizon, blunt boned like a crouching beast, is Pen-y-ghent, used by the road-builders as a marker to fix the line of sight. As I say, exquisitely simple. I was well and truly hooked now and wouldn't rest until I'd followed the road as far as I could go.

I wasn't the first to be drawn by the spell of the Maiden Way. Another wet afternoon saw me back in Colne library and in among the sinister sliding shelves which contain the Proceedings of the Lancashire and Cheshire Antiquarian Society. Volume 31 for 1913, *The Roman Road from Ribchester to Overborough* by William Harrison, FSA. Overborough was a Roman fort at Nether Burrow, near the confluence of Leck Beck and the river Lune, about as far north in Lancashire as you can get without clashing spears with the Cumbrians or those from North Yorkshire. But just how does our Roman road get there with all the Bowland fells in the way? It will take more than a stroll up Jeffrey Hill to answer this question because the fells start to become seriously wild from now on. And how would the road keep straight using Pen-y-ghent as a marker, much too far over to the east for the road's course? William Harrison knows. After reaching the summit of Marl Hill the road bends and Ingleborough is used to face the road-builders. But soon after crossing the Hodder, the bulk of Low Fell gets in the way of the line of sight. 'From the nature of the ground, they were compelled to depart from one of the principles of their road-building,' says William Harrison, quoting schoolmaster, John Just. They therefore made their way north-west up Croasdale, taking care 'that this ascending line in no point approached a steep part of the mountain from which the troops could be assailed with stones rolled down upon them.' Our hairy, woaded forebears again, defending their patch. Despite my growing admiration for the Roman road engineers, I was inclined to shout, 'Good 'un on you, lads!'

And don't let anyone tell you there's no wilderness left in England. Just point them in the direction of Croasdale. Where the road bends to pass round the elbow of Low Fell, civilisation ends. That was where we left behind the couple of youths on trail bikes, that bane of the peace-loving rambler. (I dream of sticking a stout walking stick through their spokes as they ride past, like the park keepers used to do to us when we rode our push-bikes through the corporation park.) The only other discord arises from the knowledge that you have entered the territory of United Utilities – could ever a name be more at odds with the poetic isolation of this wilderness? – with Stocks reservoir visible a couple of miles from the beginning of the valley. But after that, the sense of hush that descends as you enter the long empty glacial sweep of the valley is a rare experience. Even the sheep seem to respect the silence. When it is broken by the odd distant drone of light aircraft, the plane's disappearance serves only to accentuate the quietness. The silence folds back over you like a veil. You can imagine the sense of trepidation of the Roman soldiers as they entered this valley. It must have seemed the loneliest road on earth if you were far from home and fearful of the natives. There's a raw bareness to the valley sides, even though the bracken is still very green after all the rain and the heather is just beginning to turn pink. Only a single sheep-fold stands by the beck and then there's nothing but the road clinging low down to the western flanks of the valley – just as John Just describes – before climbing northwards to the dale head. Half-way up the valley is a sandstone quarry which sets you wondering where the Romans got all their cobblestones for their roads. But as for evidence of the Roman road under all the stones and gravel of the modern track, there was none.

I had no idea what a Roman road would look like after almost 2,000 years of neglect, so after Bleasdale I headed back south again to Cow Ark where the Roman road marches off across the fields unobscured by the tarmac of the modern lanes. Just where the modern road climbs to Marl Hill I stood at the gate of a field which had just been mowed, and looked back towards Jeffrey Hill. And there, quite unmistakably, crossing the field is a raised ridge, now no more than eighteen inches high but about seven yards wide. This, I was to learn, is known as an 'agger', the Roman name for an embankment, and this is how the Romans built their roads: raised to give them a properly drained base on which was placed the actual roadway of big stones skimmed with gravel.

My excitement was out of all proportion to the modest little ripple in the fallen grass which I'd discovered. I already saw the glint of helmets and breastplates in the sun, the imperial eagle borne high. I heard the ring of footsteps on the cobbles and the murmur of voices across two thousand years of time. (Did Roman soldiers actually converse in Latin? It seems altogether too solemn and scholarly a language for idle chatter.) Across the lane from my discovery was a house, and I heard voices coming from the garden. Perhaps they could confirm that this actually was the Roman road? Not only was the lady from the old vicarage able to do this but she also showed me where the road had been recently excavated in her garden. A party from Ribchester museum had unearthed the stones used for the metalling. But apart from that, nothing else. No spearheads or catapult balls. No gaming counters or curse tablets or nit combs or phallic pendants (apparently the Roman soldier was

Marl Hill with Pen-y-ghent in sight.
PHOTOGRAPH: AUTHOR

The lovely Roman road up Croasdale.
PHOTOGRAPH: AUTHOR

very fond of concealing phallic objects about his person) – all of which you can see in the Ribchester Museum. All they found was an extraordinary number of old bottles. 'The parson's tipple?' I enquired discreetly. No. Apparently most of them seemed to have been Milk of Magnesia. The pressures of life in the country must have played havoc with the digestion in those days, though it was hard to believe on a day such as this with the air full of birdsong and the sweet smell of mown grass. The lady from the vicarage seemed rather phlegmatic about having a Roman road through her garden, and when I ventured to enquire about the possibility of ghostly footsteps marching past in the night she looked away from me and seemed to be searching for a means of escape. However, she did invite me to dig in her field whenever I liked, but to be careful to avoid the one next door which belonged to the Queen. I could see the headline: 'Roman Road Addict Locked in Tower of London Forever'.

From the top of Marl Hill above Cow Ark there is one of those views which mocks the notion that some strangers have – they're usually from the south – that Lancashire is a landscape of post-industrial dereliction broken only by tracts of bleak moorland. To the west are the fells of Birkett, Totridge and Hareden, forever alive with the moving projection of cloud and sunlight. You can pick out the road from Dunsop Bridge winding its way through the Trough to Lancaster, boldly going where lesser roads would fear to go. To the east is Easington Fell and the fell road over to Waddington where just another valley hop will take you into the urban sprawl of the Calder which is still invisible and whose congested clamour could be a thousand miles away. Pen-y-ghent guards the route northwards through Ribblehead, and to the west, Ingleborough, taking up duties as the road's sight-marker, lies straight-backed as a Roman road itself. And tucked among these rising waves of mountain splendour, the wooded pastures of Slaidburn, Newton and Dunsop Bridge, all on such a human scale and not a vast agri-business field in sight. A heart-warming, almost nostalgic scene, I should imagine, for any Roman warrior dreaming of his farmstead in Tuscany. Except – and here I was struck with the folly of projecting scenes of the present landscape back so many years – in the first century this area would most likely have been deeply forested. To the rigours of constructing stone-clad embankments would have been added the task of clearing great corridors of forest in order to drive the Roman road northwards. And just how good would have been the view of the approaching armies for our Brigante ancestors from their fastness in the hills with so much woodland about? And where actually were their camps, the Iron Age hillforts? Here was a question that finally dragged me away from the Roman road into the fells to the west.

'I like nothing better than to stray off the beaten track and into the realms of wild but stimulating speculation'

In their book *Bolland Forest and the Hodder Valley*, first published over fifty years ago, Margaret Greenwood and Father Charles Bolton speculate about the existence of one such fort at a place called Castlestead, not on the map and unknown to all but a handful of people. Now looking for somewhere like this is just the sort of wild goose chase that appeals to me, something to take me off the beaten track and in to the realms of wild, but stimulating, speculation. As you've probably concluded from all this Roman road business, anything which gives me an excuse to turn my back upon the scheduled and over-regulated world of today I embrace with all the relief of a drowning man clutching a life-belt. A Celtic encampment, perhaps even an earthworks comparable to something like Maiden Castle in Dorset, here in Bowland? The challenge to look for it was irresistible.

Greenwood and Bolton's main justification for believing in the existence of an ancient hillfort here is the name itself. 'Castlestead' means the 'place of the castle', and there's a reference to it in the survey that dates back to the reign of Elizabeth I. And they found that some of the local hill farmers continued to use the name, or did so over 50 years ago. Now even then, it strikes me that Bowland, or in particular the fells north of Chipping, must have been a darned sight more isolated than they are today. As Greenwood and Bolton write, 'Anyone who has the courage and endurance to set out on foot and explore the hills that surround the steep valley of the Burnslack brook will see the line of Castlestead. It is an artificial rim high up on the steep face of the hill.' Courage and endurance! Crikey, they make it sound like climbing Everest.

The success of most enterprises in life is not to be measured by what you achieve in the end, but by the discoveries you make on the way. The quest for Castlestead was no exception to this rule. On first arriving at Burnslack I saw a hen harrier. This splendid raptor with a wingspan of 4½ feet was quartering the slopes of Burnslack Fell close to the ground, a male with pale grey plumage and black wing tips. I'd have probably thought it was a gull had it not been pointed out to me by Shirley at Burnslack house, a bit reluctantly at first because she's fearful for the birds' safety. She told me at the time we met that there were only seven breeding pairs in the country and six of these were in Bowland. Although they are protected and the penalties for harming them are severe, their scant regard for the local grouse make them unpopular with gamekeepers. For the sheer thrill of catching sight of this rare creature I'm for ever in Shirley's debt. She'd also heard of Castlestead and pointed me in the direction of a field low down on the slopes of the fell. It was a square area, slightly raised and enclosed by ditches, but whether or not they were man-made I couldn't tell. As a defensive position it was ideal; tucked under the protective arm of the hill to the north and east, it commanded a wonderful view to the south as far as Pendle Hill and the southern Pennines, a fine view over the Fylde and a glimpse of Furness across Morecambe Bay to the north-west. I wandered about, not knowing what I was looking for, but enjoying spotting the flowers of yellow tormentil and blue speedwell and

A leafy lane near Chipping.
PHOTOGRAPH: AUTHOR

listening to the skylarks trilling overhead and the falling cadences of the curlews. No annoying traffic sounds at all, just the hum of the bees in the thistles. But it didn't feel like a fort (don't ask me what forts feel like) and Greenwood and Bolton's description of 'an artificial rim, high up on the steep face of the hill', didn't fit at all.

Still, the best discovery was on the journey home along the lane leading past Saddle End towards Chipping. Whoever is responsible for protecting and encouraging the wild flowers in this area of Bowland deserves a medal. The lane is full of foxgloves, with fat bees emerging from their spotted throats. There's red campion, with flowers as rich a pink as I've seen, and birdsfoot trefoil, whose egg-yolk yellow flowers are like tiny-snouted butterflies. The tormentil smiles through a rich green bed of bilberry leaves where the berries are just beginning to form. And everywhere meadowsweet, rich and thick as cream and smelling like powdered milk. In a ditch near Jeffrey Hill, where I was looking for traces of the Roman road, I came across a plant that filled the whole hedgerow with an intense green earthy smell and when you crushed the leaves it resembled nothing so much as smelly socks. Did the tramping Roman army wear socks? I don't know, but I bet they'd have recognised the plant. When I got home I looked it up. With its tiny purple flowers I think it may have been woundwort or even betony, known to the Romans as a cure for headaches and liver complaints and as a safeguard against witchcraft. Today we've lost much of our knowledge and lore of plants. It's that perspective thing again. If we will go thundering down the motorway at 70 mph, what do you expect? It doesn't seem so long ago that people strolled down country lanes, because there wasn't a lot else to do on a summer Sunday afternoon, and they could recognise and name the wild flowers that grew. The yellow birdsfoot trefoil has no fewer than 70 local names.

When I was a young man and lived in Foulridge, I sprained my ankle playing football and the old lady next door, Mrs Hartley, went out picking comfrey and made me put the hairy leaves down my socks. And very itchy they were but they cured the sprain. We may be able to watch live Premiership football now on a Sunday afternoon or speed along the motorway to the Trafford Centre, but what we gain from progress on the larger stage we lose on the smaller. And the intensity of the pleasure, as my stroll along the lanes of Chipping proved, can be just as great and satisfying. What is it Hamlet says? 'I could be bounded in a nut-shell, and count myself a king of infinite space.'

Then suddenly there was something to mar my idyll. In the field at the other side of the hedgerow I spotted a man in a camouflage jacket with a shotgun. Then there was another, and another. I counted seven in all, fanned out across the field and all strangely silent. But that didn't last. There was an absurd tootling wail from a horn and a man in a red anorak suddenly appeared with a set of hounds, their noses welded to the ground and their tails winding like clockwork. It was the local foxhunt, God bless us! No horses, but men on foot with armaments. But the dogs weren't having much luck. Another wail from the trumpet and an exasperated cry from the man in red as he tries to instil some order into the hopelessly deluded hounds. There's an urgent cry from a curlew, warning the fox perhaps, as I hope curlews do, and the men trudge off rather dejectedly over the hill. Good old Mr Fox has outwitted them all. But, of course, the incident reminds me that this is hunting country and has been since Stone Age man knapped his first flint. And who am I to interfere with tradition, however unspeakable the practice in the modern day when the killing is purely for pleasure, whatever the protestations of the farmers about foxes killing lambs? And as for the argument that foxes kill the game birds which the rich businessmen need to shoot come inglorious August, well, I'll leave you to work out my feelings about that.

I'd failed to find Castlestead but seen plenty to engage me. Not least, I think I spotted an Ancient Briton. Stopping off for a drink at the Tillotson Arms in Chipping, I stood at the bar and right behind me sitting in a chair and gazing steadfastly in front of him like someone on a bus was a giant of a man with a shaven head, earrings and a neck like a tree trunk. He wore a red vest with barbed wire tattooed round his prodigious biceps. Not a bit like the poor Celt being impaled by the spear of the horseman in the museum. He scared me to death. And I thought: If the men of Bowland have always been like this, it's a wonder the Romans ever got beyond Ribchester.

Another day, and I still haven't had enough of Burnslack. The surrounding fells exert a strange magnetism, bringing on a need to climb them, look over the top and see what's beyond – conquer them both physically and visually. It was not just the Romans; I discover the colonialist in me, too. Most of the fells up Burnslack are closed to the public for the shooting fraternity, but there's a grand path up Saddle Fell. And the landscape on the top, just past where the path forks west over Wolf Fell, belongs to another world. It's a lost world of matt black peat hags like inky lakes out of which climb strange atolls of peat sculpted by the wind. And in between, where the heather has been burned as if by star fire, stems bleached pale as bone reach grotesquely to the sky. But make your way the short distance across the moortop where the cotton grass bobs its wild dance in the wind and the view northwards suddenly leaps into view. Down below there's the sweep of a lonely valley full of shifting light and shade as the clouds fly eastwards from the sea. And beyond, range the fells, jostling like Adam's new world to be named. But I don't know any of them yet except the Three Peaks, those ancient gritstone-capped bastions of resistance to ice and water and even time herself, basking in the sunlight and the glory of their mountain status. Wonderful. Awesome, even. And it occurred to me that this is where all true Northern Spirits belong. This is our native home, where our ancestors gazed out from their hillforts and buried their dead under cairns of stone so that their spirits could wander the fells. And today, when we chance to glance up from our busy lives in our narrow valleys or crowded cities, and we catch a glimpse of these distant northern fells, this is the place to which our hearts and souls repair.

The journey back south down Saddle Fell is as good as any as an introduction to Lancashire. Marching south beyond the Calder Valley are the hills of the southern Pennines with the wind farm clearly visible above where I live in Cliviger. (Why, oh why did they have to make the turbines white?) Below is unlovely Burnley, looking quite lovely today in the sun with her imperfections ironed out by over 20 miles of distance. Over the wooded edge of Longridge Fell lie Accrington, Blackburn and Preston, with the glint of the sea on the Fylde coast visible round the corner of Parlick Pike. And to the south-west, the Lancashire Plain, with the glass towers of Manchester glinting through the warm blue haze. Pendle, straining to became a mountain herself but just failing, rises to the east, with Clitheroe beneath with its smoking cement works, white, obtrusive and, by all accounts I've heard, obnoxious.

Knowing that all these destinations and more lie before me, I feel daunted by the prospect. All those people, all those lives crowded into the valleys and plains. And yet these hills so empty. Not a figure in sight to interrupt the restless, shimmering waves of bronze moorland bents as if the whole fell was on the march like an army. Only when I'm back on the road and driving home do I meet the real armies, the true successors to the Roman legions. These are the latter-day Ribble Valley colonists, having conquered the markets of the cities and made their plunder, hurrying home in their Mercedes and four-wheel drives to their burglar-alarmed villas in Bowland. If my experience is anything to go by, I sincerely advise you not to take to these roads around teatime or they will cut you down as ruthlessly as any Asturian horseman riding down a Celt.

Back home I climb the small hill at the back of the house to watch the sun set over the fells I've just trodden. I've been doing this for the last 20 years (nothing metaphysical here, just a dog to be exercised), but today is the first

Atolls of peat.
PHOTOGRAPH: AUTHOR

time I've ever walked upon those fells. I now know their names – Totridge, Fair Oak, Saddle, Wolf and Parlick – and they've suddenly become personalised. (My dog once killed a neighbour's hen and I thought she'd be very upset. But she told me, 'It's all right. I hadn't given it a name.') Until you personalise and familiarise things, they don't seem to matter so much. After today these fells have really started to matter to me. This doesn't mean they've lost their mystery. Fells and mountains will always remain untamed. But I feel that I've mapped out the horizons of my life better, by being there and naming. I've bonded more completely with the landscape in which I live. I can be said to belong better and my roots with my Lancashire home are all the stronger for the experience. It's something I'd recommend to anyone.

But that view northwards from the top of Saddle Fell into the lonely valley of Bleasdale and the fells beyond had left me wanting to reach out further to the very northern limits of Lancashire hill-country. I'd always believed Pendle Hill to be the highest hill in Lancashire. It isn't. It's Ward's Stone, by a mere four metres. I had to go. You can't write a book about Lancashire without really getting on top of your material.

I once had a thoroughly unpleasant experience travelling through the Trough of Bowland. My wife and I were journeying in the car to Lancaster and were beginning the climb out of the Trough at Lee Bridge when a motorcyclist raced into view in the rear mirror. He was dressed like a goon out of one of those futuristic films where they are employed by some wicked totalitarian power to menace the innocent – I recall particularly a sinister black helmet and visor. He drew alongside the car and began waving violently, his features contorted with rage. Taking him to be one of the locals deranged by the isolation of living in such wild parts, I checked the door locks and drove on. But he wasn't to be thwarted and he slewed in front of the car forcing me to stop. He then sprang out and began pounding on the window, snarling malevolently. By this time both I and my wife were scared to death and expected him to produce a shotgun. (My imperfect memory of the situation had him waving a gun at us. But that couldn't have happened, could it? This was Great Britain in the 1980s, not some war-torn South American republic.) I kept the window firmly closed and slowly the source of his agitation emerged. He was a gamekeeper, and apparently someone answering to my description (bearded, bald, *Guardian*-reading liberal, into civil liberties and possibly animal welfare) had been spotted helping himself to his precious pheasants. Now, as we'd witnessed on the way up, these pea-brained creatures require very little encouragement to end their own lives by throwing themselves under the wheels of passing cars, so it struck me as being no great tragedy that a few more were being lost to larcenous humans. But it was clearly a waste of time arguing with him. I'd a tough enough job explaining to him that I was not the felon he was pursuing but simply an innocent passer-by off to deliver a bottle of sweet sherry to a maiden aunt in Lancaster. He eventually left us, muttering darkly about beards and stamping his jackboots. But the experience had unnerved me, and I've never been able to travel that road without a certain feeling of trepidation.

Now it so happens that the route to Ward's Stone starts at about this point on the road. And if you consult the latest OS map, there would appear to be several shorter options along which you could take the car rather than the somewhat circuitous footpath from the main road which involves a walk of

Beware! Road through Trough of Bowland.
PHOTOGRAPH: AUTHOR

around eight miles to and from the summit. Should you be tempted to try any of these alternative routes, I urge you to remember the above anecdote. The routes are unfenced tracks, maintained, I presume, at great cost, and used by the hunting fraternity to drive along in their SUVs before staggering out several yards to the nearest shooting butts to discharge their shotguns and fill the quiet skies with lead and feathers. Far be it from me to disparage such time-honoured activities, especially since the land is owned by the Duke of Westminster, reputedly the richest man in England, and one with whom only a fool would want to be involved in any form of litigation.

But enough of such banal considerations. Let's get on to Ward's Stone, the very rooftop of Lancashire. The stone itself is an obdurate lump of weathered gritstone, grey and sutured like a skull. In fact, it resembles nothing so much as Lancashire's very own sphinx, and I'm surprised it has never been adopted as a visual expression of our indomitable spirit. It gazes out resolutely northwards. Follow its gaze and you can see where Lunesdale and Ribblesdale finally meet and shake hands after their journeys through the hills. Beyond, the northern fells roll and pitch, seeming to range across the whole breadth of England. And the peaks of the Lake District rise out of the mists of Morecambe Bay until they lose themselves in the grey haze of the sky.

I'm glad I took the trouble to visit Ward's Stone. I'll long remember the family of kestrels hovering out on the edge of the hill at eye-level, busy hunting among the fissures of broken rock which litter the summit. And there was the route of the Roman road which had brought me so far in the first place, disappearing northwards alongside the Lune. In one way it seems my journey northwards was complete.

To see what a Roman road really looked like I recommend a visit to Blackstone Edge just north-east of Littlebrough, where the modern road to Halifax swings north to climb the hill. It joined Ilkley (also a Roman fort) with Manchester and is unique for its well-preserved paving stones. The cobbles are set to either side of central slabs worn into a groove down the middle by the brake-poles of carts descending the hill (though this is disputed by some, not least a member of the Lancashire and Cheshire Antiquarian Society writing in 1883 who believed only such wear could have been caused by cart wheels, since they measured the same distance apart as the space between the runs in the Roman gateway at Pompeii. Yes, he'd measured them both!). In all, the causeway is 15 to 16 feet wide but must have presented such difficulties to negotiate because of its steepness that it was finally abandoned in favour of a zig-zag track still visible to the north of the paved section. You'd have thought that a major piece of engineering from almost 2,000 years ago could at least be properly maintained. Alas, it is an indication of the low esteem in which some hold our historical heritage today that the paving stones have become so hopelessly overgrown as to have become virtually invisible in some sections. But there's worse. Many of the stones have been defaced and some actually removed. It would appear that some of our fellow Lancastrians are in the habit of taking their strolls in the countryside equipped with

lump hammers and cold chisels, just in case they come across any ancient monuments to which they can add their name. To Steve, '81, John '97 and Lee, who managed to carve his letters six inches high (thank God he wasn't called Nebuchadnezzar), I would recommend an enforced spell picking up litter on Hadrian's Wall, all 70 miles of it. However, what can you expect from the rest when officialdom ignores the site, and whoever built Broad Head drain vandalised the road by driving a concrete sided gully across it?

But whether you care about Roman antiquities or not, it's worth climbing Blackstone Edge for the view west and south across the Lancashire Plain. You can stand on the peat beds, which are like islands of hailstones where the white pebbles of quartz have been left after the millstone grit has been eroded away. We watched a golden plover sitting amongst the cotton grass piping plaintively. His sad song could have been a lament for lost civilisations. The sheer immensity of effort to shape and lay the stones across such a tract of remote moorland speaks of a civilisation powerful, organised and confident of its own durability. Ah, but where are they now? *Ubi sunt?* As I look out over Hollingworth Lake under a bruised and brooding sky the glass towers of Manchester rise arrogantly. Fifty years ago they weren't there and the Manchester of my youth was a smoke-blackened Victorian city. What will it be like in another fifty years? Moorland can make you melancholy, especially when the clouds hang low. And we'd wandered along the moortop into darkest Yorkshire. And there to the south, an extraordinary sight. A vast procession of insects of all shapes and sizes crawling along the roof of the moor, their droning filling the air in an angry corridor of sound. Yes, the M62, a universe away from these silent, timeless moors. I was glad I was where I was and that its so easy here in Lancashire to step off the conveyor belt into the wilds, into history. We should all do it more often.

CHAPTER THREE

VIKING TREASURES

ONE OF THE GREATEST HOARDS of buried treasure ever found in this country was unearthed from Lancashire soil. The Cuerdale Hoard was a Viking treasure chest containing almost 10,000 silver coins, ingots, chains, armlets and rings. In all, the weight of silver was 44 kilograms. An account of the discovery is likely to bring a sparkle into the eye of every schoolboy and tears of envy to every metal detectorist.

The day was the 15 May 1840, and it was around six o'clock in the evening. Workmen were repairing the banks of the river Ribble about half-a-mile downstream from the Tickled Trout near Cuerdale Hall when one of them struck a lead-lined box and watched as pieces of metal spilled from it. In a thoroughly charitable gesture he alerted his fellow workmen and they were soon filling their pockets. The account of what happened next displays a little less charity.

> At first the finders began to fill their pockets with the coins, but upon the arrival of the hind, or bailiff, of the landowner, they were required to empty their pockets and give up all but one piece each which they were allowed to retain.

However, one enterprising fellow succeeded in concealing 26 coins in his boots without the bailiff noticing. It wasn't the only part of the treasure which went missing. As the *Preston Chronicle* of 23 May 1840 reported:

> Some odd pieces of the booty have found their way into the hands of a few individuals and are, of course, highly treasured. Indeed, the numismatic collectors and connoisseurs are quite in a furor about the matter, and the spot where the treasure was found has, since the discovery, been more zealously scratched than any dunghill in the best populated poultry yard.

(I invite you to discover the words 'numismatic' or 'furor' in any modern piece of local newspaper reporting, to say nothing of anything so splendidly sniffy as the farmyard metaphor at the end. They don't train 'em like that any more.) The treasure was taken to Cuerdale Hall where it was sealed in a box before being deposited in Pedder's Bank in Preston. Thence it was claimed by Queen Victoria for the Duchy of Lancaster. (Not an ounce of royal charity there.)

The *Preston Chronicle* reporter chose his words very carefully, especially when he used the word 'booty' to describe the hoard. Experts who had studied the coins found that they had come from all over the Viking world: Arabic coins from the Middle East, Papal and Frankish coins from Europe and bullion from Ireland. Now while the majority – some 5,000 – were minted by the Vikings themselves at York, and many others were the proceeds of legitimate trade with merchants from the Byzantine Empire in the Baltic, how else, except as plunder, do you account for over 1,000 coins minted in the Mercian and Wessex kingdoms of the Anglo-Saxons, the deadly enemies of the Vikings?

Today, the lion's share of the coins have disappeared from where they were found here in Lancashire and into the British Museum in London – a modern form of cultural looting which we seem quite happy to allow. I had thought to go down there and report back on how our treasure was being looked after. But I confess to a real aversion to London, that conflated mass of humanity with not a hill-top in sight to allow the soul to breathe. I wonder how many other Lancastrians feel this way? I once spoke to a sheep farmer in his dalehead farm. He was past middle-age and the furthest south he had been in his life was Derby. When I asked him what he thought of the world beyond his dale, seeing it as he did only through the images from his television screen, a look of pain crossed his weather-beaten brow. 'Hellish', he said. 'It's hellish.'

A mere 32 of the coins from the Cuerdale Hoard have been left behind and are on display at the Harris Museum in Preston. (An attendant I spoke to seemed to think there may be one or two more in the basement. None in his boots, I hope.) They aren't very inspiring, and if you read this and then go to look at them, you may wonder what all the fuss was about. They have the rather dull, grubby look of unpolished pewter or the colour of a well-used galvanised bucket which everyone had in their backyards before coloured plastic took over the world. I reckon that had they been in the keeping of the Bacup Nat, someone would have come along and given them a good polishing. You just have to imagine how they would have appeared to the workman in 1840, spilling out in their thousands at his feet. And, of course, you have to ask: How on earth did they get there?

Since 1840 people have speculated as to what so much wealth was doing buried in the banks of the Ribble. In her book on Viking treasures in the North West, *A Silver Saga*, Fiona Philpot says that there would have been enough money to raise a Viking fleet and pay a band of warriors, about

£300,000 by today's standards. She also points out that the Vikings buried their hoards close to certain landmarks such as trees and rivers before setting off on long journeys or in times of trouble. But a failure to recover the treasure would seem to suggest that some terrible disaster overcame its owners. Perhaps some overwhelming defeat in battle?

One such battle which occurred at about the time the Cuerdale Hoard was buried was the Battle of Brunanburh in AD 937. And many people, especially those whose origins are local, would like to believe that the battle took place here in Lancashire.

In 937, Lancashire was on the border of two kingdoms, three if you include Scotland. We would have been situated in the northernmost limits of the Anglo-Saxon kingdom of Mercia, with the kingdom of Strathclyde to the north and Viking Northumbria to the north-east. All that remote and sparsely populated fell country I'd been so happily tramping not so long ago would have formed a wild frontier. Now the Battle of Brunanburh was fought between Aethelstan, the West Saxon grandson of King Alfred the Great, and a massive allied army of Vikings, Scots, Welsh and Strathclyde Britons led by Anlaf the Dane and King Constantine of Scotland. The fight was for nothing less than the kingdom of Britain: Aethelstan to unite it under Saxon rule, the Vikings and northern Britons to keep their independence. We know so much about it because it is the subject of an Anglo-Saxon poem, and a very bloody poem at that, which in the Anglo-Saxon tradition gloats over the fall of five kings, including the son of King Constantine and seven jarls. Because the outcome was a victory for Aethelstan, it could be argued

Brunanburh? Off the long causeway, Burnley.
PHOTOGRAPH: AUTHOR

that we became the Christian country that we are and not just a bunch of heathens waving hammers and worshipping Thor and Odin. And local proponents of the theory that Lancashire would be the ideal meeting place for these armies, seize upon the name Brunlea or Burnley, as the actual site of this momentous conflict of Brunanburh. And who but a member of the Lancashire and Cheshire Antiquarian Society would bring the full weight of his amateur scholarship to bear to support the idea.

After delivering a paper to the society on the subject, James T. Marquis brought a party of members to Burnley in 1909, furnished them with a map of the battlefield, and then proceeded to describe the events of 937 in the most minute and bewildering local detail. Bewildering because the Anglo-Saxon poem offers little or no topographical detail about the battle. But Mr Marquis was determined not to let the absence of a few historical facts prevent him from bringing the ancient battle to life in the most vivid detail:

> Aethelstan placed Thorolf on the left of his army, at Roo-Ley, to oppose the Welsh and irregular Irish under Adalis. In front of Brownside (Brunside) was Egils with the picked troops, and on Egils' right, opposite Worsthorne, Aethelstan and his Anglo-Saxons. Across the original Long Causeway, which leads to the other causeway over Blackstone Edge and on to the south east of England, with the burh entrenchments immediately at his back, was the valiant Turketul, the Chancellor, with the warriors of Mercia and London opposite Round Hill and Mereclough ... Aethelstan and Anlaf were fighting in the centre for the possession of Worston, when the Chancellor, Turketul with picked men including the Worcester men under the magnanimous Singin, made a flank attack at Mereclough and breaking through the defences of the Picts and Orkneymen got to the Back o' th' Hill. He penetrated to the Cumbrians and Scots, under Constantine, King of the Grampians. The fight was all round Constantine's son who was unhorsed. The Chancellor was nearly lost, and the prince released, when Singin, with a mighty effort, terminated the fight by slaying the prince. On Round Hill, down to one hundred years or so ago, stood a cairn called High Law. When the stones were made use of to mend the roads, a skeleton was found underneath. That, I believe, would be a memorial to that fight.

You can see from the sheer eminence of the protagonists why Marquis, who lived in Colne, would wish to appropriate the site for the nearby town of Burnley, a humble Lancashire textile town never before accorded any importance in the nation's history. I am surprised that none of the PR wallahs in our town halls of today has ever exploited this. Signs on the M65, perhaps? 'Welcome to Bloody Burnley. Site of the Battle of Brunanburh.'

But what sort of a person was James T. Marquis that he could manage to fill out the sparse details of the poem until they took on such a startlingly localised reality? Just over 20 years ago when I first took an interest in this story, I found and spoke to Mr Marquis's granddaughter. She revealed that he was a bank manager by profession and the family stood in great awe of him. She recalled that if they met him in the passageway of the house and he was without a coat, he wouldn't speak to them until he was properly dressed. One can only marvel at the wild undercurrents of imagination that might be at work under the most staid exteriors of our fellow men.

Many advocates for the Battle of Brunanburh occurring locally offer the Cuerdale Hoard to support their belief. Here, they say, was the treasure chest of the confederate army, buried in haste as they fled. Unfortunately, none of the thousands of coins found at Cuerdale can be dated later than those of Louis the Blind, Emperor of the West Franks between 901 and 905. For this reason, experts believe the hoard was buried around 905, more than 30 years before Brunanburh. Poor Mr Marquis will be turning in his grave at this news. But never mind, J.T., Burnley needs all the allies she can get, and a wander round Rowley today can only be enhanced by your exhilarating speculations, even though, rather then being the revered resting place of kings, the council have turned the area into a landfill site for the town's refuse. Hmm.

'Tea-time rush hour: sword-waving Viking hoards would hold no terrors for me after this!'

I could not allow the opportunity of writing about the Cuerdale Hoard pass without a visit to the place where the treasure was discovered. Unfortunately the nearest convenient place of access was from the Ribble bridge by the Tickled Trout and its adjoining filling station. Any attempt to park your car thereabouts is met with threats of wheel-clamping and extortionate fines. The whole area is an extension of motorway Britain, with its ruthless regulations and pitiless self-interest. I simply wanted to park my car for half-an-hour while I walked to the spot where the treasure was found and stood and dreamed of tenth-century Britain. Fat chance. I finally had to park on a housing estate half-a-mile away at the top of Brockholes Brow then trek down the hill inches away from a never-ending stream of maniacal motorists determined to ignore the speed limits. Yes, it was the teatime rush hour. Sword-waving Viking hoards would hold no terrors for me after this. And by the time we reached the bridge to head away on to the river bank, to the south side where the treasure was found, it became clear that the footpath had become totally submerged. After days of torrential rain the Ribble was in full spate, brown as thick Yorkshire tea brewed in the peaty fells, with polystyrene and plastic bottles flying past on rafts of driftwood. So we had to take the tarmacked path on the Preston side, part of the Ribble Way. Whoever maintains the riverbanks today should take a leaf out of the book of those who conserve the country lanes in Chipping Vale and encourage the growth of native species. Instead the banks have become overrun with the invasive Indian balsam, pretty enough in pink at this time of years, but a brute, a bully of a plant that will take over to the exclusion of all else and whose long, sappy stems dwarf the cranesbill cowering in their shadow. And I was amazed to see how much ragwort has been allowed to seed, a poisonous menace to livestock which has been outlawed. It's time someone got to work on the Ribble's banks; you never know, they may be rewarded by finding another treasure chest.

There was nothing to see of the site of the discovery from the other side of the river, only a party of swans who had abandoned the swirling torrent and were standing disconsolately marooned in a nearby field. On this occasion, place could not offer any historical resonance and we would have to rely upon the meagre rows of tarnished coins in the museum to remind us of one of the most exciting discoveries of treasure from Viking Britain here in Lancashire.

But there's one other treasure from Viking times not to be overlooked. Not coin this time, but stone. A hogback Viking gravestone, carved to every inch of its surface and undoubtedly the finest of its kind to be found anywhere in Britain. And to see it you need to travel to Heysham.

The approach to Heysham from the motorway is a hideous jumble of pylons, power lines and transformers assembled like the ranks of a mechanical army. Signs to the town disappear in the commercial imperatives of ferry terminals, gas terminals and the vast complex of the nuclear power station. As a consequence we soon got lost and ended up in the power station car park, dwarfed by the two giant blockhouses, clean as a pin and smoke-free, but nevertheless sinister, to our simple minds, in the knowledge that the violent forces which fuel stars and galaxies are being mucked about with to bring us electricity to watch *Eastenders* and drive hairdryers. Hubris or what? As we fled, we had to stop alongside two diesel locomotives hauling heavy metal chambers. I became convinced that we had become lethally irradiated, and we hurried off to find our Viking grave before our hair began to drop out.

But the modern world hadn't done with us yet. We had to run the gauntlet of new housing developments as we followed the signs to Heysham village: estates, all pantiles and Tyrrolean finishes, red-brick drives and gaping, empty conservatories, not a ha'peth of individuality to set us apart from anywhere else in dormitory Britain. But this was nothing to the rank awfulness of the village green which is dominated by what looks like a '60s toilet block: two urinals separated by a featureless concrete verandah for which I could discern no purpose unless to torment our aesthetic sensibilities. Or perhaps it was for a band to play music while you wee? Handel's *Water Music* would be a tasteful option. Then there were the stone monoliths to guide you into the car park. Massive lumps of featureless limestone brought down from Holme Park quarry to the north where tedious limestone invades our native sandstone. They should take them straight back. If plonking ugly boulders all over the place is the only way our planners can think of to stop people parking their cars on the grass, it's time someone plonked one or two of them on their heads to help their brains to work. But there's nothing to stop the owner of the nearby house from parking his wagon and a few oil drums outside his house and doing some running repairs. Nothing must interfere with the

Englishman's inalienable right to park his vehicle outside his door, even if it is a ten-ton truck.

But hope that Heysham had a soul rose at the sight of all the flowerbeds in bloom. Ignoring the bizarre announcement that the bed of yellow begonias was sponsored by Hydrocarbons Resources Limited, I loved the beds of lavender and red begonias and the blue and white petunias. And at last, with the toilet block and boulder avenue left behind, here was Main Street, pretty as a picture postcard with all its hanging baskets and whitewashed cottages selling nettle tea. All journeys to heaven pass through purgatory, we're told, and here was heaven at the bottom of Main Street. St Peter's church gazing out across the infinitely stretching sands of Morecambe Bay to the mountains beyond. Quite the most beautiful and inspiring location for any church I've seen, even the dramatic cliff-top churches of the Aegean. But then, wormwood. The bitterest disappointment. The church is closed for the day, our Viking tombstones locked away inside the sulky shadows.

I stood inside the porch and ranted. Viking oaths, I am ashamed to say, burst from my lips. I went to the vicarage and pleaded with the vicar's wife to be granted the key. Five minutes, that's all I needed, just to see it. But Christian charity was in short supply at the vicarage that day. Understandable, perhaps, with all the theft and vandalism that seems to go on these days. A new Dark Age. Our churches under siege from the heathen hordes of pilferers. Everything under lock and key and electronic surveillance. I returned to the

Main Street, Heysham.
PHOTOGRAPH: MALCOLM GREENHALGH

churchyard, moodily kicking the ancient sods underfoot. But then, a miracle. The church door opened and out spilled the vicar and his congregation of one from evensong. I renewed my appeals, this time to the reverend one. He looked doubtful. But then an angel sprang forth in the shape of his one faithful parishioner. She offered to take the keys and show me round the church. God Bless Mary Wright!

Mary is as sprightly as a sandpiper. When I met her she'd lived 74 of her 76 years in Heysham, and her knowledge of all things historical connected with the church overflowed like silver from a treasure chest. For the next hour she gave as generously with her time and learning as any scholar saint. First the Viking tombstone.

St Patrick's chapel, Heysham.

PHOTOGRAPH: AUTHOR

Rock tombs like mummy cases. Heysham.
PHOTOGRAPH: AUTHOR

Nothing could have prepared me for that first glimpse of the hogback stone. Mary unlocked the chancel door and there it was, the warm sandstone glowing in the half-light of the security lamp. A six-foot length of arched stone, two feet thick, every inch carved with strange beasts and primitive figures of men. If ever inanimacy can be said to have a presence, here it was. Here was an object of reverence, albeit from a heathen culture; it spoke of mankind's belief in an afterlife, his attempts through myth and legend to reach beyond himself to a sense of the Eternal.

The Viking hogback gravestone is cut to resemble a Danish or Norse house. The sloping sides of the top are like the sides of a roof and are covered with tile-like patterns. In the case of this one at Heysham the two gables are in the shape of bears and the whole roof is supported by four human figures. An individual house of the dead, I'd say, reminded of the phrase used to describe the Bleasdale Circle. Mary took me through the whole complicated symbolism of the elaborate carvings which cover the walls of the 'house'. The birds, the horse, the wolves, stags, snakes and fish. The dragon and the tree of life. The figures of Sigmund and Sigurd from the Norse Volsung Saga. She believes that the Vikings who left this stone – and it was found in the churchyard 200 years ago and stood outside the church until 1964 – came here from either Ireland or the Isle of Man. The gravestone belongs to one of Lancashire's Viking settlers and clearly a very important person. We spent a long time bobbing from one side of the stone to the other, kneeling on the floor to trace yet another piece of carved symbolism: the presence of a fish, an early Christian symbol. Mary indicated that the carver had perhaps come in to contact with Christianity and was hedging his bets over entry into the afterlife. But did she feel in any way uncomfortable about having such a pagan monument inside her church? Some did, she confessed, but not her. She thought God might be amused by the Vikings' stories, which is, after all, what they were, and they could do nothing to undermine her Christian faith.

Mary then took us up the hill onto the promontory to show us the ruins of St Patrick's Chapel. Their most remarkable feature is the rock-cut graves thought to date from the eight century. Six graves with human shapes like mummy cases are carved out of the giant rock which hangs over the edge of the promontory looking out across the sea. Today they are filled with rainwater which in its dark surface reflects the distant movement of the clouds. It made me think of the words from the Bible: 'And now we see through a glass darkly ...' and I wondered at the ultimate destination of those who were laid to rest here over 12 centuries ago. Valhalla or a Christian heaven? Or, looking across the bay to the Lakeland fells and reminded of Wordsworth, simply 'Rolled round in earth's diurnal course, With Rocks and stones and trees'?

Mary believes the rock graves belong to an even earlier pagan age and she points out the mounds on the headland covered with brambles where the blackberries are just beginning to ripen. These are the barrows, she tells us. It's an eerie feeling to look out across them and glimpse the top of the nuclear power station in the distance. It scrambles the message the place gives out, your sense of time.

Heysham is an uneasy balance of past and present, a strange juxtapositioning of ancient mysteries and crass modernism. Standing upon Heysham Head you capture it all. The ancient ruin with its tombs which are as inscrutable as the scrawls in the sand left by the retreating tide. Then above you, overlooking the barrows, the modern houses ranged incongruously along the cliff top. And finally, the sprawling nuclear plant at the opposite pole to the ancient Cumbrian mountains, a breathtaking monument to the arrogance of modern man who can pilfer the stars for his energy and yet produce a deadly waste which he doesn't know how to get rid of. Heysham is a fascinating contradiction.

CHAPTER FOUR

THE RISE AND
FALL OF AN ABBEY

I HADN'T FINISHED with carved stones and all those mysterious images sent down through time to us by our distant ancestors. They start to become a lot clearer with the advent of Christianity and the symbols which are recognisable to us all today. But for a long time, as Christianity began to find its feet, the old gods shuffled along behind in the shadows.

Stand in the graveyard of the parish church in Whalley and you'll be surrounded by the usual sad reminders of the departed. 'In Loving Memory.' 'Gone to Rest.' Words on headstones, picked out perhaps in gold, but still words. Words are the coinage of expression today, the way we release our deepest feelings. 'Beloved husband.' 'A treasured son.' But among all the Victorians' decorous expressions of grief, their polished marble monuments, are three shockingly incongruous intruders. Three ancient stone crosses, weathered to a grainy coarseness, every sandstone pore invaded by lichen, but covered in primitive carvings. Not words but strange whorls and spirals, animals and human figures, worn almost to the edge of extinction but hovering on the verge of visibility. Ghostly images from the distant past waiting for us to reach out and try to understand them.

And that's what you do. You find yourself tracing them with your outstretched fingers, like a blind man reading braille; following the faded outlines where, once bright and sharp, the chisel cut and the human breath of the carver condensed upon the cold stone. It can be an almost religious experience, touching the past like that.

But what are they? On the tallest of the crosses, the one furthest from the church, a series of panels rise up the eight-foot high shaft. First there are grids of interlaced patterns, then a four-legged creature reaching back as if to eat

Strange whorls. Viking cross, Whalley churchyard.

PHOTOGRAPH: AUTHOR

its own curled tail, then a human figure with raised arms with what might be serpents at his feet, then a bird, and finally, more interlocking patterns. If you step into the church and buy a guidebook for £1.50, it will tell you that these are Celtic crosses which the monks of Whalley Abbey thought dated back to St Augustine at the end of the sixth century. But they are more likely from the tenth century. The booklet confidently interprets the carvings as Christian symbols. The figure with the raised arms has a sort of halo and is said to be Jesus, and the bird is a dove, symbolising the Holy Spirit. The animal is a Scandinavian image and emblem of eternity taken over by the early Christian church and known as 'the Dog of Berser'. The Dog of Berser! The very name seems to bring the chill wind of paganism into the warmth of the sunlit churchyard. Suddenly I'm no longer quite so happy to run my fingers over the rough beast. The name has released some latent reservoir of superstition in my nature and for all the Christian guidebook's efforts to sanitise and sanctify the cross by turning these images into Christian symbols, I'm afraid I don't believe it. These crosses seem to me to contain defiantly heathen symbols, as out of place in a churchyard as an armed Viking in a monastic cloister.

I have no doubt that my peculiarly emotional reaction to the Whalley crosses will bring a pitying smile to the lips of any level-headed archaeologist. But I'm not an archaeologist, and this book is not principally a history of Lancashire. It is intended more to be an expression of the fascination, delight and excitement to be discovered in this county of ours by anyone prepared to take the time to wander through some of its more unusual places. If you are looking for a scholarly account of the Whalley crosses, as well as the Heysham hogback tomb and the Cuerdale Hoard, I'd recommend Ben Edwards' *Vikings in North West England*. Its line drawings and careful descriptions are particularly helpful in enabling you to trace and recreate the worn carvings. But don't expect many answers as to what the symbols mean. To the cautious archaeologist these crosses are 'eccentric monuments' and The Dog of Berser simply a 'quadruped'. Nothing to raise the pulse here. Their true meaning remains locked in stone.

The way that Christianity was able to absorb the earlier pagan symbols is seen at work again inside the church. Undoubtedly the most prized possessions of the church are its choir stalls. They were rescued from the abbey next door at its dissolution in 1537. It's thought that they were carved for the abbey in about 1430, and the seats or their ledges, the misericords, and the canopies above, contain the most intricate carvings of foliage, beasts and human figures. But what are we to make of them? Above the abbot's stall is a face, a real loblolly with bulging eyes and gawping mouth. And next door another grotesque head with leaves spewing from his mouth but an expression, this time, of much more unsettling malevolence. And here he is again under the choir stall seat and across the aisle, this time as a tricephalos or three heads in one. He's popping up everywhere like the bogeyman of a child's worst nightmares, a Gothic monster, disgorging his leaves, his leering eyes challenging you to dare to ignore him.

He is, of course, the green man, that perplexing expression of the pagan imagination which embodies so many ideas alien to the modern mind, from the Celtic cult of the severed head to the dark and demon forces of unredeemed nature. Today, from our cosy suburban perspective, we can't begin to imagine the terrors fostered by the forest in the superstitious mind. Bend down to look under the choir stalls of the north aisle and you'll fine the wodwo or woodhouse, the wild man of the woods, his body scaly with leaves, waving his huge club. But the pert damsel he is confronting doesn't seem a bit put out. Because, by this time these pagan forces have been tamed, banished like the medieval gargoyles to the windy corbels of the church roof and rendered comic and absurd, no longer to be feared but laughed at. So perhaps the abbot could afford to indulge his carvers and ignore the hairy buffoon above his head with his fantastic curling eyebrows and moustache. You can't help, though, but detect a certain subversiveness about the carving, a deliberate attempt to poke fun at the pomposity of the abbey hierarchy seated below in all their finery. The spirit of non-conformist defiance at work among the ordinary folk of Lancashire even in medieval times?

There's another tiny little cameo to illustrate the clever way in which the church tolerated paganism the better to modify it and bring it under its own control, a process which began when many of the first churches were built on pagan sites and which can still be seen at work today in Whalley church.

Green man, Whalley.
PHOTOGRAPH: AUTHOR

At the north-west end of the church is a small carved statue to the Roman god, Mars. What is a heathen god of war doing in the church of the Prince of Peace? Some of the local parishioners, I was told, have asked that question and were unhappy with the statue's presence. So quite ingeniously someone has stuck a wooden cross upon the stone and turned it into a tiny Christian altar. It seems that the same spirit of shrewd magnanimity which allowed our green man into the chancel is still in evidence 500 years later.

The ruins of Whalley Abbey next to the church are one of the modest delights of Lancashire. Protected from the busy conurbation to the south by the leafy knoll of Whalley Nab, roads and the railway pass close by bearing commuters to the towns but nevertheless leave it serenely undisturbed. But that is just as it should be. The word monastery comes from a Greek word meaning to live alone. It was a place where monks lived in seclusion from the world. They should reinvent the idea. Only I'm sure they'd be overrun with people wanting to join them.

Today you enter the monastery grounds through the north-east gatehouse with its great oak doors ribbed with iron-nailed batons to keep the world out. The battlements make it look more like a medieval castle but above the archway is a niche which probably once contained a statue of the Virgin Mary, to whom the abbey, like other Cistercian foundations, was dedicated. But later, if you visit the small museum, you'll find a brightly painted wooden statue of the Earl of Sussex, the doer of the king's dirty work when Henry VIII took possession of the abbey in 1537. This statue replaced the Virgin Mary, symbolising the assertion of the king's secular power over the Catholic Church. I mention this to remind myself that passing through the gateway I'm stepping back 500 years into Tudor Lancashire. It helps if you ignore the sign for Walls ice cream and the outlet for designer spectacles housed in the building next to the café and gift shop. Someone has to pay for the upkeep of the ruins, I suppose. But by and large there is an other-worldliness about the carelessly cobbled courtyard with its herbaceous border, and when you step inside the precinct walls the centuries peel away. It's rained remorselessly all morning, guaranteeing that I have the place all to myself for the old stones to exercise their magic. Shall I go clockwise or anti-clockwise round the ruins of the abbey church? I decide to go widdershins and risk bad luck; it feels more medieval, and anyway there's barely a stone of the church standing to fall down on my head. (More than can be said of what happened in 1356 when the central tower over the crossing was nearing completion and a stone from the bell tower fell and killed poor Ralph of Pontefract.)

All that remains of the abbey church now is a ground-floor plan set out in foundations of masonry, some original, others added to complete the picture for modern eyes. It gives an excellent impression of the church's size, which was as big as Ripon Cathedral. The central tower rose to a hundred feet, which is three times the height of the sturdy gatehouse. It must have been a very impressive structure for an abbey for such a relatively small number of brethren. You can stand in the foundations of the choir from where the stalls I'd just been looking at in Whalley church were removed. And in the floor of the transepts are cracked and weathered tombstones which moss and groundsel are patiently prising apart. But despite the worst efforts of

Barely a stone standing. Abbey church, Whalley.

nature, you can still make out the names of the monks round the sides of the gravestones. There's brother John Walton and brother Thomas Wood. And in the ambulatory to the north side of the altar there's a tombstone bigger than the rest and bearing the coat of arms – a lion on a shield – of the de Lacy family who gave the land to the monks when they came here from Stanlaw in Cheshire in 1296. A skeleton was found under here when it was excavated, and I'm beginning to feel a personal involvement now because my neighbour in Cliviger (if time had not accidentally separated us by 200 years) was Dr Thomas Dunham Whitaker who did a lot of excavations here back in 1798 and found many more skeletons under the presbytery; which brings things to life, in a contradictory sort of way, doesn't it? We're not just dealing with stones any more but human remains.

The once magnificent church is indeed razed to the ground and I begin to feel strangely guilty by association. You see, I have some of the stones outside my house. I found them in the garden walls, strange branching curves of stone that were once part of the tracery of windows. You can even see the narrow rebates on the inside of the arcs where the lead to hold the windows was poured. The only explanation for their presence is that Dr Whitaker, who had the hall next door and was vicar of Whalley, must have half-inched them. But to have them carted 15 miles just to hide them in retaining walls doesn't sound like the actions of one of Lancashire's most eminent and respected historians. Were they still tainted with papistry for this stern Church of England vicar? Now I treat them with the respect I feel they are long overdue and they stand outside my window in tribute to the local craftsmen who made them and whose skill could draw such soaring ecstasy from uncouth stone.

The rain today is perfect for melancholy reflection on time and human mortality. It drips down like history itself, pricking the puddles into life, a hundred trembling circles which grow then disappear for ever. And now I've moved to the monastery buildings and am sheltering under the thick arches of the sacristy. Here the walls still stand and the ivy-leaved toadflax clings everywhere, nourished by the ancient lime mortar. This is where they kept their sacred things. There's an alcove in the wall where they may have stored the sacred vessels, silver and perhaps gold, the first thing the Earl of Sussex removed to take to his master the king at the Dissolution. The abbey would have been immensely wealthy and the church's treasures would have been one of the first things Henry would have wanted to get his hands on (after Miss Boleyn). What stories these stones could tell that are now festooned with grizzled spider webs and blackened with the soot that once fell with the rain from the Lancashire skies. What sermons.

The doorway which leads from the cloisters into what was the chapter house and the two windows on either side are elaborately carved. But what are these strange shapes, crusty with pale green lichen, reaching up the curve of the arches and grown almost amorphous with weathering and time? At first I took them to be flowers but they lack any kind of symmetry. They are humped like snails with stretching heads, clawing their way up the stonework.

The silent cloisters of Whalley Abbey.
PHOTOGRAPH: AUTHOR

Some grotesque product of the Gothic imagination or merely mine? (My headmaster at school once told me that I had a diseased imagination.) And at the apex of the windows, what are the things with arms outstretched which seem to be welcoming the climbing creatures? Humans or insects? Worn stonework again teasing the mind. At either side of the chapter house door are human heads, one so badly damaged as to be unrecognisable as such. The other, while featureless with age, still manages to convey some meaning by the urgent thrust of the head. 'Look,' it seems to say, gazing sightlessly towards the empty cloisters, 'all human effort comes to this. Over a hundred years it took to build our abbey. Our church took half a century. Here above me are the dormitories where we slept on straw and the steps where we trailed down in the small, cold hours of the night to sing our prayers in the church. Through this doorway is the chapter house where we had to come for confession and correction of faults. Across there in the south range of the cloisters is the warming room, the only place apart from the kitchens where a fire was allowed and we could get warm in winter. And next to it you see the stone arch of the lavatory where we washed our hands and feet before eating our simple meals in the refectory beyond.'

But such lives of austere piety didn't last. By the time Abbot Paslew arrived, life at the abbey had become more ostentatious and indulgent. The 20 or 30 monks had a staff of 90 or so servants to look after them. In 1520, Paslew is thought to have spent £500 of the abbey's £900 a year income on food, drink and entertainment. Witness his kitchen which still stands today with its two huge fireplaces for spit-roasting, to say nothing of his own extensive lodgings nearby. Paslew, with his retinue of 20 servants, lived like a grand ecclesiastical lord.

But the best way for you to see for yourself the kind of opulence which existed in monasteries like Whalley before the Dissolution and which must have excited the envy of Henry VIII and his church commissioners, is to visit Towneley Hall in Burnley where some of the abbey's vestments have been brilliantly preserved.

I must have seemed like a medieval peasant as I rested my backside on one of the hall's old cast-iron radiators (no misericords here) and gawped at the sheer sumptuous splendour of the chasuble in the display cabinet in the room at the top of the stairs. Worn by the abbot when he celebrated mass, this huge sleeveless coat shimmers like liquid gold. And set in a sea of shining gold threads are crimson pomegranates of embroidered silk. As the notes explain, 'The richness of the gold would be emphasised during celebration of the mass by the play of light from flickering candles and shafts of sunlight.'

It's probably churlish to observe that in the next case, containing an equally spectacular dalmatic – a garment worn by the deacons who assisted the priest during mass – the play of light was non-existent because the tiny bulbs which illuminate the case had all gone out, leaving me peering blindly into the shadows. When I pointed this out to one of the attendants, he chided me. Didn't I realise that these precious relics would be damaged by the light? If they were to survive for another 600 years they must be carefully looked after. I was tempted to say that there wasn't much point in preserving them for so long if during that time no one was able to see them. I'm convinced that the dismal state of the illumination was directly responsible for most of the visitors I saw spending little more than three seconds flat examining these monastic treasures before groping their way past in search of something more illuminating. I must also quibble at the number of noisy attendants shouting at one another and barking into personal intercoms, to say nothing of all the children haring about the place waving sheets of paper and engaged in some kind of noisy historical treasure hunt. I think we've taken things too far these days. By all means let's encourage children and others to take an interest in history and culture by making our museums and libraries less stuffy. But to turn them into fairgrounds where no one can concentrate without hordes of noisy humanity trampling all over the place and destroying any mood of quiet contemplation, strikes me as a backward step. Lock them in the chapter house and discipline them, I say. Right, bee removed from bonnet, let's move on.

The other most striking thing about the abbey vestments takes us back to the visual and symbolic world of the churchyard where we began. On the back of the chasuble is a huge embroidered cross, or orphrey, with biblical scenes embroidered in coloured silks and silver and gold thread. It is a visual account of the life of the Virgin Mary. There's a panel showing a rather pregnant Mary next to a very old and grey-bearded Joseph, who I must say is looking rather shell-shocked. Then there's a nativity scene with a delightfully coy and doe-eyed ox, and Joseph again with his hand on his heart, still protesting his innocence. Baby Jesus is not so much wrapped in swaddling clothes as bound with ropes lying in the manger. It's all charmingly naïve and one wonders at the ingenuous piety of the embroideries who came from professional workshops, mainly in the City of London, and included men as well as women. But a much more dramatic scene depicts the massacre of the innocents and makes much use of red-dyed silk in its gruesome illustration of babes being run through with swords, one child impaled high upon the lance of a soldier, with a river of blood coming from his stomach. Knowing how gory-minded kids are these days, I felt like stopping them as they rushed past and pointing out the scene for them to enjoy. But you can't be too careful nowadays and I might be accused of deviancy by one of the attendants who was already looking suspiciously at me for loitering for so long in such a dark room and taking such interest in embroidery.

I wondered how many ordinary people got the chance to see these pictures back in the fifteenth century. The most lavish details are on the back of the chasuble, prominent when the priest turned towards the altar. All right for the monks to see from their choir stalls. But they would be educated and literate and know their Bible stories. What about the lay brothers who were recruited from the illiterate peasantry to do the manual and agricultural work around the monastery? Their biblical education came from all the visual imagery of carvings and stained glass. But they were confined to the nave at the back of the church during the services and would only see the stunning vestments of the monks if they processed past, which I don't know whether they did. Maybe the sheer ornate magnificence of the vestments was intended more to reflect the wealth and power of the monastic institution then for any didactic purposes.

I don't really think that the ordinary people of Lancashire would care much when the king's men came and sacked Whalley Abbey. They probably helped by carrying off the stones to plug a few holes in their farm walls, much like Dr Whitaker's men 250 years later. They might have missed the alms which the monks were obliged to give out to the poor at the north-west gatehouse, the best preserved of Whalley's monastic buildings and easily ignored because it's further down the road towards the railway viaduct. But the monasteries held a quarter of the land in the country and they had such wealth and power that they were the medieval equivalent of a modern global corporation but with the added irksomeness of being able to tax people by making them pay tithes. The only organised rebellion against the closure of the monasteries came from what has become known as the Pilgrimage of Grace, and this is what finally put the nail in the coffin of our Abbot Paslew.

The Pilgrimage of Grace doesn't seem to have been a Lancashire thing at all. It arose in 1536 out of discontent at Henry VIII's reformation of the church and attempts by his minister, Thomas Cromwell, to increase government control in the north of England. The arrival of Cromwell to collect taxes and dissolve some of the smaller monasteries triggered the revolt. Some 30,000 rebels gathered in York and, supported by the archbishop, set out to march on London demanding a return to papal obedience and a Parliament free from royal influence. But they were tricked into thinking that their demands would be met and, after disbanding, 250 men were executed, including three abbots. Paslew, the Abbot of Whalley, seems to have been implicated because some of his monks gave assistance to rebels from nearby Sawley Abbey. Paslew was hauled off to Lancaster, found guilty of treason, and executed. Only then was the Earl of Sussex sent to Whalley to take possession of the abbey and its treasures. The monks were dispersed, some finding work as parish priests. On the floor of the chantry chapel in the north aisle of Whalley parish church is a tombstone with a foliate cross marked XS, possibly that of Christopher Smith, the last prior of Whalley Abbey. In a rather touching story it's recorded that Smith, being 80 years old and decrepit and having been a monk at Whalley for 50 years, should be granted a stipend of £6 or £7 a year as a parish priest. The tombstone now in the north wall of the church is probably not that of Abbot Paslew as some would have us believe.

> '... the arrival of Thomas Cromwell to collect taxes and dissolve some of the smaller monasteries triggered the revolt'

One neglected monument to the ill-fated Pilgrimage of Grace is to be found above a gate in the south-west corner of Cliviger parish church, the eccentric classically styled structure built by T. D. Whitaker and something of a monument to the doctor's intellectual conceit. Again the light-fingered Whitaker was probably responsible for moving it there from Whalley. It is a cross-head showing a heart set upon a crucifix and bearing the five wounds of Christ. This was the emblem of the Pilgrimage of Grace. I'm glad it's there. It's one of the few historical relics in the village that has escaped the scourges of modernisation or neglect, and I'm thinking not least about the recent shameful destruction wreaked upon Dr Whitaker's house, The Holme. There's rarely a day passes when I don't walk under the cross and think of the doomed rebellion and the unfortunate Paslew. Rather unfairly the abbot martyr doesn't merit an entry in the *Encyclopaedia Britannica*, nor a word of mention in *Chamber's Biographical Dictionary*. (He *does* now gets mentioned in one sentence about Whalley on wikipedia.) Only this lichen-stained cross and the magnificent chasuble in Towneley connect us with the vainglorious Lord of Whalley Abbey.

I came across a more insubstantial reminder of the abbey's past when I last visited the parish church. John Boothman was doing a stint at looking after the church during afternoon visiting hours and as we spoke about the tombstones John suddenly revealed that he'd once seen a ghost in his house in the old west grounds of the abbey. John was 75 and the encounter occurred 38 years before when he was alone in the house preparing it for his forthcoming marriage. As he was busy scrubbing the floor he was struck with a sudden stabbing, cold sensation. He looked up and through a glazed door in the house saw a monk glide past, head down as if meditating. 'He wore a black cowl and the rest seemed to be white,' recalls John. Now, in the small museum just inside the abbey grounds there's a life-size reconstruction of a Cistercian monk wearing a white habit and a black hood, just like John's description. The ghost disappeared through the wall along a ginnel in the direction of the abbey. John seemed very sanguine about the experience, so much so that he and his wife have happily occupied the same house ever since but without any further visitations.

The black and white monks are in evidence today in the abbey grounds. A handful of rather elderly specimens mingle with ladies in bright hats and suits of pink and powder blue. There's a do at the Conference House and on such occasions a group of retired local teachers dress up and give talks and conduct tours of the abbey. As we sit outside the small café in the sun enjoying tea and the sublimely sticky parkin that's made at the abbey, one of the monks glides past towards the bookshop. Several minutes later he emerges in a smart modern suit. He seems to be smiling somewhat ruefully at this strange transformation. If only the past were half so easy to recreate as changing clothes. I know they can do amazing things with computers. Only recently on TV I watched two people walking through the ruined courtyard of a Roman villa while the computer reconstructed the buildings around them. But this depends upon us knowing just what Roman villas were like. It seems to me that there's no such knowledge of the landscape of historical Lancashire except what we can piece together from tantalising clues. For example, after only 20 years at Whalley the monks who came here wanted to pack up and leave, because in 1316 they obtained a grant of land at Toxteth and Smithdown in Liverpool. The reason they gave was that the countryside was too bleak and there weren't enough trees to provide timber and fuel. This is almost impossible to believe when you visit the Whalley of today.

'the Ribble valley is a truly blessed spot'

We climbed up onto the slopes of Whalley Nab to look down on the abbey and the town. The summer is ebbing away and the leaves of the trees are darkening with the tannins of autumn. But even at this time of change it's hard to imagine a more fortunate and bountiful place. We pass banks of ripening blackberries, and the elders are offering us bunches of berries black and bright as birds' eyes. The river winds past and earlier we stood by a weir and watched the water transformed from a glassy smoothness to a turmoil of white ice as it broke on the stones below. And beyond is a small eyot where the willow saplings bend in the breeze and the ducks dabble. This is the Calder, 'a fair river ... wherein is taken Salmon trout with other good fish'. And looking beyond the boundaries of the town the pastures of the Ribble valley are laid out in a rich tablecloth of plenty. It is truly a blessed spot.

But all this is to ignore the way the modern world has superimposed itself upon the landscape like a crude but indelible stencil. And this is what makes it so impossible to visualise the scene 800 years ago. The square stone tower of the abbey gatehouse is visible beyond the trees, but beyond that marches the sprawling Victorian railway viaduct. They've made two of the arches, on either side of the road, into Gothic arches, in a sort of brief genuflection towards the ancient abbey. But for all the fancy, overlapping brickwork, the viaduct is still brick. And red brick at that. It's so brash you could almost admire it. That Victorian self-confidence that couldn't believe any age could surpass its own; that ripped the soul out of so many of our medieval churches and replaced it with their own version of medieval; that recreated and 'improved' upon the classical age. It's there in the viaduct. Gothic Accrington brick, for God's sake!

The sins of the modern age surround the abbey, squeezing out all sense of the past. Stand for long on the bridge over the river to see if there are still fish there and you'll die of exhaust fumes from the traffic. You wouldn't think there was a by-pass. But it's hard to blame people. Who wouldn't want to drive through the charming main street with its cosy-looking pubs and antique shops rather than be bullied along a soulless by-pass by lorries and young executives with deadlines to meet? But you should be able to amble along the river more easily past the abbey grounds. Instead, the east gates are locked and if you try to dodge round you find yourself among exclusive mews house properties. Not friendly old Lancashire any more but twenty-first-century Britain, divided by wealth and by automatic gates. Whalley, to use the inflated language of the estate agents, is a much sought-after place to live. A fashionable dormitory for today's go-getters. We gawp through the window of one estate agent who had a two-bedroom terrace – the sort they are giving away down the road in Burnley – for sale at £162,000. And we laughed out loud at an advert in one window for a chambermaid. The antique shops say it all: raffia-seated church hall chairs, once ten a penny in every junk shop, dressed up as antiques. Whalley has become rather gentrified these days. (I suddenly recall Florrie Birtwell who was 95 at the time I met her and lived in Calder Vale by the river, telling me about how excited she was at the age of 14 to be going to work at the local cotton mill. For her, life's greatest pleasure had been the Whit walks through the town and picking primroses in the country lanes near Wiswell on a Sunday afternoon.) Today, the cars arrive outside the school at 3.15 as the parents come to pick up their children. Enough money laid out in polished metal and smoky exhaust pipes to satisfy the greed of Henry VIII. History, instead of being something to set the pulse racing, has become a commodity, a means of marketing a place and selling a lifestyle. How the first monks of Whalley Abbey would have shook in their hair shirts had they known what they had started.

Another clue to the conditions that would have met the monks when they first arrived in Whalley comes from documents which survive relating to the Abbey of Sawley just seven miles away within the Yorkshire border and founded earlier, about the middle of the twelfth century. In an appeal to the Pope by Edward I to allow the abbey to be granted tithes due to the church at Gargrave, the king describes the parlous state in which the monks found themselves. The abbey, he says, is 'situated as it were in the most castaway and remote parts of all our kingdom towards the Irish sea, and moreover in a country wonderfully wooded and hilly, and, on account of the too great frequency of storms, for the most part barren and unfruitful.' This translation comes from Thomas Whitaker's *History of Craven* and leads the doctor to speculate upon these complaints about the Ribble valley. Despite writing 200 years ago, he fearlessly dons the mantle of the weather forecaster:

> Pendle, Longridge, and the Fells of Bowland, have, in the interval of five centuries, lost nothing of their attractive power over the vapours of the Irish Sea; yet the environs of Salley now produce crops of wheat, which seldom fail to arrive at maturity. But there were at that time probably many swamps, now drained, and great tracts of woodland, now cleared away; the former of which would augment the exhalations, and the latter arrest and detain them, in their first ascent.

However quaint the terminology, it all amounts to a familiar Lancashire story. Rain, showers, drizzle, and more rain.

Calder–Ribble confluence.

The remains of Sawley Abbey.
PHOTOGRAPH: MALCOLM GREENHALGH

But what are we to make of these conflicting accounts of the landscape of 800 years ago? First Edward I tells us the land is wonderfully woody and next the monks of Whalley are wanting to move because they can't find enough firewood. Whitaker thinks the Ribble valley will be full of swamps as well as trees and Edward says it's for the most part barren and unfruitful. All very confusing. But this excursion into the marshes of historical literature is not a complete waste of time. According to Edward I, one of the reasons the monks of Sawley find themselves in such a depressed condition is 'on account of the cruel and inhuman spoliation of their movables, and the horrible burning of some of their places which the evil-disposed army of the Scots ... lately effected.' From a Lancashire of sacred stones and monastic tranquillity we must move on to one of castles and defensive paranoia.

CHAPTER FIVE

NORTHERN FORTRESS

WHEN I USED TO DO WORK for the BBC and had to go down to the loathed London, I often used to say that I'd come down from my fastness in the hills. I was only half-joking. I've always regarded the Pennine hills as my sanctuary, my fortress from which I could look down in secure detachment on the rather silly and self-important preoccupations of London. I know it's supposed to work the other way round and we are seen as the weak-minded hillbillies, cut off from all the major social and cultural trends and the mighty huff and puff of Parliament. Well let them think that. We know different. We have perspective. Lofty, empty hills and wild skies lend a sense of proportion to the petty affairs of men, so that champion of the Northern hills, Wordsworth, can dismiss the metropolis as a 'monstrous ant hill on the plain of a too busy world' and every true northern spirit will cry, 'hear, hear!'

Geography and climate have meant that Lancashire has always been something of a fastness, flanked by sea to the west and defensive mountains to the north and east. You feel that in its darker past travellers journeying northwards must have approached it with some nervousness, like entering a corral, a place of no return. And long before they stuck those impertinent and obtrusive mobile phone masts on every hilltop, we would have our signal stations like those the Romans built where fires could transmit news of an intruder almost as quickly as it takes to send a text message these days. Now far be it for me to destroy the cherished belief that we Lancastrians are the friendliest folk around. This may have been the case after the Industrial Revolution had thrown us all so close together that we couldn't help but mind one another's business, and when getting on was easier than falling out. But my instincts tell me that before this, like all fortress folk, we were probably exceedingly wary of strangers, especially if they were bent on sacking our abbeys or burning our hay ricks and stealing our cattle. This may help to account for why our country was for many years a sort of no man's land.

At the time of Domesday in 1086, Lancashire didn't even have a name. North of the Ribble it was largely split between Yorkshire and a region called Amounderness, a bleak-sounding name for an area corresponding to today's Fylde. And considering the compendious size of the Domesday Book – I have a translation which runs to 1,300 pages of small type – Amounderness merits but a tiny portion, a mere page. The conclusion must be that until this time there was very little land deemed worthy of settlement. In fact, before the Norman Conquest, the north of our county had been part of the earldom of Northumbria, ruled by one Tostig. He was the brother of the unfortunate Harold, who, equally unfortunately sided with the king of Norway and was defeated and killed by his brother at Stamford Bridge before Harold marched south to meet the fateful arrow at Hastings in 1066. After the Conquest, when the Conqueror William doled out the country to his knights and favourites, Roger of Poitou was given the land between the Ribble and the Mersey (described in just two pages in Domesday). Much of this land was used for hunting, and according to Domesday this included the Blackburn Hundred, which stretched from Walton-le-Dale to Pendle, and consisted of many leagues of woodland, formerly the royal estates of Edward the Confessor. Later, Roger became the overlord of the whole of Lancashire, his estates being known as the Honour of Lancaster.

The first thing that the Normans needed to do once they'd conquered England was to secure this wild northern frontier land of ours from rebellious natives who clearly didn't like the idea of Frenchmen just walking in and taking over (early anti-European feeling here), and also protect the borders from the ever-predatory Scots. I'd like to think the locals gave the Normans some grief, none of that renowned Lancashire friendliness (Oh, come in Roger and sit you down. I'll put the kettle on.) Around 1070 there was a period of rebellion which the history books refer to as 'The Harrying of the North', when we northerners put up some stout resistance against the Norman occupation. And to quell the rebellions, castles began to shoot up like brollies at Wimbledon.

We all have a good idea from our primary school days of what a Norman motte and bailey castle should look like, but the real feel of their location, their fortress vantage over the surrounding countryside, can be sensed by a visit to one. And there's no better place then the Lune valley north-east of Lancaster where you have a choice.

I started off at Castle Stede between Hornby and Melling, just a few miles south of Over Burrow, where our Roman road from Ribchester arrives. Having conquered the high and lonely passes of Croasdale and the Bowland fells, it now eases its way through the Lune valley. I mention this because where the Romans had been the Normans often followed. They had the same defensive instincts of all conquerors, establishing their forts and castles at river crossings, with uninterrupted views of the enemy's approach. Castle Stede is

Castle Stede's motte and bailey.
PHOTOGRAPH: AUTHOR

no exception. It stand above and right next to the river Lune at Loyn Bridge, the only crossing point of the river between Lancaster and Kirkby Lonsale. The hillside rises up above the river where a knoll of trees marks the motte or mound upon which the keep of the castle was built. What is startling is that as you approach the site through a stile off the road you are met by the twentieth-century equivalent of a Norman defensive outpost, a Second World War pillbox. It is quite astonishing to think that after a thousand years of human progress we still have to resort to settling our territorial ambitions by warfare. And if you are in any doubt about that still applying today, you don't have long to wait before you are buzzed by a NATO jet roaring overhead up the valley.

At Castle Stede someone has attempted to restore access to the bailey with a small stone-walled walkway across the outer ditch. But once inside the bailey all is empty pasture. But if you climb a small retaining wall you can scramble up among the trees and stand on the mound where the castle keep once stood. The motte is about thirty feet high and maybe sixty feet across. But all the trees prevent you from getting a good view of the surrounding countryside. You end up staggering about snagging your feet on fallen branches and brambles. The mound is littered with rabbit holes and other signs that the soil has been disturbed. I often think what archaeologists rabbits and moles must be, scrabbling about in the earth among its hidden secrets. Your mole may be a nuisance hoofing up your lawn but if you root around amongst the soil he turns up you can find all sorts of things: bits of pottery and clay pipe, ancient nails and even flints – all peace offerings from the diligent mole. I have a shoebox full of interesting objects presented to me by moles and I rarely pass a molehill without dabbling my toe around in it to see what I can find.

But today Castle Stede is keeping its secrets. Clearly the best time to come here is in winter when the trees are bare and you can look right up the Lune valley. Today I can see the cows in the meadow below, many of them lying down, occasionally reaching lazily for the odd blade of grass and chewing contentedly. In the distance I can see the square tower of Melling church peeping above the trees in the sunshine. It's such a peaceful scene it soon dispels all notions of the warlike purpose of the castle. Perhaps it's only through war that we can enjoy peace.

Only when you leave the castle and climb down into the open fields below and walk along the banks of the Lune do you see the wisdom of the site as a defensive position. Wrapped in the arms of the swift, brown river to the west, to the east the northern fells provide a protective bastion, leaving the

The Lune valley stretching northwards.
PHOTOGRAPH: AUTHOR

vista of Lunesdale stretching northwards. You'd feel secure here in whatever time, and my wife and I spend a timeless moment picking up pebbles from the riverside, blues and pinks and yellows which darken when they come into contact with the water, all wonderfully smooth and sculpted by the river. I found one which Barbara Hepworth would have been proud of, with strange holes like eye sockets and irresistible to run your fingers round. Of course, it's now at home on my windowsill along with my molehill offerings. Then we found flat pebbles to skim across the water until they danced and bounced all the way across the river to the willows in the opposite bank. Ah, simple, childish pleasures. The pleasures of peace.

Closer to Lancaster at Halton is another motte and bailey castle. It's up on the hill behind the church. But before you climb up there it's well to have a look at the Viking cross in the churchyard. Our old friend Sigurd from the hogback tombstone in Heysham is there, gorily roasting the heart of the dragon Fafnir on a spit. The cross depicts the whole story from the making of Sigurd's sword to the slaughter of its creator, Regin, when Sigurd is warned by two birds that he is about to kill him. (Apparently, eating dragons enables you to hear the conversation of birds.) The cross serves as a bloodthirsty introduction to the treacherous and warlike times of medieval Lancashire which the Lune castles exemplify. As you climb the hill up the main road to the castle you begin to notice that so many buildings seem to be crenellated, an architectural reminder of the siege mentality which must have dominated these parts. Even as a young adult of the Cold War and the Cuban missile stand-off, I find it hard to imagine living your life with such insecurity.

They're proud of their motte and bailey castle in Halton. You can tell that because they've stuck a flagpole on top. The motte is small but perfectly formed, and you'll enjoy standing on the top and getting an uninterrupted view, this time of the wooded banks of the river with Ingleborough and Leck Fell flanking the Lune valley to the east. The strategic significance of Halton to an area troubled by invaders from the north was obvious. But seven centuries on and the town has fallen asleep. Only the restless guttural roar of traffic from the nearby M6 disturbs the peace as people, untroubled by history, pass between two nations once so bloodily at odds.

Before the Conquest Halton, not Lancaster, was the administrative centre of the area. But in the early 1090s, after William Rufus expelled the Scots from Cumbria and established the Anglo-Scottish border where it is today, the whole of Lancashire was concentrated into the hands of Roger of Poitou and Lancaster became his headquarters. You only need to stand on Castle Hill in the town to see the advantages of this new site as the centre of what was to become the Honour of Lancaster and the county as we know it today. It not only commands a view of the Lune to the north and the Fylde to the south, but in addition it looks across Morecambe Bay to the lands of Cartmel and Furness, parts of Lancashire stolen from us in 1974 without the shedding of a drop of blood but merely the ink from the pen of bureaucrats. Surely a new slant on the old adage, the pen is mightier than the sword.

After the empty acres of the Lune valley I was rather looking forward to the bustling confines of Lancaster. Now this may sound strange coming from someone who exults in his lonely Pennine fastness. But then I have a particular weakness for the delight of Ye Olde John o' Gaunt pub in the centre of the city opposite the city museum. The John o' Gaunt is all jazz and clutter, scumbled walls in nicotine yellow with framed beer mats, green button-back seats in gentlemen's club leather and a dark green roof done in syrupy gloss. A message on a blackboard reads, 'The liver is evil and must be punished'. There's a rare intelligence at work here for a pub. They have malt whisky nights on a Monday, and a notice tells you that chess sets are available from behind the bar. You can eat baguettes with feta cheese, basil and tomatoes and the pint of Timothy Taylor's Landlord I had was to dream about. You're as likely to meet a prof from the university swatting up on his Beowulf as a middle-aged escapee from Essex wearing a baseball cap and enthusing about Jelly Roll Morton. It's university meets Bohemia and it's a great novelty to anyone used to pubs with horse-brasses and bogus coal fires

Cheers! Ye Olde John o'Gaunt.

or one-armed bandits and Sky TV. It's a real city pub in a setting which is still small and intimate enough to be a market town. I love it and have booked my seat in the corner to retire into.

Within easy staggering distance of the Old John o' Gaunt is the museum. The armchair explorer is spared trekking up Roman roads and fossicking in ancient churchyards by a visit here. The artefacts on display capture perfectly the excitement and mystery of our early history. Just inside the foyer is a fine Roman milestone which dates back to the Emperor Hadrian. It's 9 feet high and was found at Caton. The inscription says it's four miles (*milia passum*, or thousand paces) to Lancaster. (They took big strides, these Romans. People bent on conquest often do.) I'd never thought of these huge columnar milestones besides the Roman roads when I set out from Ribchester a couple of months ago. How I'd have scrabbled around more in ditches and walls looking for fragments if I had. Half of this business of discovering your own past is knowing what to look for. Upstairs, and the first room you walk into, you are confronted by four huge stone heads, thought to represent the seasons, and part of a third-century mausoleum. There was a stool nearby and I needed it to take in the awesome impact of these carvings. They are huge, fat, gravelly faces with great empty eyes. They have such presence, convey such a mute challenge, obdurately stationed under the quartz halogen spotlights, the sandstone still tinted green with lichen, sparkling with mica.

But no amount of modern enlightenment will reveal what was going on inside the heads of the men who carved them. They're haunting. Even when you turn your back on them and move on, you can feel their primitive power reaching after you.

Nearby is a Roman altar to a river god of the Lune. Do you mean to say that while we were skimming pebbles the other day at Castle Stede we were being watched by a river god? And did we do nothing to propitiate it? For such gross neglect can we expect death by drowning next time we cross a river? I try to make things right and, to the consternation of the other visitors, read out the words on the altar like a spell: '*Deo Ialono contrebi sanctissi.*' To the most holy god, Jalonus Contrebis. There, that should do it. I hope.

And then something creepily disconcerting. The Quernmore Dark Age coffin burial. Two canoe-like halves of hollowed-out oak pegged together to enclose a body. But the only thing that remained when it was opened in 1973 was a pile of hair and some toe and fingernails. And there they are, laid out for you to contemplate mortality. Hair and fingernails. And nothing else. Weirdly, the hair still shines, as if it had just been brushed. But it has changed colour, long, tangled locks of red, stained by the acid soil and the tannins from the coffin. And the fingernails are revolting, thick, black excrescences. The rest of the body, it appears, had dissolved in the acid peat of the soil in the thirteen hundred years that it had lain there.

You are ready to be consoled by the subdued choral chants coming from the next display after that. The plainsong confers a strangely other-worldly atmosphere to the section which deals with early Christianity. There's the cast of an Anglican cross from the priory church next to the castle (I'll give you one guess as to where the original cross is). It is decorated with whorls and interlacing chains and, most fascinating of all, runic inscriptions. The runes are strange, twig-like glyphs, more the sort of thing that I in my overheated imagination associated with curses rather than prayers. But apparently they read, 'Pray for Cynibald, son of Cuthberect'. I don't know who can translate this sort of thing, but I'll bet they get in to The Olde John o' Gaunt! There's part of a stone throne discovered in a grave at St Patrick's chapel at Heysham Head. It's in the shape of a huge bird's head, a rather glum looking creature with a raptorial beak and a very beady eye which follows you all the way past and into your dreams. The museum is an inspiration for anyone seeking to discover an exciting new dimension to Lancashire's history without stepping off the beaten track. I can guarantee that after a visit you'll never shop again in Lancaster without wondering what other marvels lie undiscovered beneath the foundations of Woolworths and British Home Stores.

High upon its hill, Lancaster Castle is a spectacular defensive stronghold. It may have been built to keep intruders out, but today they're just as concerned about keeping people in. As much as half the castle is now a prison and the only flag that flies from its keep is a blue and white affair which denotes Her Majesty's Prison Service. As you approach, it's a forbidding and unwelcoming prospect, all portcullis doors and barred windows and stone balconies decked with wrought-iron spikes and razor wire on the roof. A young man is posing in front of the prison gates while his girlfriend takes his picture, sufficient of an odd affair to make me wonder what the caption will be when it finds its way into the family album. 'Our Kev was 'ere, 2000–2004'? This might be the gatehouse built in 1400 by Henry IV, Duke of Lancaster, but I get none of the customary vibes from our great and glorious history, only a sense of the misery of incarceration. In the damp and rat-infested dungeon of the well tower, the 80-year-old witch Demdike died while awaiting execution. And George Fox, the Quaker dissenter, was imprisoned for believing that all men were equal in the eyes of God. Am I the only person to find the statue of John of Gaunt in the niche above the gateway slightly ridiculous? It was placed there in 1822 and shows the old warrior in his armour, one hand resting on his sword, the other on his hip. To me, he manages to strike a posture of effeminacy rather than belligerence. Perhaps the sculptor got him mixed up with Edward II.

If you pass the gatehouse in the direction of the church, you come to the courtyard into which they brought the prisoners to hang them. The last person to be disposed of this way, in 1910, was a young man called Thomas Rawcliffe. There's a picture of him inside, scowling like a truculent schoolboy in a schoolboy's cap. People used to come in their thousands to stand in the churchyard and watch the executions. The boys from the local grammar school were even given a day off to come and watch. It was thought to be an edifying spectacle which would discourage evildoing. Today there's a wind blowing off the sea making the rope on the flagpole tick like a pulse. The first fallen leaves of autumn are rustling across the cobbles like the restless spirits of the dead, sent from the gallows to their graves in unhallowed ground beyond the churchyard.

We paid to go on one of the half-hour tours. We were the only ones, and our guide was a somewhat formidable figure dressed in a black full-length coat reminiscent of a Boot Hill undertaker. But I bucked up a bit when she announced that she was a member of the Guild of Virgins, until I realised that I must have misheard her and it was the Guild of Vergers, an office to do with the priory church next door. We were conducted through the civil and criminal courts which still convene at the castle before being shown into Adrian's Tower, named after the emperor Hadrian, mistakenly thought to have had a hand in its construction. Here, in the claustrophobia of five-feet thick walls, it is a veritable museum of official sadism, a collection of chains, manacles, scold's bridles, lunatics' chairs and other restraining apparatus belonging to a time when any deviation from the norm was usually treated with incarceration and ultimately death. There then followed a conversation of the kind, 'But don't you think things have gone too far the other way these days?' normally associated with *Daily Mail* editorials. I thought it wise to remain silent, especially since we had now passed into the prison cells and our host was opening one of the massive oak doors and encouraging us to step inside to sample the dank, airless and totally black interior. The tour was interesting, but probably not to be recommended to those of liberal leanings likely to suffer from depression when confronted by man's long history of inhumanity to his fellow man.

We next stepped across the way to the priory church. If you like nothing better than to hear the heavy creak of an oak door and enjoy the sniff of venerable mildew which is the first step to exploring an ancient church, Simon Jenkins' guide *England's Thousand Best Churches* is indispensable. In the book, Lancashire merits only a very disappointing eleven entries, only half of which are medieval, the rest being largely Victorian. Compare this with, say, Norfolk, where there are 65 fine churches listed, most dating from the middle ages. I think this says a lot about the relative poverty and sparsity of Lancashire in those times. We have to wait until the Industrial Revolution before the surplus wealth of the rich and successful could be lavished upon fine public buildings. Also, being of a somewhat macabre turn of mind, I've often wondered about how badly we suffered from the ravages of the Black Death. I can't believe that we would have escaped from a disease which wiped out over a third of the population of fourteenth-century England, unless our isolation and fortress mentality did enough to insulate us from the rest of the stricken population. But I can find no documentary reference to the

> 'Our guide was reminiscent of a Boot Hill undertaker'

Great Plague, no grim little skeletons tucked away in the darkest corners of the churches I've so far visited. It's a fitting quest for a wet Saturday afternoon in January and would make an engaging topic of conversation over tea afterwards.

Jenkins likes the priory church in Lancaster. He finds it more interesting than the castle. This can only be because of the choir stalls which he believes are some of the most remarkable woodcarvings in the north of England. The canopies contain some of the most intricate carvings of foliage and heads imaginable and date from around the time of the Black Death. But I must say that while admiring their astonishing detail and complexity, I was somewhat disappointed by their appearance. There is a grey patina of dust on them which deadens the wood and renders them dull. The ladies of the parish have done their best, and in the 1960s set colourful modern tapestries into the back of the seats to set off the wonderful carvings. But for me they only accentuate their dullness. We spoke to Howard, the head verger, who had been vigorously mopping the tombstones below the chancel steps and seemed to show a remarkable talent for domesticity for a male. He told us that he regularly dusted the canopies above the choir stalls but that you had to be very careful in case bits dropped off, so fine was the workmanship. I wonder if some sort of lighting behind the gables and shining through the tracery would show them off to better effect? The hinged seats of stalls, or misericords, remain down, perhaps a wise precaution to discourage inspection of the carvings beneath. Many of the faces have been broken off, allegedly by Cromwell's men, but one in particular is quite shocking to anyone with a certain moral injunction of St Paul still ringing in their ears. It shows an angel indulging in a very un-angel-like activity, one normally associated with pubescent boys. I should never have realised what was going on had Howard, with all the glee of a mischievous angel himself, not been so eager to point it out. Quickly returning the seat to its chaste position, I couldn't help but hear the snicker of rude choirboys down the ages echoing in the holy shadows.

Simon Jenkins himself is very rude about Lancaster and her planners. Sampling the view seawards from outside the church, he observes only 'a wilderness of warehouses, roads and estates'. It's hard not to agree with him. On the afternoon I was there, the raucous cries of football supporters from the stadium below were rising into the air, noises which made our soldiers the most feared in Europe during the middle ages and still strike fear into the hearts of the natives of the Spanish costas. It is indeed a badly contained sprawl of haphazard development, of featureless flats and warehouses and wastelands of nettles and brown docks. In the distance the giant cellblocks of Heysham power station are darkly silhouetted against the shimmering sea. Only the occasional loitering gull lifts the eye to Morecambe Bay and the

> 'The snicker of rude choirboys echoes down the ages'

Author's wife relaxes outside priory church.
PHOTOGRAPH: AUTHOR

mountains beyond to raise the spirits. Returning from the castle down the hill, you can enjoy the pleasing jumble of handsome three-storey Georgian houses with smaller cottages tucked between them. The doors are all equally handsome and tastefully painted, and I wondered whether there'd been some planning edict which had ensured this sensitive conformity.

The Judges' Lodgings, with its cobbled frontage and gilt coat-of-arms above the doorway, is fine, but then you are back into the town and confronted by Lancaster's greatest *bete noir*: traffic. The old A6 runs straight through the town and though it is only one-way, the streets are so narrow and the buildings so tall, the noise is amplified to levels only exceeded by the main runway at Manchester airport. In doing its best to disperse this congested nightmare as quickly as possible perhaps, the pedestrian crossings have all been set to such intervals before they turn to green that you can stand and wait while whole empires rise and fall. If impatient people die while trying to dash across, as many more must expire while just waiting. Once across the A6, the town centre is mercifully pedestrianised. It's a warren of shopping streets, cosy or claustrophobic, depending upon your love of shopping. I hate the activity and so find Lancaster too congested. The square in front of the museum – Lawks! I'm back at Ye Olde John o' Gaunt again! I wonder why? – lacks any of the real generosity of size that you'd expect from a thriving, busy city. There's barely room for the pigeons to take off without flying into you. Perhaps it's the town's defensive heritage. Closing ranks in face of the enemy. Fortress Lancaster.

CHAPTER SIX

A FURNESS FORAY

O NCE AT LANCASTER it's tempting to make a quick dash across Morecambe Bay, or, in consideration of the well-publicised dangers, a tortuous journey round the coast road, to see what was stolen from us in the local government reorganisation of 1974 and whether or not we should care. Cartmel, of course, is now in Cumbria, and with Simon Jenkins averring that the priory church there is the most beautiful church in the north west, perhaps it was time for me to make a belated protest against this act of bureaucratic larceny.

Equinoctial storms are sweeping across the bay today, bringing dark curtains of rain which are turning to hailstones in the cold exhalations (to borrow a word from the good Dr Whitaker) of the Lake District mountains. In a brief interval of dazzling sunshine we stand in the churchyard to examine the curious tower with the belfry set at 45° to the square tower beneath. There's an opaqueness to the limestone which even the sunlight cannot bring alive. It is pale and dead, like cement, reminding me of those glum imported boulders in the car park at Heysham village. Maybe we're spoilt for stone in Lancashire with our warm Pennine sandstone, invigorated by sunlight and the gloss of rain. No wonder people steal our stone. You can't keep a decent set of flags these days without some lout coming along in the night and prising them up and sending them off on a lorry to the Home Counties. It's become one of the county's major exports.

The church at Cartmel is all that is left of the Augustinian priory founded there towards the end of the twelfth century. It survived the suppression of the monasteries because the parishioners managed to convince the royal officials that it was also the parish church, which they would rather like to continuing using. Part of the fun of a visit to the priory church is to try and discover what else you can find of the priory buildings. Most obvious is the gatehouse

Cartmel Priory and its curious tower.
PHOTOGRAPH: MALCOLM GREENHALGH

to the west of the church which leads into the market square. Unlike the north-west gatehouse at Whalley, where the stone vaults are impressively displayed, at Cartmel they've been clumsily rendered over and the ceiling is just a grey and dingy mess. Back at the church you can stand near the graveyard and see ghost doorways in the south wall which would have given access to the church from the monks' dormitory. And just round the corner by the porch are two of the corbels which would have supported the lean-to roof of the cloisters. But it's when you step inside the seventeenth-century porch that you find the wonderful early Gothic doorway which would have led from the cloisters into the church. It is old, dating from the last years of the twelfth century. Tiers of tooth-carved stones arch elegantly from the columns at either side of the door. (Is this a serpent which coils out of the arch to the right?) The doorway is an uplifting entry into the church and a preparation in style for the arcades in the chancel with the beautifully lit triforium striding out above like the cloisters of heaven. In fact, they've placed white angels blowing trumpets beneath every arch, very pre-Reformation. But they seem to be made from paper and are very frilly, and their presence arrests the eye from its journey along the fluid ripple of stonework. And, alas, they made me notice the modern radiators in the gallery behind, which rather broke the medieval spell I was under. But I mustn't quibble. They are obviously well-intentioned.

There are plenty of carvings to enjoy on the misericords. There's a scary winged and clawed demon baring its teeth balefully; a truly horrid pig-like demon with a nasty grin; a green man; a mermaid, said to symbolise the lusts of the flesh; an ape holding a flask (probably of urine), thought to be a satire on medical doctors; some savage hounds poised to strike down a hind; a hedgehog; and an elephant and castle, with the elephant looking more like a horse and making me wonder whether the fifteenth-century carver had ever seen an elephant. The stalls behind are all Jacobean and rather too formal for my liking, although they do shine nicely. Jenkins thinks the walls of the chancel cry out for limewash to cover the bare stone. This is plain nonsense because the stone is a lot warmer and more attractive inside, being tinged with the ochre of ironstone. The east window is huge, apparently modelled on that of the Minster at York. Unfortunately it's fairly empty of stained glass, and today the trees outside wave rather eerily and out of focus in the translucent panes: wild nature clamouring for redemption and trying to get into the sanctuary. The most beautiful coloured glass is in the Town Choir on the south side of the chancel. They form a Jesse window, a collection of bearded patriarchs in solemn conversation, thought to comprise the lineage of Jesus. Christ himself is in the centre, shown in glory wearing a gold crown and carrying a mace. The blues of the glass are not as striking as the cobalts in the east window, but it is the golds of the garments, the green of the leaves and the ruby red background which make this stained glass so beautiful. When you learn that it dates from 1340, your sense of wonder intensifies.

Sepulchral drama.
The Harrington tomb.
PHOTOGRAPH: AUTHOR

But I like the Harrington tomb best of all. John Harrington was the lord of the manor who died in 1347. (Just in time to avoid the Black Death!) His tomb is set into the wall at the south side of the sanctuary. In fact, the wall has been removed and the tomb is under an arch where it's best inspected from the side chapel. It has life-sized effigies of Lord John and his wife surrounded by elaborate carvings of saints and angels. The couple, he with a lion at his feet and she with a dog, stare upwards to a painted roof or tester showing the figure of Christ in glory. Her face is worn to a pale blank; he is frowning, annoyed perhaps that his nose has been chipped off. My wife, strict on matters of sexual equality, observes that her ladyship rests several inches lower down from her lord and master, reflecting the inferior status of women in the medieval scheme of things. But what interested me most of all were the minor players in this medieval sepulchral drama. Round the bottom of the tomb are tiny, dwarf-like figures. These are bedesmen, clergy, or perhaps in this case monks, endowed – as so often before the Reformation – to pray for the souls of the departed. Hooded, they huddle in groups reading from prayer books at their knees, a carved cameo of grief, their stooping figures and worn, expressionless faces conveying perfectly a poignant sense of emptiness and loss. Another suggestion is that they might be canons singing over the souls of the deceased. The Harrington tomb was opened in 1832 and some of the objects enclosed can be seen on display in the south transept. They include the leg bone of a hawk.

I thought I might have found a reference to the Black Death in some of the tombstones set into the floor of the church. Many are carved with a skull and crossbones. In the nave they are so worn that only the eye sockets remain, trapping the deep shadows. But all the burials date from the early eighteenth century. It seems that the district must have had a mason of a particularly morbid temperament and this must have been his trademark. Interestingly under the crossbones is carved an hourglass. In one grave, the hourglass is on its side. A shortage of room? Or did the deceased die prematurely, before even the hourglass had time to run out?

We had a chat with the elderly lady in charge of the bookstall and asked if she minded Cartmel and the Furness peninsula being stolen from Lancashire. 'No,' she told us in an accent you could cut like a Bury pudding, 'I'm still a Lancashire lass at heart.' I wish I'd had the chance to ask her what she thought of the restaurant we passed on the way back to the car. Sheltering from another vicious attack of hailstones, we studied the menu outside. You could have butternut squash and tangerine soup, chips done in peppered parmesan, scrambled egg, smoked eel and hyssop froth, something or other with 'a hint of woodruff' and a selection of bottled aromas. And if that wasn't enough for your finely tuned tastebuds there was always the 'Cubism in foie gras' to try. At £95 the bill hits like a lump of Lakeland slate. At last I'd found the reason why we let Cartmel go.

On now, further round the coast road to Furness Abbey. And again it's stone which makes the first and lasting impression. We're back to sandstone again, but this time it's red, flushed with the iron deposits of the Furness peninsula. Founded in 1127 the abbey was one of the most important Cistercian abbeys in the north of England after Fountains. The monks mined the local iron ore and owned great areas of land in Lakeland and the Pennines where they grew rich from the wool trade. They had a port at Piel Island and exported to Ireland as well as across country and into Europe. Like Sawley they did not escape the depredations of the Scots, especially after their victory over the English at Bannockburn. Furness was attacked in 1316 and 1322. But in the second raid the abbot of Furness, John Cockerham, entertained Robert the Bruce at the abbey and agreed to pay him a ransom against any further attacks. The abbey was one of the first to be dissolved, in 1537, and the buildings are said to have been pulled down even while the monks were still living there.

The commissioners didn't do as thorough a job of dismantling the abbey as they did at Whalley. Today, huge walls tower skywards at either end of the church. You can gain some impression of the size of the central tower from inspecting the remains of the piers which supported it. The site was so boggy that the abbey had to be built on a raft of oak, a piece of which can be seen in the visitor centre. Red gargoyles have been set dramatically against the white walls, and the effigies of the barons of Kendal lie upon the floor clad in full armour, injured only by time and not battle, their wimpled ladies at their side. Even supine they look tall and imposing and I have to quell a quirky instinct to lie down besides one of them to see how tall they were. One lies with his legs crossed and is immortalised in Wordsworth's

Furness Abbey's dissolving stonework.

Prelude. The Romantics were apparently great visitors to Furness, revelling in its atmosphere of picturesque decay. The presence of the knights is a reminder of the close association of piety and chivalry in the medieval mind. But this was the age of the Crusades when there was no such thing as the modern dichotomy between war and the Christian religion. In any case, with Robert the Bruce and his men on the loose, the abbey would be glad of the patronage of a few knights. It also gives me the justification for this detour to the religious houses of Cartmel and Furness when I'd set out in search of north Lancashire's castles.

A walk around Furness Abbey helps in an understanding of Whalley's less complete remains. Much of the east range still survives with its book cupboards and elaborately carved archway into the chapter house, whose walls and finely ornamented windows, unlike Whalley, still stand. But the limitations of the red sandstone are all too apparent. It is soft and porous and with time it has let down the efforts of the medieval craftsmen. Whatever elaborate workmanship once crowned these arches is now sadly worn to a series of amorphous lumps. No games here, tracing the outline of thrusting heads or strange lithic beasts. I'm afraid I'm disappointed and it's the stone that's to blame. Perhaps it's an acquired taste, this red sandstone. But I'm finding the colour too oppressive. It reminds me of the red brick of our industrial towns and has the same depressing effect. And the fact that the walls tower above you in the rather narrow sanctuary intensifies the oppressive, claustrophobic effect of the stonework.

It's a good job I met Tom to lift my spirits. He was the only other person in the abbey when I was there and he was up a ladder cleaning the stonework with a wire brush. Tom was 63 and he had been cleaning the lichen and moss from the abbey stonework for the past six years. He's measured out his life in the countless wire brushes he's been through. Nowadays he's at it seven days a week, often starting at 6 a.m. in the summer. When I strike up a conversation with him he's soon down his ladder and showing me around. He proudly points out the floor of the nave where he's spent most of the summer on his hands and knees. It makes a real difference. The lichen is pale and unsightly if it's left. You can see it at its worst where he's not allowed to work high up on the walls, creeping and dribbling down, a kind of eczema on the skin of the stone. Tom befriends those who come down from the nearby hospital seeking comfort and peace in the tranquillity of the setting. It's as if, even as a ruin, the abbey is still fulfilling its spiritual function. He's a Barrow man and I took to him as a fellow Lancastrian. But I didn't love his abbey like he did. Perhaps it would take many more visits, coming sometimes like Tom does at three o'clock in the morning on moonlit nights, the time when the monks would have been rising from their dormitory to shuffle down into the great church to say their prayers at the beginning of the monastic day 800 years ago.

CHAPTER SEVEN

A QUEST FOR THE GREEN KNIGHT

SETTING ASIDE the spiritual havens of our monasteries, an insight into the more outlandish nature of our region in medieval times comes from an unexpected source, a poem. *Sir Gawain and the Green Knight* was written in the late fourteenth century by a poet whose distinctive dialect and geographical references are decidedly north-western. Sir Gawain's journey in quest of the Green Knight to whom he must submit to a beheading which he, a year earlier, had inflicted upon the giant at the court of King Arthur, is into the Pennines. It is a winter journey and takes us into a landscape which is part of the soul of every northerner, something uncomfortably harsh but at the same time remotely beautiful. It is a world away from the smooth sophistication of the courtly society of the south, and, with its insistent alliteration and hard northern vowels, the poem rings with the crack of ice and bursting mountain torrents, and the almost brutal honesty and uncompromising integrity of the hero himself, Gawain.

Gawain's journey north to honour his tryst with the Green Knight in his green chapel takes him through North Wales and Anglesey and across the River Dee into the Wirral. There he has to contend with the full panoply of beasts and monsters from our medieval church carvings made flesh.

> Sometimes with dragons he fought and with wolves also,
> Sometimes with wild men who dwelt amongst the rocks,
> Both with bulls and bears and wild boars
> And giants that pursued him over the high fells.

To suggest that the Wirral and the lands around were overrun by dragons and giants in the fourteenth century is, of course, far-fetched, but only as far-fetched as a story of a green man who, as soon as his head is struck off with an axe, pops it back on again, mounts his horse and rides off into his northern fastness. The point the poet is making to his audience, comfortably ensconced in their baronial halls or maybe even in their well-appointed monasteries, is that this region of England he is describing is fraught with dangers, if not supernatural, human. So bad was the reputation of the Wirral for harbouring armed bands of outlaws, that in 1376 a petition was sent to the Black Prince from the citizens of Chester urging the disafforestation of the area, which would mean the abolition of the protection which the royal forest afforded miscreants. It is difficult to conceive what this landscape must have been like, especially today when the only things that have sprung up to replace the forest are the monstrous steelwork and pipelines of the chemical plants around Runcorn, and the only dangers to life which now exist come from inhaling too deeply anywhere within their vicinity.

Gawain's journey through this region in search of the Green Knight's chapel seems to have been a very haphazard affair and has left scholars of the poem quite dizzy with speculation as to where his travels actually took him. He certainly seems to have left the plains of North Cheshire and strayed into the wild hill country to the east, to judge from the description of the landscape through which he and his horse struggle.

> They journeyed by slopes where boughs were bare,
> They climbed cliffs where the cold clung;
> The clouds were high but ugly thereunder,
> Mist hung on the moors, melted on the mountains;
> Each hill had a hat, a huge mist-hackle;
> Brooks boiled and broke by banks about
> Bursting white on stones where they plunged down.
> Wondrous wild was the way by woods they went.

This is familiar territory to all who have clambered the cloughs and tramped the moors of the Pennine hills in winter. As a daily observer of Pendle Hill, I can vouch for the regular appearance of 'mist-hackles', that cap of cloud the hill often wears which is like the raised hairs on the back of a giant animal. But most scholars plump for the Peak District on the Staffordshire/Derbyshire border for where Gawain finally meets up with the axe-wielding Green Knight, though why he should have got as far as the Wirral only to turn back south again, I don't know. If for no other reason than regional chauvinism, I prefer the suggestion of Dr J. P. Oakden, a Manchester University man writing in 1930, that Gawain journeyed further north to Clitheroe where he spent Christmas as the guest of the lord of the castle before travelling on New Year's Day to the nearby Green Chapel, successfully to honour his tryst with the Green Knight and emerge unscathed from the giant's axe-blow.

Today Clitheroe Castle stands fortress-square upon its limestone outcrop above the town. From Main Street people must have looked up and felt reassured. Here was somewhere to scuttle to in times of trouble. From below

Clitheroe's grizzled castle keep.
PHOTOGRAPH: AUTHOR

it looks dark and solemn, absorbing the sunlight. None of the wistful romance of Camelot and Arthur's court, but something more in keeping with the grim reality of Gawain's lethal quest. His life is on the line; a sense of dread has dogged his every footstep up here. Up North where it's savage and wild.

I climb up towards the keep. The rock is a maze of saplings. Ivy clings to the stone, the security of this castle rock. They've spread chippings over all the rock gardens to suppress the weeds, stifling unwanted life, again with stone. Everything, it seems to me, is a statement of obdurate intent. The steps that climb to the top are thick as doorsteps. But there's no welcome mat. This is a fortress.

Only at the top do you lose the sense of oppression when the sky splits open in a yellow grin. You're there on the bailey wall and there's a walkway where you can inspect the land around as far as the rim of the sky. The Ribble valley is a soft bowl full of light. And there's Longridge Fell, dark with woodland, pushing the Hodder and Ribble together until they meet at Mitton, where they discover how much they have in common, and join up to spend the rest of their lives together. Behind you is the defensive bulwark of Pendle Hill, its northern slopes a soft scoop of mellowing brown. Eastwards is the Aire Gap, but before that a plume of cement dust rising lazily from the cement factory, mingling with the pale smoke from the chimney and dispersing, conveniently, across Waddington Fell. (When it rains, do the sheep there get concrete coats?) Below, Clitheroe rests, confident in its middle-class prosperity. Today is the autumn equinox, and the summer has grown stale and tired but is

Pendle from Downham Green
PHOTOGRAPH: AUTHOR

hanging on, which is all life can do. To the west where the clouds are silver in the dropping sun the first fires of winter are being lit in the terraces of Low Moor and the smoke shakes itself free of the chimneys and drifts away over the yellowing fields.

Turning away from this seductively peaceful scene I enter the castle keep. It is grey and grizzled and the walls are eight feet thick. Inside it is grimly claustrophobic, no more than fifteen yards square. I'm hemmed in by rough stone. Nevertheless, this is still a place of trysts, perhaps not quite in the Gawain tradition, but boy and girl stuff. Inside one of the stone alcoves a love-lorn youth has written a poem in felt-tip pen which begins, 'My heart still aches with love for her ...' It is lengthy and heart-felt and is a warm, human presence amongst all this cold stone, this grim history of war and hatred. Thank you Mat, whoever you are. I hope your words melted her heart. Sir Gawain's honour is tested in the castle when he is tempted by the lord's wife in her husband's absence. He resists and departs to meet his fate at the hands of the Green Knight. The poem tells us that his chapel is not more than two miles away, so I set off down the hill towards the Roman road which runs north from Ribchester towards Elslack and then on to Ilkley and York.

I hope to pick up the Roman road just north of the village of Worston, but the sign I follow leads to a busy by-pass and the footpath has morphed into a cycle-way which heads off alongside the road. But then it gives up, as cycle-paths always do, and I'm left trudging along the by-pass verge with juggernauts hurtling past and mothers pointing me out to their children in passing cars: 'Look at the funny man, he's actually walking!' My OS map definitely shows a footpath here, so it must be out of date. Once more the humble pedestrian has to defer to the imperatives of motorised transport. The road has been driven through a hill, and there's a cliff face with a notice warning me of falling boulders, and on my other side is the tarmac full of thundering lorries. I am, it seems, between a rock and a hard place. If Gawain's quest was ever brought up to date, these are the hardships he would face, not steep hills and tumbling waterfalls but the concrete jungle of today. One interpretation of the Green Knight fable is that it is an environ-mental parable. The Green Knight is Nature and our contract with it has to be honoured. The denuding and over-hunting of the forests was already an issue back in the fourteenth century. Who could have dreamed that it would all end up in this nightmare? I pick up a piece of high-class rural refuse. It is the latest edition of something called *Country View* that someone has tossed out of their Range Rover. 'On Target,' it halloos on the front cover. 'The Duke of Northumberland on why country sports play a vital role.' Go blam 'em, your Lordship!

I make a dash for the nearest field and look out towards a limestone hill. It's Worsaw Hill, which the erudite Dr Oakden reckons Gawain would have passed. But I'm not happy. This landscape is far too comfortable, with its rolling pastures and wooded knolls. There's nothing 'wondrous wild' about this. But the limestone is interesting because it means caves, and when

Gawain meets up with the Green Knight he emerges from a cave, 'whirling out of his lair with a fell weapon'. I inspect the limestone hillsides for caves but only find one barely big enough for a rabbit to live in, never mind a green giant. I also find a dead sheep crouched under a log in a splutter of torn wool. Overhead a kestrel hovers, ignoring my presence. The rest of the sheep ignore me, too. And why not? Am I real? A bloke wandering around fields clutching an edition of the *Early English Text Society* looking for a green man. Touched or what? The stink of the dead sheep drives me away upwind. And then a piece of luck. I find the Roman road, the 'agger' I learned to recognise at Cow Ark, plainly visible across the field. I follow it, buoyed by a sense of adventure. But I soon arrive at a gate marked 'Private' and have to make a detour. Oakden writes of plenty of barrows in this area. Nowadays they are impossible to recognise amongst the well-groomed pastures and managed coppices. I end up in a wood where many of the trees have been marked for felling. Chainsaws these days, not axes. Imagine what it would be like if Hollywood got hold of the story: 'Gawain and the Green Giant Chainsaw Massacre'?

I'm back on the road that leads to Downham. Somewhere beside it, or under it, lies the Roman road. I pass a house called Greendale which does teas. Should I knock and ask if the Green Chapel is nearby? They probably get people like me all the time, asking for Postman Pat. On the right as you enter the village is Downham Hall. It holds the key to the village, the rather disconcerting quietness that meets me. The pub is closed, the forecourt bare. The main street, whilst undoubtedly picture postcard, has a lifeless tidiness to it. It doesn't look lived in. There's no clutter like you expect wherever people gather. No individuality. I was reminded of a poem by Robert Graves about a visit to a dying man. It's called *It Was All Very Tidy*. Smoke rises from some of the cottage chimneys, and it's as grey as the rather grizzled limestone many of the houses are built of, as if some planning regulations had obliged them to match, to fit in with the greyness of Pendle Hill which fills the background. I know it's picturesque in summer and people love to come here in their hundreds to picnic by the river and feed the ducks, but today we're on the threshold of winter and the mist-hackles rise over Pendle Hill, and Downham to me seems as welcoming as a north wind and a face full of sleet. And I wonder if it is all because of the dead hand of feudalism. 'The lord of the manor owns everything as far as the eye can see,' a resident told me ruefully. 'All the houses, the pub, the post office. They all belong to the Assheton family up at the hall.' Now here's an issue to debate over a long winter's evening. Does the controlling hand of an autocrat, whether it be a lord of the manor or a National Park or the pernickety watchfulness of the National Trust, improve our rural heritage by curbing the wilder excesses of the individual? Or does it lead to the sort of sterile, rather precious prettiness that met me in Downham, turning it into the kind of place you traipse round on a Sunday afternoon when you've nothing better to do before hurrying home with a sign of relief to your often untidy, sometimes chaotic, but always real

The Green Chapel?
PHOTOGRAPH: AUTHOR

life at home? Maybe I'm doing Downham a disservice. Perhaps I visited them at the wrong time, a Friday afternoon, when everyone disappears to do their shopping at the supermarket in town. Maybe in a couple of hours they'll all rush home, throw open the door of the pub and spend the rest of the night in rustic revelry with a knees-up in the local tithe barn.

I visit the post office to ask if anyone has heard of a Green Chapel hereabouts. Probably to get rid of me they send me up onto Downham Green. This is on the north side of the village where the Roman road passes. I tramp up through plashy pastures and am rewarded by fine views of Ribblesdale. The clouds are brewing dark over Waddington Fell. Ingleborough is melting into the sky. Pen-y-ghent has already disappeared and the rain arrives. I spend an awkward couple of minutes trying to stuff my rather cumbersome copy of the Gawain poem down the front of my trousers to keep it dry, hoping I'm not being observed. My quest is over. There is nothing remotely like the harsh and rugged landscape of the poem here. It's wishful thinking to say the poet had this place in mind, and it all goes to show that you should take what scholars and historians write with a pinch of salt. Like the Green Knight, everyone has an axe to grind.

But it's not been a waste of time. As I drive back home along the Clitheroe by-pass, an astonishing sunset is pouring down Ribblesdale. The beams of light are trapped under the blanket of dark cloud, and flanked by the whale-grey fells of Bowland the valley is an intense blood-red corridor. If ever Armageddon comes, it will look like this. I have to get off the road, and pull into the car park of a McDonald's to sit and gawp at the sky. The by-pass is heaving with traffic and people are breaking their necks to get into the restaurant, as if it offered the most irresistible experience of their lives. And suddenly I know why I am spending so much time wallowing in this history of ours, why I prefer chasing shadows across the landscape to the brazen reality of the modern world. It is because the very vagueness and uncertainty of our knowledge of the past, of what it was really like and what really happened, enables you to fill in the details from your own head, your own heart. It is a void to fill with your own fictions and fantasies, your own dreams of mystery and romance and chivalry like Gawain's. And it's the most complete and satisfying experience I can think of to pass your later years. It's probably not history as scholars would have it and for people writing more serious-minded books. But for me, it sure beats haring along by-passes in heavy traffic or queuing up for a Big Mac and some French fries served up in a cardboard cup.

CHAPTER EIGHT

THE RICH MAN
IN HIS CASTLE

ONE OF MY FAVOURITE Lancashire people is Titus Thornber. Whether it's that dignified, patriarchal Christian name or the small, rather modest exterior which belies immense knowledge, or the fact that at 92 when I last met him he seemed to encompass with his historical knowledge so many generations of Lancashire life, I regard him as a model Lancastrian. His grandparents moved from Rimington on the edge of the Ribble valley into Burnley during the great expansion of the cotton industry in the nineteenth century, and the family became manufacturers and mill owners. Titus was a brilliant scholar at Burnley Grammar School, where he came under the influence of the famous historian and schoolmaster, Walter Bennett. Instead of pursuing a natural bent for history and archaeology he became an engineer and after graduating from Manchester University worked in the vast wartime works of Metropolitan Vickers.

But there was always something of the maverick in Titus' soul, and finding the huge drawing office at the engineering works stifling his individuality and polymath instincts, he returned home to Burnley to an isolated farmhouse on the edge of the moors to pursue an unconventional life as farmer, inventor, author and historian. What Titus found around him was enough to set his enquiring mind off upon its journeys. It may have only been Burnley but it was the nutshell I quoted earlier which made him a king of infinite space. His book on the subject of the Pennine parish of Cliviger may sound parochial, but in it you'll find enough geology and the movement of great glaciers or history and the doings of the kings and queens of England, to satisfy the most expansive mind. And he was never happier than when whatever he was studying could combine the two aspects of his intellect, the historical and the scientific or technical. And there's no better example of this than his discoveries about the lime workings on his doorstep at Shedden Clough, workings which helped to bring about the revolution in house building in the sixteenth and seventeenth centuries and which will take us to some of Lancashire's finest ancestral homes.

Titus is too frail to venture out and so I made the journey to Shedden Clough on my own but armed with what I'd learned from him about the lime workings. The presence of the limestone under the cover of surface silt and vegetation is entirely due to glaciation. It was moved down from the limestone regions of Upper Ribblesdale and Craven in the form of pebbles and boulders on the back of the melting ice 10,000 years ago. What intrigued Titus was just how the early lime-workers retrieved the limestone from the mass of boulder clay with which it was congested. Prior to the discovery of a method of extraction Lancastrians had to rely upon limestone being imported into the county by means of packhorse ponies, a very expensive method which made its use as a building material and agricultural fertiliser difficult. The solution came from a much maligned but abundant Pennine resource: rainwater.

The rain clouds are ranking in the south-east down the Calder valley of Yorkshire. To the east, Boulsworth Hill crouches darkly, exhaling its damp breath. Shedden Clough is just off the ancient prehistoric route-way down the spine of England that links the two Calder valleys of Yorkshire and

Limestone 'sheddings'. Shedden Clough.

Lancashire, known as the Long Causeway. Near here is where that local bank manager turned historian J.T. Marquis believed was the site of the Battle of Brunanburh; and packhorse traders have used the route for centuries. It has even been suggested that this may have been the itinerary of the Norman Barons de Lacy in their journey from their headquarters at Pontefract to their stronghold of Clitheroe Castle. As you arrive at the top of the Clough you can soon begin to see that something unusual has been going on. The land is dotted with spoil heaps covered in bilberry plants, but between them run reed-filled channels linking hollows or ponds which in turn feed outlet goits. These are the 'hushings', an ingenious method of collecting water into reservoirs which could then be released down the hill to flush away the moraine and collect the limestone. The unwanted boulders were piled into 'sheddings' which cover the landscape beneath in an unnatural maze of conical foothills and islands of shattered stone. Scattered among the sheddings are the kilns, beehive structures of lichen-covered sandstone which look like the remains of amputated mill chimneys. Here the limestone was burned with coal or wood, both in plentiful supply locally, to produce the lime. In earlier days Titus mapped the entire operation and dated its commencement to 400 years ago, the method only becoming obsolete after the opening of the Leeds and Liverpool canal into Craven in the late eighteenth century (the building of the canal had been promoted in large part to bring cheap limestone from Yorkshire).

Titus reckons that the availability of cheap lime plaster gave the impetus to the expansion of stone-built houses in the area. As he points out, without tapestries on the walls the lords in their stone castles and manor houses were worse off than the peasants in their wattle and daub huts, simply because of the condensation that living surrounded by stone walls would produce. Rendering the stone with lime plaster would insulate it and result in something more comfortable and habitable. And with the arrival of stone buildings we have much more durable structures which, with a bit of luck, to say nothing of a lot of money and family prestige, could survive into the present day.

Sir Richard Bernard Cuthbert de Hoghton, 14th Baronet de Hoghton, is proud of his pedigree. It is painstakingly laid out in the brochure you get when you visit his seat at Hoghton Tower, high on a hill four miles west of Blackburn. Other ancient and noble Lancashire families will have theirs on display in meticulous copperplate upon their ancestral walls. They're like military medals, awarded for long and ruthless campaigns down the ages to seek favour at royal courts, marry advantageously or swoop to acquire a neighbour's land who may be unfortunate enough not to provide a male heir. In Tudor times, when the present Hoghton Tower was built, status was measured by the amount of land you owned. And if you could cap this with a fine mansion or manor house filled with a great hall, a minstrels' gallery (preferably housing a few resident minstrels), bedrooms with elaborately carved four-poster beds with feather mattresses, and a mausoleum as big as a cowman's cottage in the village church or churchyard, your respect and admiration throughout the county would be assured. The feudal system, disintegrating as it was, was still all about hierarchy, more so in Tudor times when a general price inflation meant that yeoman farmers, with agricultural surpluses to sell at a good profit in the local markets, were getting richer and more uppety and could begin to afford the trappings of wealth and prestige themselves. It must have been a continual battle for the knights and baronets, Lancashire's gentry, on the one hand to keep up with the Joneses – in this case the mighty earls of Derby, the pre-eminent Lancashire aristocrats – while at the same time watching their backs for all the upstart minor gentry and gentlemen who were busy scrambling up the social ladder behind them.

Hoghton's finest hour, from which to judge from their brochure you may be forgiven for thinking they'd never quite come back down to earth, was the visit in 1617, of the king himself, James VI of Scotland and I of England, or 'his sapient majesty' as the author rather fawningly describes him. In many ways it was every host's nightmare. Because the king didn't just bring a few mates, like the Duke of Buckingham, the Earls of Pembroke, Richmond, Nottingham and Bridgewater. He also brought lords Zouch, Knollys, Mordaunt, Grey, Stanhope and Compton, plus dozens of lesser notables. In fact, he brought the whole court. And if that wasn't enough, he brought his standing army as well. No wonder Hoghton has never recovered from this three-day squat. The poor Sir Richard Hoghton (yes, the 'de' seems to have disappeared for 300 years only to re-emerge with the 9th Baronet in 1862) seems to have spent time in debtor's prison as a result of the massive junket. The menu for Sunday dinner is preserved. It included beef, mutton, veal, venison, duck, turkey, capons, swans, chicken, goose, rabbits, tripe pie (Lancashire traditionalists will be delighted to learn), herons, curlew, quails, partridge, plovers and pigeons. The woods around Hoghton must have been silent for years after this massacre. And this was just for the king's table. Goodness knows what the army and other riff-raff dispatched. It was during one of these gastrofests that the king is reported to have knighted a side of beef, Sir Loin, an act of such absurdity that one can only conclude that the wine list must have rivalled the excesses of the menu.

A much less ostentatious visitor to Hoghton a generation earlier might, just possibly, have been the young William Shakespeare. The 'lost years' of the young Shakespeare, after he left school and before he appeared on the London theatrical scene, is a happy subject of speculation for Shakespeare scholars. It's thought that his mother, Mary Arden, would have had connections with the well-to-do Lancashire families because of her own Cheshire roots, and when Shakespeare's father was in trouble for his Catholic beliefs, to send young William to the west Lancashire stronghold of Catholicism might have been thought a good idea. Whatever the truth, a young man using the name William Shakeshaft seems to have spent a couple of years under the wing of Alexander Hoghton as a stage manager in the theatre company which may have performed in the banqueting hall at Hoghton Tower. This was before the persecution and torture of Edmund Campion made Hoghton unsafe and the young bard had to flee to Rufford Hall. But don't take my word for it. I understand that learned seminars drawing the great and the good of Shakespeare scholarship to Lancaster University have still not reached agreement on this shadowy period of the young poet's life. It would be nice to think that our county had at one stage in her history touched the hem of the world's greatest playwright. It is a slender arrow in our defensive armoury when we are accused of being a cultural backwater. Could the bogs, flats and fens of Prospero's island in *The Tempest* have been inspired by the west Lancashire marshes? Could the once splendid library at Hoghton have furnished the raw material for the histories? I, for one, would like to think so.

Hoghton Tower today stands high on its hill, so close to Blackburn but a thousand years away in all its historical resonance. Even with the covering of autumn trees you can see how the site of the original stronghold was dictated by the imperatives of defence. It commands the surrounding countryside, though the imposing cliff face to the north can't be properly appreciated for the dense trees (though it's worth a detour to see the splendid railway viaduct below the Tower). In the past the trees around were said to have been so thick that they couldn't be penetrated by the noonday sun. The approach from the south is grandiose, nearly three-quarters of a mile of driveway with wide manicured verges, steadily climbing the hill until you arrive at the gatehouse, imposingly castellated with supporting towers at either side. A weathered carving of what I took to be a man with a lion's head wrestling a serpent stands above the archway, though I was later informed that it was biblical and depicted Daniel in the lions' den. But as soon as you enter the outer courtyard, all grandiosity is forgotten. It's like entering an ancient Oxford college; it's intimate and on a human scale. Perhaps the ambition and vanity of the builders were curbed by the limitations of the mound on which the castle stands. Thank goodness. It feels friendly and welcoming in the warm pink glow of the stonework and the trim gardens of lavender and evergreen hebes. The flags are laid in diamond shapes and the cobbles in a circle, warmly inclusive. It seems a genuine retreat from the violent and hostile forces outside, and if Shakespeare really was here, I'm sure he would have felt safe, his youthful mind free to grow and flower. The inner courtyard where the family live is even more enclosed. But it's bare and rather cold in its immaculate stony perfection. For a moment or two you crave a Tudor black and white gable to break all the grey monotony. But then it was a fortress, still on the northern frontier of England, and this is where the great keep was built after the Conquest, before it was blown up during the Civil War when its store of gunpowder caught fire leaving, one might think, rather a lot of spare building stone. The double and triple mullions and a famed oriel window look out onto the courtyard but we were not allowed inside because the building closed for the winter at the end of September.

If all of this stone is too much for you, a craving for timber frames can be satisfied by a visit to Rufford Old Hall on the west Lancashire plain. Where stone was not so readily available the forests must still have been able to offer an abundance of wood. And between the dark oak frames with their quatrefoil panels, the lime mortar would provide the white infill which gives Rufford its typical Elizabethan character.

The Hesketh family emerged from medieval obscurity by acquiring land through a mixture of judicious marriage and inherited fortunes. By early Tudor times they fulfilled another requirement of social advancement in Lancashire. Thomas Hesketh found favour with the all-powerful Stanleys, the earls of Derby, and an office in their household at Lathom, four miles south of Rufford. I understand that the expression 'networking' is a modern term to describe the way in which today's go-getters make it their business to cultivate the acquaintance of those whom they think will be of use to them. Well, nothing's new. Throughout Lancashire's history the same family names keep cropping up, the same minor aristocrats forming a nobs' network of power and influence, helping one another to get on and maintain their wealth and status at the top of the local social hierarchy. So when Thomas Hesketh dies, leaving what appears to have been as much as '1,400 lbs of gold and silver plate', it is Sir John Towneley of Towneley Hall in Burnley who turns up as overseer of the will, carting the treasure off to Whalley Abbey where it was to be held in trust for Thomas's heir, Robert Hesketh. Another overseer is Sir Thomas Southworth, who rebuilt Salmesbury Hall (the modest ruins of the old hall are down by the banks of the Ribble) in a very similar style to which Robert was to use his fortune to built Rufford.

The Tudor age seems to have been a great age of building and rebuilding for the halls of the Lancashire gentry. Perhaps they were reasserting themselves as the old feudal bonds of society were collapsing. Or perhaps they simply had too much money and were determined to show off. That they were never satisfied with what they had got and were forever altering without always improving, will come as no surprise to observers of today's people with money. And if the alterations were not just designed to reflect their status, they were, more understandably, made to improve comfort. Whatever the reason, the visitor to these old halls will find themselves perplexed about what bit belongs to what age. For example, visiting Rufford, where the way in is a bit of a muddle, we found ourselves taking a first look at the building from the garden at the south side of the house. Nowadays restoration must always be pure. I know a plasterer who, when asked to restore some old property in the hands of the National Trust like Rufford, didn't complain when he was given handfuls of horse-hair to put into the plaster. But when he was handed a bundle of twigs to rough up the plaster between coats because that was the way they used to do it, downed tools and left, mumbling a few medieval curses. They had no such precious scruples about restoration in the past. The south wing is a curious mix of timbering, stone and red brick. It somehow manages to look disappointingly suburban, like the back of some modern-day mansion in

Henley-on-Thames. But the yew topiary of two giant squirrels which guard the approach to the former doorway, is cheery – something you can't always say about yew. And I enjoyed the sculptures – a hefty-thewed bronze maiden protecting her modesty from the attentions of a fig-leafed Pan. An arm of the Leeds and Liverpool canal slips sluggishly past the avenue of beech trees, giving the setting a more down-to-earth feel. (Good for perch, a hoary old angler told me.) Today sweet chestnuts strew the path beneath our feet, spiny as cacti. Many have split open to reveal furry white tongues holding clusters of nuts which I thought I'd try. They were rather soggy but nutty enough. 'Just like you,' observed my wife and companion through life.

Once round the west wing I revised my first impression of the hall. Here, the combination of the original timbers of the Great Hall of 1530 and the red brick north wing added in 1662 is strikingly handsome. This is red brick as I feel it should be: mellow, warm and subtle, none of your brash cardinal red like the Accrington brick of Whalley viaduct. Inside, the Great Hall is astonishing for its open timbered roof, supported by hammer beams resting on braces with carved spandrels (I've always wanted to use that word). At the ends of the hammer beams are carved angels soaring out overhead, but winglessly because these celestial appendages have unfortunately succumbed to woodworm. The angels are an odd ecclesiastical addition to the domestic architecture and they may have come from one of the monasteries at the Dissolution. It's typical of these old Catholic houses, how many devotional

Rufford Old Hall. Strikingly handsome.

PHOTOGRAPH: AUTHOR

and biblical carvings find their way into the furniture, especially the four-poster beds. The other striking thing about the hall, besides all the armour which is a reminder of how they often begat and maintained their wealth, is a huge moveable screen described as having 'outlandish finials'. These are spires carved from a single piece of wood and elaborately decorated with a twisted mass of rams' horns. It is quite grotesque and reminds me of nothing as much as those hideous threshing tentacles out of *Alien*. I suspect that the carver was somewhere on the teetering brink of insanity. And talking of insanity, high on the roof is something I tried my best to ignore when I first saw it from outside. It is a lantern added by the Victorian owners, it's said, to give extra light into the hall in order that their children could play billiards. It is hard to contemplate the levels of self-indulgence that the wealthy could afford, especially during periods of almost universal and abject poverty suffered by the ordinary people of Lancashire.

For all its amazing workmanship Rufford Old Hall was not good enough for the Heskeths who by 1760 had a new hall built, a neo-classical mansion, half a mile down the road. A hundred years later the family inherited a 5,000-acre estate at Easton Neston in Northamptonshire, where they have lived ever since. However, this has recently been put on the market for £50 million by the latest Hesketh, the motor racing baron. I am indebted for this piece of information to one of the tirelessly civil stewards, those middle-aged and elderly handmaidens of the National Trust who volunteer their weekends to stand in dim rooms and dark corridors answering silly questions from people like me, with a smile and a measure of enthusiasm few of us deserve. It seems to me that today the National Trust are as niggardly as families like the Heskeths were extravagant. While one of the stewards proved her weight in gold to the organisation by beating out Beethoven on the Steinway in the dining room for our edification, Barbara, another, told me that their only reward for their stint as guides, apart from a few travel expenses, was a refreshment allowance of a cup of tea and two biscuits. They certainly couldn't afford to eat in the tea room, she told me. At £3.10 for a small bowl of rather flavourless but what was described as 'sustaining' soup, one began to wonder just who the soup was intended to sustain, the consumer or National Trust Enterprises Limited. At Rufford the tea room is a converted stable block, and surrounded by flagged floors, a black-leaded range and skillet pans, you can convince yourself you're dining with the servants. That's until you become aware of the fiercely middle-class marketing that goes on. It is the usual gentrification of the once humble, with ginger beer for sale in wine bottles and peach tea. Even under threat of being put to one of the Great Hall swords, I will not enter their gift shops and go anywhere near their beeswax candles and potpourri. (Clearly I still haven't forgiven the National Trust for failing to offer any concessions to the over-sixties on the door.)

On the way home we decided to take a look at the new hall. It is a Georgian affair with pillared porticoes on every side, only two storeys but making up in sprawl for what it lacks in height. Every inch of stonework has been painted in a clotted cream colour and it resembles nothing so much as a giant confection. It has, of course, been sold and turned into dozens of mews houses, each with its BMW or SUV parked outside. With discreet globe lighting dotted amongst the apron of beech and laurel hedges and the whole contained in acres of parkland, it is the ideal domestic retreat for today's socially mobile classes. But it is all horribly sterile and eerily quiet, with not a hint of riff-raff in sight until we arrive. We leave before too many curtains start to twitch and telephone calls are made to the local constabulary.

Once you've got a taste for these Lancashire halls it can become a bit of a compulsion to visit as many as possible, especially with the closed season approaching and workmen arriving to conduct their authentic restoration by lashing the plaster undercoat with twigs. Speke Hall is on the Mersey estuary near Liverpool airport. It is another timber-framed house and was built by the Catholic Norris family in the sixteenth century, not without a degree of understandable paranoia. One of the first things that can be observed as you cross the moat bridge is a peep hole in the eaves to the right of the door from which the occupants could spy upon their approaching visitors. And inside, the bedrooms are riddled with priest-holes. In the Green Bedroom there's a ladder in the cupboard to the side of the fireplace where an illegal priest could be hidden in a space around the chimney breast, which, for a believer in Hellfire, must have been uncomfortably warm. There is an overall sense of confinement about the house which gives an authentic feel of life in the Elizabethan house for its Catholic occupants. There are low-ceilinged corridors with heavy panelling and creaking floorboards, lit only by the leaded windows which look out onto the dark inner courtyard. The house-dwellers must have suffered from seasonal affective disorder throughout the year.

The shadowiness of the interior isn't helped by the two giant yew trees in the courtyard, massive, sombre creatures with their waxy crimson berries, curiously named Adam and Eve. The courtyard is cobbled with small irregular pebbles, a real contrast to the geometrical perfection of the paving at Hoghton Tower. The yew trees exude a baleful dampness and I can already feel my rheumatism starting to play up. The stone-tiled roof is bright green with lichen and they look to have trouble with ferns growing in the courtyard to judge from the number of amputated clumps. Despite the black and white timbering it is cheerless, and I begin to wonder what the Norrises did in the long winter evenings. The answer is to be found in the Great Parlour in the overmantel above the fireplace. Here is a carving of Sir William Norris, 1524, and his nineteen children. He did actually have the children by two wives and here they are, both looking adoringly at him while he gazes out magisterially, very bearded and slightly reminiscent of the green man, that ubiquitous image of medieval fertility. The room was abysmally dark, and I had to ask to borrow the steward's torch as I attempted to count all the

Speke Hall. Besieged.

PHOTOGRAPH: AUTHOR

children packed into the panelling. 'You should come back in summer when the light is better,' I was helpfully instructed. It seems that here was another instance of the National Trust's legendary meanness. There was only one light in the room because the only other power point was being used for a fan heater to keep the unpaid stewards warm. What on earth do the National Trust do with the £6 (no concessions for elderly grumblers) entrance fee? I had observed a notice outside advertising a special ghost tour of the house for Hallowe'en, another successful fund-raiser for the National Trust, to judge from the 'sold out' notice printed across it. The shadowy atmosphere of Speke Hall is no doubt a happy haunting ground for ghosts. But when I ask a splendidly forthright Liverpudlian steward whether she had ever seen any ghosts in the building, she told me, 'I'm very sensitive to atmosphere. I once stayed at an hotel in Scotland that was haunted and the sweat ran off me. But there's nothing here. I'd have felt it if there had been.' Oh dear. Is it too late to get our money back?

Outside in the daylight I wander through the gardens that fill the old moat and are surrounded by small yews which stand like sentries across the lawns. At this late season the garden is full of fragile, faded colour. The red embers of the sedums, the delicate tissue pink of the hydrangea flowers, a sudden crimson burst of flame from the mahonia leaves and the last roses of summer fading now against the serene longevity of the house itself. But Speke Hall is besieged and not just by its own shadows. The modern world presses in from all sides. To the landward side the sprawling landscape of dreary modern warehouses and freight terminals spawned by the airport. Jets lumber into the air, heavily laden with passengers on cheap flights to Europe. And across the Mersey, the sinister sulphury light of the flames from the oil refinery flicker in the grey sea gloom. No wonder the impression you leave with as you look back at the hall is of a building shrinking within itself under the wide sky. This is history in the twenty-first century, isolated and forever pushed into insignificance by the irreverent and relentless tide of material progress.

My final excursion of the season takes me to a hall built right at the end of the Elizabethan period. Gawthorpe Hall near Padiham was the home of the Shuttleworth family who had lived at Gawthorpe since the fourteenth century. One of the earliest members of the family was christened with the worst-looking forename I have ever encountered: Ughtred de Shuttleworth. (Now I write this down, the surname doesn't sit so elegantly with it either.) Clearly the Shuttleworth mums and dads didn't share my prejudice, because Ughtreds keep on breaking out like rashes in the family down the ages. The thought of 'Come on in, our Ughtred, your tea's ready,' echoing around the north parterre begins to sound like something out of *Blackadder*. Happily the name did not survive into the present time with our predilection for abbreviations.

But there's nothing disharmonious about the hall itself. On the contrary, Gawthorpe is the most extraordinarily symmetrical and compactly handsome of buildings. A central tower around which the words *Prudentia et Justitia* are clearly visible is a reminder of where the Shuttleworth fortune came from. It was new money arising from the success of Sir Richard Shuttleworth as a London barrister and Chief Justice of Chester in 1589. Around the tower – slightly off-centre, but we're all human – is the most sharply elegant of structures. It is built from warm, mellow sandstone, well suited to the late October afternoon of my visit, with the leaves of the trees thinning to trembling medallions of gold. There's no shortage of light entering the frontage of Gawthorpe, with rows of criss-cross leaded windows rising in bays to the full three-storey height of the building, which is topped by an ornate parapet. There's none of the somewhat rickety olde worlde charm of the timber-framed Speke. It is as if the Age of Reason has already arrived, and just as Newton was to reduce the universe to mathematics, so the architect

Gawthorpe Hall, a slide rule palace.
PHOTOGRAPH: AUTHOR

of Gawthorpe has used the fundamentals of rectilinear geometry to create his house. There's no hole-in-corner Catholic fear here, but the bold Protestant confidence of being on the right side of the law and of the Establishment. But is it all too methodical and well ordered? All too perfect? Round the other side, the building is much plainer and keep-like. Of course, it's facing north, the outlandish north, with the grey presence of Pendle Hill, a surly reminder that all is not sweetness and light, that darkness and superstition play their part in man's nature whatever the age. Nevertheless, here's an ornamental garden designed in a semi-circle with radiating spokes of variegated shrubs which end in spherical domes of privet and truncated cones of box, all very geometrical again. A garden designed by a mathematician and not a poet, a lover of order and not of uncouth nature. And look at the ornamentation which the designer has permitted himself! On the roof, stone balls raise their perfectly rounded heads like bald sentries, while below, on top of the stone rails which surround the ground floor, are obelisks, strangely hatched. And then, wildest of fantasies, on the balcony of the parterre, bizarre onion-like shapes, positively Moorish, and yet they too are unable to escape the constraints of mathematics and the dreaded straight line, and instead of being smooth and rounded they are sharply cornered. You find yourself remembering those doodles you and your classmates used to do on the front of your rough books at school and how they were supposed to reveal your psychological self. All curves and swirls and you'd grow up to be a hippie and believe in flower power and free love. But all straight lines and sharp corners and you were emotionally crippled and would grow up to be a bank clerk or a judge who wore his wife's tights under his gown. I suppose it helps to know, as I found out later from reading the guide book, that the garden as well as the parapets above were redesigned by the Victorian architect, Sir Charles Barry, the one who designed the Houses of Parliament. And look what a funny lot they are who work there!

The most interesting room in the house, and quite the most crazily ornamented, is the dining room. The panelling is influenced by the Italian Renaissance but above it is a Jacobean frieze which casts off all the inhibitions of the world outside and really lets rip. There are twisting sea-monsters and frolicking mermaids, staring dismembered heads and winged beasts or griffins perched on spindly legs, all entangled in a vegetable cocktail of frantic foliage and plump exotic fruits. Here is the medieval age again, poking its grotesque head above the wainscoting and sticking out its tongue at all this talk of mathematics and order before dancing round the dinner table with its trousers down. I'm glad. It shows that the people who built this slide rule palace hadn't lost their sense of fun.

The last Shuttleworth to live at the hall was the Hon Rachel Kay-Shuttleworth who died in 1967, and it's her collection of embroidery which dominates the first floor of the building. A few months ago I'd have given anyone a rather cool reception if they had suggested I visit an exhibition of embroidery. But the splendid ceremonial attire of the abbots of Whalley in Towneley Hall are still fresh in my mind, so I'm happy to forget about football – Burnley FC have a training ground you can see just out of the window at Gawthorpe – and take up embroidery, or at least admiring it. There's work inspired by the frieze in the dining room and undertaken by the Shuttleworth sisters – cushions where griffins crouch fiercely entwined in a forest of twisting stems and leaves. A lot of winter evenings – light available – must have been profitably spent working on these sumptuous creations, the sisters retiring to bed with a sense of fulfilment instead of that leaden feeling of frustration and guilt you get these days after an evening spent slumped in front of the telly. Some of the work, brought from overseas, is nothing short of stunning. A fallak or Persian tablecloth of cerise and green with gold metal thread upon a background of pale ice-blue silk. Another table-cover, this time from India, in silver grey with a surround of dazzling metallic silver braid. One Indian piece has emerald green beetle wings embroidered into it which flash out magically from the back of the display cabinet. I'm astonished that we have such a treasury upon our doorstep and I'd never seen it before.

Contrasting with the dazzling metalwork and the satins and floss silks of the embroidery is the sepia solemnity of the portraits in the Long Gallery. Here's a who's who of seventeenth-century court life. There's the Duchess of Cleveland, a mistress of Charles II, with enough facial shadow to suggest that she might have taken up shaving at an early age. But any suggestion of masculinity is dispelled by a rather wet and pouting bottom lip which had me hurrying past all of a dither to observe the king himself looking darkly handsome with a distinctly contemptuous gaze in my direction, as if he was resentful of such scrutiny from the lower orders. They're a haughty lot, these aristos, especially the Earl of Oxford, dressed in a most foppish assortment of garters, frills and furbelows, and even some silk tassels that look as though they've been borrowed from Lawrence Llewelyn-Bowen's lounge curtains. But, while casually turning a well-shaped calf towards the painter, tight-lipped, he looks down his long aquiline nose with all the hauteur that down the ages the aristocracy have reserved for the likes of you and me. Across the corridor in one of the bedrooms, one scrupulous authenticator has placed a chamber pot under the four-poster bed, leaving me in no doubt, after seeing these portraits, about what job I should have been given in even the most minor of aristocratic households.

Close to Gawthorpe Hall is the site of one of east Lancashire's most important historical buildings, that's if you measure importance by the influence exercised over the surrounding area. Ightenhill manor house was one of the manors of the Honour of Clitheroe held by the de Lacys and consisted of a deer park, lucrative vaccaries (cow farms), and stud farms. That it was significantly more comfortable than Clitheroe Castle, with a great hall and chambers and even a chapel of its own, meant that the de Lacys would use it often as they broke their journey north from Pontefract Castle. In fact, so well appointed must it have been that in 1323, no less than the king himself, Edward II, arriving to deal with a spot of bother with rustlers from Yorkshire, stayed for eight days. (You can almost hear them gnashing their teeth with envy over at Hoghton Tower.) Now visits to Burnley have never figured prominently on royal excursions, and with medieval kings second only to God and the Pope in the great chain of being, you might have thought there would have been some lasting evidence preserved of this important building. I consult my OS map in vain. I hurry for assistance to the reference library in Burnley where maps are heaped upon me like royal bed linen. We find a reference to the site of the manor house on a large-scale map, lost not in a forest of deer but on the edge of a huge new housing estate, its exact whereabouts only being indicated by its proximity to a pylon carrying overhead power cables.

It's not without a sense of irony that I set out in search of a medieval manor house by way of the National Grid. The housing estate is brown brick, many houses with shallow bays with leaded lights and tiny gables above, otherwise known as Barratt Tudor Vernacular. At the northern apex of the estate there's a small plantation, put there, I can only conclude, to rob the residents of the spectacular view and, to judge from the discarded cans of lager, give their teenage offspring cover to indulge in early experimentation with alcohol. Over a stile and there's the grotesque pylon towering over an enclosure where the walls have all collapsed and the only indication of any possible earthworks is a slight unevenness to the surface grassland. A carrion crow on a fence post looks balefully at me as I make notes, then fans out its tail and leaning forwards starts to caw derisively. 'If you think you can make something of this lot then I'm a vegetarian.'

I can cite a modern instance of how the most substantial of historical buildings can disappear with startling rapidly. The Holme in Cliviger, once part of the manor of Ightenhill, was built in 1607 on the site of an earlier timbered building, and was, as already mentioned, the home of the renowned Lancashire scholar and historian, Thomas Dunham Whitaker. In 2001, while empty of occupants and up for sale, it was attacked by arsonists. Subsequently it was plundered mercilessly for its building materials. Practically the entire roof disappeared, along with ancient oak doors, carved oak fireplaces and even stained glass, probably from Whalley Abbey. What had stood secure for 400 years was cannibalised in less than 18 months. It stands now a heartless shell, a dismal ruin which would take a king's ransom to restore, if ever it should happen. What on earth does this say about our cultural priorities? It was a listed building. Councillors and planners were aware of what was going on; police were urged to watch over it; but still it was destroyed. What does it say about our regard for our history and our stewardship of our historical heritage? There can simply be no excuse for what has happened to The Holme and everyone associated with its downfall should hang their heads in shame.

With no one to look after it when it was abandoned by the de Lacys, Ightenhill manor house fell into disrepair and was plundered for its beams and masonry. The only thing that remains which no one could take away from here – though I'd be watching the housing developers and planners, if I had anything to do with it – is the view. You can see just why this was

The dismally ruined Holme.
PHOTOGRAPH: AUTHOR

chosen as the site for an important manor house. It looks out northwards beyond the crossing of the river Calder to where Pendle Hill sprawls lazily in the afternoon sun. East is the Aire Gap and the hills around Skipton. West, round the hillside of Portfield prehistoric camp, lies Whalley Abbey and the valley of the Ribble. This, not today's urban valley to the south where Nelson, Brierfield, Burnley and Accrington lie, is the valley which shaped our early history before the Industrial Revolution. It is now the abandoned valley. On the hillside towards Pendle lie the dormitory estates of the valley's new inhabitants. The people who live there can earn their corn in Manchester and beyond, not filling the great barn with fodder for the draught oxen or brood mares or mending the fences around the deer park. Today's agricultural activity is confined to a man on a tractor drawing a tanker which fires a viscid spout of slurry onto the fields. His hay is packed in giant bales which lie in untidy piles like the fat, black, shiny eggs spawned by some monstrous insect. The only horses I can see are two shaggy-maned ponies dressed in winter coats, a far cry from the iron-grey stallion brought here from Henry de Lacy's stable at Pontefract Castle in 1304. This is the valley down which the king and his attendants journeyed in 1323 on their way to Wigan to mete out justice to the local lawbreakers. And it was no doubt the route taken by the tumbrels which bore the Pendle witches from their hovels under the shadow of Pendle Hill to meet the hangman at Lancaster Castle in 1612.

What became of Ightenhill Manor?
PHOTOGRAPH: AUTHOR

CHAPTER NINE

'THE GOBLINS OF WITCHCRAFT'

WHILE THE GENTRY were busy showing off their new stone houses with their fancy Italianate ceilings and elaborately carved four-poster beds to their friends, the ordinary peasants of Lancashire were living in much the same conditions as they had tolerated since Saxon times: wooden-framed huts with mud walls, earth floors and a thatched roof with a hole in, through which the smoke from the fire eventually found its way after depositing layers of soot and ash over the interior. The occupants must have looked permanently like kids at a bonfire. The gradual loss of their strips of land and the enclosure of waste land which deprived the peasants of their customary grazing rights was one reason for the slow drift of people from the countryside to the towns. Arable land was replaced by pasture for sheep as the woollen textile industry in Lancashire continued to grow. But plenty of work was still available on the land to the young and able-bodied. Only if you were old, infirm or dull-witted did keeping body and soul together prove more difficult. Henry VIII had got rid of the monasteries as a source of almsgiving for the poor. Voluntary contributions to the welfare of the poor were encouraged throughout Elizabeth's reign but it wasn't until 1601 when the Poor Law was passed that compulsory taxation was introduced in every parish for their upkeep. But parishes were slow in levying the new poor rate and in Lancashire, which was still something of a backwater and one of the poorest of England's counties, it must have taken many years for help to trickle down to the needy. As a consequence beggars must have been a common sight up and down the parishes and their persistent and sometimes aggressive importuning of other folk was a constant thorn in the side of the authorities.

This is the background to what is, to the liberal conscience of the twenty-first century, one of the most shameful episodes in Lancashire history. But to put it in further context we need to return to the man (though he regarded himself as more of a god) whose appearance at Hoghton Tower later in 1617 inspired such lavish hospitality and the elevation of a lump of beef to the Order of the Garter, the king himself, James I.

James I was a profoundly superstitious man. Once, when he'd nearly drowned at sea, he believed it was because he'd been cursed by a witch. Not only had he personally examined a witch who had in her possession a dead body for the purposes of enchantment, but he'd written a book on the subject which contained an account of the ceremonies used by them, the way to detect them and how they should be punished. As Dr Johnson so dramatically observed of the period, 'the goblins of witchcraft still continued to hover in the twilight'. He goes on to point out that to adopt the king's superstitions was a ready way to gain his favour. In the first year after James came to the throne in England (he'd already been king of Scotland for twenty years), 1604, Parliament enacted a law which decreed that anyone who 'shall use, practise or exercise any sort of witchcraft, sorcery, charm or enchantment whereby any person be destroyed, killed, wasted, consumed, pined or lamed in any part of the body ... shall suffer death.'

'not broomstick navigation but beggary'

It was in the shadow of Pendle Hill that the Lancashire witches plied their trades, by far the most successful of which was not broomstick navigation but beggary. A description of one of them, Anne Whittle, better known as Chattox, survives:

a very old, withered, spent and decrepit creature, her sight almost gone, her lips ever chattering or talking, but no man knew what.

Another, Elizabeth Device, daughter of Demdike, was an equally nightmarish figure. She suffered from violent and uncontrollable fits. She had such a terrible squint that one eye turned up and the other down: 'one on t' pot and t' other up t' chimney', as one homespun description would have it.

Now add to these frightening appearances the knowledge that they'd been seen scratching around the graveyard at the New Church after midnight and about their persons they just happened to carry a few teeth, the odd scalp and an old finger bone, or a clay effigy which in the heat of the moment you couldn't help but believe bore a striking resemblance to yourself, and you begin to see just how successful they must have been at begging and how eager the people accosted by them must have been to open their purses and get shut of them.

It was after one such incident that their activities came to the attention of the local magistrate. On Wednesday 18 March 1612, Alizon Device, Demdike's granddaughter, was begging near Colne when she met a peddler from Halifax named John Law. When he wouldn't unloosen his pack after she had begged some pins (Pins? Now what on earth would a witch want with pins?) she cursed him. Within a few yards Law had collapsed of a seizure and was carried paralysed to an alehouse in Colne. Law's son was called, who accused Alizon of bewitching his father and the girl confessed before the magistrate, Roger Nowell, at Read Hall, between Gawthorpe and Whalley.

Nowell was already building up quite a charge sheet against the Pendle witches. Christopher Nutter, a yeoman farmer, claimed before he died that he had been bewitched by Chattox when he tried to eject the family from their hovel on his land at Greenhead. Richard Baldwin's little daughter had become ill after he'd ordered Demdike and her daughter from his premises. 'Get out of my ground, whores and witches', he'd cried. 'I'll burn the one of you and hang the other!' And when John Nutter of Bull Hole farm called in Demdike to use her skills as a herbalist to 'mend' a sick cow and it died next morning, Nutter accused her of bewitching the beast.

When Alizon Device confessed to Roger Nowell she told him that she had lamed the peddler John Law after a black dog had appeared to her and asked: 'What wouldst thou have me do unto yonder man?' 'Lame him!' she had said, and before Law had gone 200 yards he fell down lame. This black dog, she told him, was her familiar. It had come to her two years earlier and asked for her soul. Thereupon, went her confession, 'the said Blacke Dogge did with his mouth sucke at her breast, a little below her Paps, which place did remain blew halfe a year next after.' No doubt then, scrupulously following the king's instructions in his *Daemonologie*, Nowell availed himself of the opportunity to inspect the witches' mark upon the body of the 17-year-old girl.

In these accounts, meticulously preserved because they were recorded by the clerk of the court, Thomas Potts, at their trial in Lancaster, you get the impression of a dark door being opened upon the superstitious shadows of a bygone, medieval age. This talk of curses, blood-sucking familiars and the Devil's mark is a world away from the cool mathematical precision of the façade of Gawthorpe Hall which had been built a decade earlier. But, alas, it is only a façade, for within the edifice of Jacobean society the echoes of age-old superstition ring along its corridors, and people shiver and cower in the shadows of the darkest period of all, the dark before the dawn of the Age of Reason.

'trumped-up charges'

But why did Roger Nowell, the magistrate, an intelligent and educated man, go in for all this superstitious claptrap? Why, like us today, could he not see that a middle-aged peddler, puffing up a hill towards Colne and accosted by a frightening self-confessed witch, might be a prime candidate for a stroke? Or that a mark upon a girls' breast might be more easily explained as a birthmark or a mole rather than the diabolical attentions of a blood-sucking hell-hound?

Well, I think the answer may lie in politics, that age-old art of knowing which side your bread is buttered on. As has been suggested, Roger Nowell would be doing his best to keep in favour with that arch-believer in the black arts, the king himself. And if you consider that Nowell was probably in fairly bad odour with the powers-that-be for presiding over a district well known to be a hotbed of outlawed Catholicism, you can begin to understand, if not forgive him going along with all this nonsense and ordering, on 14 April, Alizon Device, Demdike, Chattox and her daughter Anne Redfearn to be bundled into a cart and trundled off on the twenty-six-mile journey through the Trough of Bowland and thrown into the gaol at Lancaster to await the August assizes.

'A gallows full of twitching witches'

And if you require further convincing of the nonsense of the trumped-up charges set before this most famous of all witchcraft trials, you need look no further than the events of a week later at Malkin Tower on Good Friday, 10 April. Described as a black sabbat, according to Thomas Potts, 'there was a meeting of all the most dangerous, wicked and damnable witches in the county farre and neere'. The truth was, it was a lunatic enterprise by the prisoners' families, one a girl of nine, the other a half-witted lad, to spring the four prisoners from Lancaster gaol by killing the gaoler and blowing up the castle. You can imagine old John o' Gaunt rocking with mirth in his grave at the thought of these bundles of rags assailing his stronghold with its five-feet thick walls.

Nevertheless, seven of those present at Malkin Tower were arrested and in turn hauled off to Lancaster. Among them was the most enigmatic figure in this whole sorry saga, Alice Nutter. Potts describes her as 'a rich woman who had a great estate'. I can only assume that she was there ministering to the needy in the way that the well off had been enjoined to do before the introduction of any proper parish welfare scheme; she was an early form of voluntary social worker.

The trial in Lancaster attracted thousands and had such moments of high drama as would have had today's tabloid press drooling in the gallery. There was the moment when Chattox of the chattering lips broke down and confessed; when cross-eyed Elizabeth the epileptic had to be dragged out of court when they brought her nine-year-old daughter in to give evidence against her. And there was the appearance of her brother, Jem, in such a bad state from his spell chained in the dungeon and suffering so badly from the after-effects of the attention of the gaoler, Master Covell, an adept at extracting confessions of his own, that Jem couldn't stand unaided. Or the court room confrontations between Alizon Device and the man she had bewitched, John Law, the peddler, still lame from his seizure.

At the close of the fifth day of the trial the jury brought in a verdict of guilty against ten of the accused. Only old Demdike escaped the noose by dying earlier in the dungeons.

So, the Pendle district of Lancashire rid itself of a serious social nuisance in one fell swoop. It got rid of two families of lice-ridden beggars and half-wits who had been terrorising the honest, god-fearing citizens for two generations, in a fraction of the time it would take a modern social worker to compile a case history. It did its bit to ensure that medical and veterinary science remained in the Dark Ages by insisting that blood clots endemic to middle-aged peddlers who over-exert or over-excite themselves, or liver fluke in cattle, were the outcome of spells and sorcery. Likewise, it did nothing to encourage the early birth of that much-abused modern science of psychology, of which it takes very little understanding to know that if you're so hideous and deformed that people shrink when you go by, and you haven't a cat in hell's chance of filling your belly by any other means, pulling faces, jabbering and cursing at superstitious folk until they are scared enough to give you a crust or two to make you go away, is as good a way as any of staying alive. And if you should just happen to carry around a few old bones and teeth and word should get around that you make a pretty mean likeness of people in clay, this would do as much to enhance your reputation among credulous folk as a modern-day diploma in quackery. Add to this a bit of good, hard evidence such as a strategically placed wart or a supernumerary nipple which could serve as a Devil's mark; add a judicial system prepared to take the evidence of lunatics and nine-year-old children, and content to take seriously the confessions of terrified and intimidated peasant illiterates cross-examined without the benefit of a defending solicitor, and you've soon got a gallows full of twitching witches for Thomas Potts Esquire to chronicle the dire deeds of as a terrible warning to the rest of England's peasantry not to stray from the straight and narrow.

The Witch's Grave, Newchurch.
PHOTOGRAPH: AUTHOR

It's Hallowe'en and I decide to set off for Pendle Hill to see what rags of superstition remain after 400 years. In actual fact, Hallowe'en has its origins not in witchcraft but in the 2,000 year-old Celtic festival of Samhain, marking the end of summer and the harvest and the beginning of the Celtic New Year on 1 November. Rather appropriately, this is the first night after the clocks have been turned back and I feel a sense of urgency about getting up the hill and back before it turns dark. When I set out from the Burnley valley Pendle is lost in mist, a grey matrix which lasts through Fence and up into Newchurch. Only the occasional autumn bush burns through the grey like a yellow flame. Half a dozen rooks rest on a telephone wire, rocking threateningly. Past the gift shop with its trio of stuffed witches outside and then suddenly at the top of the hill, the mist is gone and Pendle is smiling benignly under a blue sky.

At Barley the picnic site car park is packed. They're even picnicking on the green in the late golden sunshine, middle-aged and elderly folk with silver thermos flasks and Tupperware containers full of home baking. Forget the instant takeaways from the snack bar; this is old-fashioned prudence and self-reliance, with money to be saved. Disconcertingly long crocodiles of elderly ramblers appear, chattering happily away. An ambulance wails past. A sprained ankle on the hill? Or worse? Elderly jaws set with determination as they trudge towards the hill. The only goblins that will trouble them are the demons of old age and a good brisk walk will help to banish them. I'd been told that Pendle would be invaded by young hooligans on Hallowe'en, racing around in monster masks and extracting trick-or-treat money with menaces. (Does nothing change?) But everything, like the season, is sedately middle-aged and respectable. A few families tramp past. One child wears a skeleton suit and two sisters wear witches' hats above pretty cerise dresses. The twenty-first century has drawn the sting of superstition and poverty. Everyone is chattering amiably, the old sense of comradeship I remember as a child on the Good Friday walks to Pendle. I speak to an elderly lady sitting by the riverside reading. Harrison Ainsworth? I enquire. Or perhaps Robert Neil? She shakes her head ruefully. No. She's been to a book sale at the Clarion Club on the way up to Newchurch. And, of course, a cup of tea and a natter. Old-fashioned Lancashire working-class solidarity hanging on by the skin of its teeth in an age of online shopping.

'The twenty-first century has drawn the sting of superstition and poverty'

Half way up the hill and I'm joined by Gary from Billinge. He's in his thirties and has a camera slung round his neck and a yellow GPS satellite navigation instrument in his hand. He explains that he's on an internet treasure hunt, something called geocaching, where from information on the internet enthusiasts look for hidden boxes from which they can remove a token and replace it with one of their own. The tokens are electronically tagged and can be traced in

Pendle, witch country.
PHOTOGRAPH: AUTHOR

their journey up and down the country via 4,000 sites, or even more abroad. He shows me how the GPS works, picking up signals from one or more of many satellites spinning round the earth and telling him just where he is. An age that takes for granted such technology must surely mean the death of all superstition.

But returning home I stop off at the gift shop in Newchurch. It's even more crowded than the top of Pendle was. People are magnetised by the assortment of the kitsch and the pseudo-occult. There's vampire make-up and broomsticks, horror hoods and rune pendants. You can buy plastic moulded green men to stick on your wall or your fridge. I pick up a furry cat, made in China, which is battery operated and will shake and scream to order. Chattox and Demdike, nose and chin meeting like pincers, appear on tea towels and you can buy the *Lord of the Rings* on DVD.

As I stand there jostled by the throng of excited shoppers, the mist that I'd met when I set out descends again. Only this time it's the fog of incomprehension. Do we keep these things alive to remind us of just how far we've come out of the shadows which led us to such shameful persecution of the innocent? Or do we buy them as a talisman to ward off that same fear and prejudice which we all know still lurks within the darkest corners of our human nature?

CHAPTER TEN

LANCASHIRE
BLOODILY DIVIDED

HISTORIANS ARE IN DISPUTE about the impact of the Civil War in Lancashire. Some think we suffered unduly because of the number of Catholics in the county – usually supporters of the defeated royalist cause. Some think that living in a backwater, we sat it out and got on with the everyday business of hunting and hanging witches. But the war was hard to ignore. When the Scots got involved, to get south they had to march down the Lune valley into the county, and when Cromwell's forces scuttled through the Aire Gap from Yorkshire to meet them, there was a bloody encounter at Preston in 1648, one of the decisive battles of the wars, which resulted in the removal of King Charles's head from his body in January 1649.

But even in the first phase of the war Lancashire was heavily involved. In the autumn of 1642 the royalists attempted to besiege Manchester, and early the next year fighting broke out along the main north–south road to secure the towns of Warrington, Wigan, Preston and Lancaster. By the summer of 1643 they had all fallen to parliamentarian forces and only the royalist strongholds of the Earl of Derby at Lathom House and Greenhalgh Castle near Garstang held out. But the siege at Lathom was abandoned the next year when royalist armies arrived under the command of the king's nephew, Prince Rupert. He was only 22 and often to be seen riding around in full armour clutching his pet poodle. (The word camp didn't exist in those days except as a description of bivouacked soldiers.) The Cavaliers took Wigan and Liverpool and ransacked Bolton, the Earl of Derby playing a prominent role which was not to be forgotten, before being defeated in Yorkshire at Marston Moor just to the west of York in July 1644. So the royalist gains in Lancashire were soon lost and even

Prince Rupert and poodle.

Lathom House surrendered, with the Earl of Derby going into exile in the Isle of Man.

So, princes clutching poodles apart, the ordinary people of Lancashire must have been used to the sight of armies on the march through Lancashire in the middle of the seventeenth century, if not being actually caught up in one or another of the sieges involving their town. But which way did their loyalties lie? This, after all, was our country's great constitutional war, about how we were to be ruled: by a king who still saw himself as an absolute monarch ruling by divine right, or by a parliamentary democracy of elected MPs. I suspect that most people in Lancashire didn't give a fig for the constitutional things so long as they got enough food in their bellies and could enjoy a few nights out in the alehouse. But it was because people were often divided down religious lines that the conflict provoked such bitter animosity.

Frank Musgrove in his impressively discursive book on the history of the north of England believes that 20 per cent of Lancashire's population was

Catholic at the time of the Civil War. That's compared to only 2 per cent elsewhere. And the Fylde was the most intensely Catholic region in the whole of England. Catholicism, being authoritarian, was associated with conservatism, so this is where the royalists could expect to derive their recruits. The puritans were generally more progressive. In the area of south-east Lancashire around Manchester and in Bolton, the people involved in the textile trade were more outgoing and less isolated than out in the boggy Fylde. They had trade links with London and the continent and were responsive to new ideas or progressive protestantism. And it was in 1643 that George Fox the Quaker began his journey through the war-torn shires of England, denouncing Catholicism and institutional religion in favour of the path of individual enlightenment, and his ideas found fertile ground in many parts of Lancashire. So you have these religious divisions which the preachers, rabble-rousers and pamphleteers of the time were happy to exploit.

It's not hard to guess where the loyalties of the Catholic Hoghtons of Hoghton Tower would have lain. An incident at Hoghton which occurred shortly after the first capture of Preston by the parliamentarian troops is described in a letter from February 1643 and illustrates the ruthless brutality of the conflict. It is quoted by the Reverend Jonathan Shortt in his *Brief History of Hoghton* written in 1880. Three captains from the parliamentarian army with their companies of about 300 men, mostly from Blackburn Hundred, were sent to Hoghton. The tower was fortified by three cannons and between 30 and 40 musketeers. After an initial parley the occupants agreed to give up the tower 'upon quarter' (i.e. upon condition of receiving mercy). Whereupon, led by Captain Starkey of Blackburn, the men entered the tower where they found a substantial store of arms and powder. To quote from the letter:

'Religious divisions that preachers and rabble-rousers were happy to exploit'

> Wherefore, he and his company going into the upper rooms of the tower to search for more arms, were most treacherously and perfidiously blown up by two of them to whom they had before given quarter, who had a train of powder laid, and when Captain Starkey and his men, to the number of above one hundred, were above in the house, gave fire to said train, and blew both him and his men, with the roof of the house up; three score whereof were afterwards found, some without arms, and some without legs, and others fearful spectacles to look upon.

But it was not only politics or religion which determined which side you took in the Civil War. For some, family feuds and personal animosity seem to have played a part. A paper for the Lancashire and Cheshire Antiquarian Society points out that the Norrises of Speke may have taken opposite sides to the Moores of Bank Hall in Liverpool because in 1630 they'd come to blows when Sir Edward Norris had struck Edward Moore with his sword, for which he'd been fined £1,000, later reduced to £250, by the Court of the Star Chamber. It's not hard to imagine, especially if you live in a close-knit community where perceived slight can be magnified and memories are long, how the outbreak of war might be seen by some as an opportunity to settle old scores.

But what of the impact on the ordinary individuals, many of whom didn't take sides but probably preferred to lie low and uncommitted until the whole thing blew over and they could get back to eking out a fairly miserable existence from the none-too hospitable climate and clay of Lancashire? It must have been a miserable and interminable nine years with terrifying bands of armed troops, often disgruntled from being unpaid for long periods, rampaging up and down the countryside looking for food and shelter, threatening and bullying, looting and raping and desecrating churches. (The misericords at Cartmel were badly mutilated by the Roundheads who billeted themselves and their horses in the priory church.) It must have seemed as if the Apocalypse had arrived to many of the God-fearing. In today's age of almost universal scepticism it's hard to imagine how the world of the ordinary individual had been turned on its head and what a state of physical and spiritual anxiety had ensued with the collapse of the authority of both King and Church. A strict hierarchy had been replaced by anarchy, order by chaos. It must have taken strong people to survive such turmoil. No wonder it was a time which saw the birth of many bizarre religious sects with strange and fervent prognostications of a new millennium.

It's tempting to speculate that the rugged, even cussed, independence that is so much a part of the Lancashire spirit was nourished during this period of social and spiritual upheaval, and that the flourishing of non-conformist beliefs that were widespread in the nineteenth century had its roots in this period. In the climate of brutality and moral decline Quakerism preached a philosophy of non-violence, but with active dissension which included a refusal to pay tithes or attend church, which was compulsory and carried a twelve-pence fine for non-compliance. The Quakers suffered persecution by the authorities and George Fox was thrown into gaol in Lancaster Castle as a dangerous political rebel and 'disturber of the peace of the nation'.

When the Scots marched south in 1648 under the Duke of Hamilton to support the royalist cause they travelled through Hornby and Lancaster, ravaging the surrounding countryside and burning fields and stealing animals for their troops. They were met by an army of northern royalists under Sir Marmaduke Langdale and engaged with Cromwell's forces with a Lancashire contingent led by Ralph Assheton at Preston on 17 August. The royalist forces outnumbered the parliamentarian by more than two to one, Hamilton's men numbering as many as 20,000. Nevertheless, after terrible bloodshed, the royalists were put to flight and 4,000 of them were captured by Cromwell's men.

But the common enemy had been the weather. Apparently it was the worst summer in living memory. Torrential rain had turned every road into a running quagmire and even the tiniest watercourse into a torrent. The infantry's muskets, which were matchlocks, must have been a dead loss. They were slow enough to reload, but with damp powder ignited by a glowing cord soaked in saltpetre that probably kept going out, a swordsman would have had time to draw and quarter you before you could fire a shot. Instead of guns, the soldiers must have had to rely for their assault upon hacking, poking and gouging with swords, lances and pikes. Now the pike was a 16-foot, some say 18-foot-long pole tipped with steel. At such a length it was almost like killing by remote control. To get some idea of how long a pike like this would be, I took my measuring tape into the garden and taped together some of my runner bean canes. My pretend pike was so long I could barely see the end without my glasses. To stay rigid it must have been quite thick and very heavy, requiring a great deal of strength to wield it. And this 300 years before free school milk! The cavalry wouldn't have stood a chance against a line of pikemen. No wonder the horses needed armour like that helmet we'd seen in the Great Hall at Rufford. The scenes of carnage on the battlefield must have been appalling, burning themselves into the memories of the people of Preston for generations. Yet there's nothing much to be seen on the battlefield, which began on Ribbleton Moor – where Ribbleton Lane crossed Eaves Brook, an area which today is all built upon – and extended all the way down to the Walton bridge. I thought I'd pay a visit to the normally reliable Harris Museum for more information, but found it was closed for three months for alterations.

'Using a 16-foot pike was like killing by remote control'

A visit to the Harris Museum is bad enough at the best of times if you park as I do in the market car park because you then have to pass through the open market to get into Birley Square. It's a giant flea-market with all the charm of an over-sized cattle shed. This is the fag-end of consumerism. The traders stand dejectedly behind their stalls of cheap jewellery and soap, sound cassettes of warbling pub turns and second-rate American videos with titles like *My Stepmother is an Alien* and *Dumb and Dumber*. It's all so tacky. There's the Brief Affairs underwear stall and you can buy one-size-fits-all bathing costumes in some vile sort of synthetic material all puckered like scales. There are undoubtedly some bargains to be had but at what price to your immortal soul? It's the most depressing place to dwell in for any length of time, a sort of slough of retailing despond. How on earth can the traders stand there all day? I didn't catch any of the usual banter you can enjoy on a Lancashire market, the sort you get in Blackburn's Market Hall or in Colne, where it's warm and bright and cheerful. There are three-piece suites and bed settees around the concrete floor, which in the dismal draughty setting of the shed look about as comfortable as a waiting room on a long-abandoned branch line. In fact, the wrought ironwork of the hall is reminiscent of an old Midland railway station, with curling leaves in green and red roses which once must have looked attractive and gay. But now it's grimy and rusty and hasn't been touched up for years and adds to the general squalor of the surroundings. (Is it an old railway station? I remind myself to look it up in the reference library at the Harris, but when I get there, that's closed for the duration too.) The whole place was summed up by the sight of a sad group of middle-aged evangelists in anoraks singing hymns without enthusiasm against the grotesque grey '60s office block of Lowthian House, whatever that might be. Perhaps they were the ancestors of the pious Cromwellians? They'd have been better riding in on horseback and ransacking the whole sorry affair.

The market, along with the dingy car park and all the grey concrete-coloured discount shops that huddle round it like street beggars, is a terrible blot on our county town. If Preston, as the administrative centre of Lancashire, can't get it right, can't show a bit of pride and class, what hope for places like Burnley or Bacup or Colne? There's such a thing as leading by example. The town's Victorian fathers would have blushed to their wing collars. Just step through the market and see how the handsome court buildings near the museum contrast with the wretchedness you've left behind. How often is it the case that the only decent architecture in Lancashire, in England, is over 100 years old? A nation in decline? Was there ever such a barometer of civilisation as our public buildings? Look at the Harris Museum, a splendid piece of neo-classical self-confidence and pride. But there's no hope for modern Preston if the square in front of the Harris that contains the war memorial is anything to judge by. The Philistines were busy setting up camp when I arrived – much worse than the army of the Duke of Hamilton. It's a month until Christmas and in their wisdom the new city fathers have invited the fairground folk to set up their tawdry roundabouts and dodgems. There's a ghastly Santa's grotto in the shape of a log cabin with an inflatable roof and toothy elves peering from the windows with the mad glaze to their eyes of never-satisfied consumers. There's a food stall which hasn't yet opened but boasts 'Made for you to eat'. An extraordinary claim for food. And the marble muses, the pantheon of scholars, artists and poets look down from the frieze of the Harris Museum at the crass, vulgar and stupid scene below in dismay. And in gold letters the invocation 'To Literature, Arts and Sciences' rings as hollow today as a fool with a stick beating on an empty dustbin. The people of Preston deserve better.

I wondered if I would fare any better at reviving some of the embers of the Civil War in Bolton, the scene of a terrible massacre by the royalists and the subsequent revenge on the Earl of Derby, who was beheaded there at the Market Cross on 15 October 1651.

The old market place is now the site of the Victorian town hall. This really is quite stunning, as impressive as anything London has to offer, and if you take into account the Crescent behind, as gracious as anything in Buxton or Bath, you have the most remarkable and elegant collection of public buildings anywhere, a poke in the eye for all our southern detractors with their dark satanic mills jibes. (To be fair to Preston, they too once had a grand Victorian town hall, but it was badly damaged in a fire just after the war, and the ground-floor stump was pulled down in the 1960s to make way for what

Victorian grandeur meets bouncy castle.
PHOTOGRAPH: AUTHOR

is quite the most ugly office block ever constructed.) The truly remarkable thing about Bolton's Crescent – used, I was proudly told, by television people wishing to create classical settings for their dramas, as if we needed the patronising endorsement of media folk to tell us how good some of our buildings are – is that it was built in the 1930s. Yes, when everyone else was sticking up those horrid little pebble-dash bungalows, Bolton, never mind the Depression or the storm clouds of World War II, was building for the future in a grandiose rush of optimism and civic pride. The architects were Bradshaw, Gass & Hope, and one can't help feeling that the latter gentleman was well named. It strikes me as being an admirable principle which the modern economic Jeremiahs could well take on board. When things are looking bad, think big and spend, invest in the future, and it will lift everyone out of the doldrums. The Crescent was completed in 1939 in time to raise the spirits of Boltonians and see them through the war.

Alas, the present city fathers don't seem to be able to summon up quite the same degree of visionary scope. For Lo! Here's another Santa's Grot, slap bang in front of the town hall and sandwiched between it and the lovely war memorial with its poignant scenes of mothers grieving over their dying sons. How long memories must be in Bolton and how grateful they must be. I read the names on the tiny wooden crosses with their poppies which had been stuck into the turf on Remembrance Day: 'John Cryer. The Somme, 1916'; 'Walter Tait, The Lancashire Fusiliers, The Somme, 1917'; 'Thank you for Freedom,' says another; and another brings us right up to date and to Iraq with simply, 'Black Watch, 2004'.

I like the Town Hall Square, Victoria Square as it's now called. Today I'm prepared to forgive Santa and his grotto plastered with advertising and the smell of hot dogs that wafts noisomely from the stall on the edge of the square. I like the way people clip clop across it, quite comfortable with all the Victorian grandeur which soars above them and not a bit put out by the stern brows of the town's patriarchs or the fearsome gaze of the mildewed lions. They chatter happily into their mobile phones. 'No problem,' they always seem to say as they go past. 'No problem.' The no problem mobile phone, the panacea for all twenty-first-century ills. Meanwhile the pigeons, themselves a means of mobile communication on the Somme, where the messages must have been rather less optimistic, soar and swoop, sending staccato shadows scuttling across the square in the afternoon sunshine. One bird has formed a queue at my feet, believing my notebook to be a slice of bread. A council workman with a mobile dustbin hurries past, capturing a crisp packet with his litter tongs and dropping it into his bin in one deft movement. A minute later and another arrives and he's even quicker because there's nothing left to pick up. They're very punctilious about litter in Victoria Square. Pity they haven't invented a little picker that works on compressed chewing gum.

Anywhere around the Mediterranean the square in front of the town hall would be a piazza and people would be standing around talking or sitting in cafes around the perimeter. But this is Lancashire and we're close to the 54th Parallel, so such an exotic usage is unlikely unless global warming really does accelerate. Today, with the fountains in full spate, sending shivering columns of ice-white water into the air, it feels more like the town hall square in Murmansk.

'They've had a lot of trouble with them,' says one passer-by, seeing me admiring the fountains. 'Litter?' I venture, more to make conversation than any knowledge of such matters. 'Naw. Probably the pipes,' I'm told. 'Not long enough.'

They know about things like pipes and how things work in Bolton. Just beyond the Square, opposite Dixons, there's a working steam engine in a big glass box. It was made in Bolton in 1886 by Hick & Hargreaves, Engineers. It has an 8-foot flywheel painted green with an orange rim and a connecting rod which is bronze with grease. I'm the only one standing gawping at the shining cogs and sliding pistons and the mesmerising governor balls swivelling like steely moons. I suspect everyone else takes it for granted. After all, Bolton is the home of Samuel Crompton whose spinning jenny helped launch the Industrial Revolution, and it was probably a hotbed of utilitarianism. Usefulness and making things work was a top priority in Bolton. You can tell this because it was the highest accolade they could bestow on anyone. Beneath the statue of Sir B. A. Dobson, mayor for four years until he died in 1898, which stands in front of the town hall, it says 'Erected by public subscription to commemorate a *useful* life.' In an age such as ours, with so much emphasis on leisure and entertainment, usefulness, I suspect, has gone out of fashion. This could explain why Sir Bernard is gazing out so sternly across the square to W. H. Smith's. Maybe he is wondering why we need 50 different publications on women's fashion and home improvements, or all those books on local history? His moustache seems to bristle with truculence. It curls like the horns of a highland cow, and I know how he did it because my grandfather did the same: soap. Every morning he dug his thumbnail into the carbolic soap and coaxed the unruly whiskers into two quiveringly indignant spikes. Then he was ready to take on the world. You might have guessed Sir Bernard would have used soap because this is Bolton, home of Viscount Leverhulme, who was king of soap and sultan of suds at Port Sunlight.

But my favourite statue of a Bolton luminary is at the other side of the square. It's Edwin Chadwick, the poor law commissioner. You can tell he had something to do with the poor because he has his hand inside his waistcoat reaching for his wallet. But it's Mrs Chadwick in the frieze underneath who grabs the attention. She's busy ministering to the poor, but in her very plain and sensible bonnet manages to look quite scary, rather like the wicked witch of the north. She seems to have one of the children in her charge in a headlock: 'Now, you know it's all your own fault, this poverty.' Edwin Chadwick was hated by the poor, which in those days was more or less everybody, because his Poor Law reforms treated destitution as a form of moral delinquency and the only way to get relief was by entry into the dreaded workhouse. This hatred is captured in the inscription below the statue. No Sir Edwin. Not even an initial. Just 'Chadwick'. And try saying that without spitting. It's said that Chadwick's Poor Law of 1834 did a lot to drive people to Chartism.

Leaving the Chadwicks to their cheerless philanthropy, I walk behind the town hall, along the Crescent, and into the museum and library. Here they have a local studies department where they're so clued up the Civil War might have taken place only last week. I was shown eyewitness accounts of the fighting in Bolton. And a bloodthirsty business it was. Just how bloodthirsty depends upon which side you were on. Reading the accounts I couldn't help but be reminded of the dictum: the first casualty of war is truth. To the Cromwellians the royalists were godless monsters. To the royalists the parliamentarians were brutal iconoclasts. But however one-sided the accounts, you can't fail to feel sorry for the ordinary citizens in the middle.

This is what happened. After relieving the siege at Lathom House, Prince Rupert, his poodle and the rest of the royalists moved towards Bolton. The parliamentarians had just arrived and on 28 May 1644, a siege, battle and subsequent sacking of the town took place which became known as the Bolton

Bolton's stunning town hall.
PHOTOGRAPH: AUTHOR

Massacre. An eyewitness account, written by a clergyman to judge from his lavish indulgence in pulpit rhetoric, describes the arrival of Prince Rupert's forces 'like a wood or cloud'. He places the royalist numbers at around 12,000. This compares with a mere two-and-a-half thousand of the town's defenders. I'll quote from the account so that you can judge for yourself the sense of florid outrage which fevers his prose:

At their entrance, before, behinde, to the right, and left, nothing heard but 'Kill dead! Kill dead!' was the word in the Town, killing all before them without any respect, without the town by their Horsemen pursuing the poore amazed people, killing, stripping, and spoiling all they could meet with, nothing regarding the doleful cries of women and children, but some they slashed as they were calling for quarter, others when they had given quarter, many hailed out of their houses to have their brains out in the streets, those that were not dead in the streets already pistoled, slashed, brained, or troden under their horses feet with many insolent, blasphemous oathes, curses, and challenges to heaven itselfe ...

The streets of Bolton have become an abattoir:

First the massacring, dismembering, cutting of dying or dead bodies, and boasting, with all new coined oathes swearing how many Roundheads this sword or they had killed that day, some eight, some six, some more or lesse. Arms, legs, yea the braines themselves lying distant from their heads, bodies and other parts.

The eyewitness then goes on to name some of the victims:

William Boulton was fetcht out of his chamber with scorne, saying they had found a praying Saint, and fetcht him to kill him before his wives face, who being greate with childe and ready to be delivered, fell on him to have saved him, but they pulled her off without compassion, and bade him call on his God to save him, whilest they cut him to pieces.

Katherine Saddon, an aged woman of 72 years old, run with a sword to the very heart, because she had no money to give, and some others killed outright after they were mortally wounded, because they stirred or answered not greedy unjust desires.

Elizabeth Horrocks, a woman of good qualities, after that they had killed her husband, tooke her in a rope and dragged her up and down, after that they had robbed and spoiled her of all she had, and threatened to hang her unlesse she would tell them of her plate and money, who was yet wonderfully preserved.

Their inhuman usage of her and some other maids and wives in the town in private places, in fields and in woods, the trees, the timber, and the stones, we hope will one day be a witnesse against them, for some of them being destracted at the present day.

And so it goes on. At last we get an insight into the horrors of war as it affected the civilian population. It's Bosnia or Baghdad, except that it's here on our own doorstep in cosy, friendly meet-me-down-at-the-pub Lancashire. I'm only relieved to see it through the wrong end of the telescope of history, where it looks so small and distant that it could be another country and not our ancestors of just a dozen generations ago.

Of course, the royalist account of the massacre was different, their own reporters embedded, as it were. And so we find 'the troops performed with much Gallantry and Resolution'. The Earl of Derby, James Stanley, was to the fore in the onslaught. According to his apologist, he was motivated by concern for his Lady and children who had been besieged at Lathom and, should the parliamentarians not be defeated, would be besieged again. He was accompanied by his own men, 'being all Tennants and Neighbours' sons, clothed and trained by that valiant Earl', which sounds to me as if they could have been fighting under some outmoded feudal obligation: You fight for me or else you'll be out of house and home.

As far as the parliamentarians were concerned the Bolton Massacre became a *cause célèbre* and the part played by the earl was not to be forgotten by the people of Bolton. Their chance for revenge came when the earl, coming back from self-imposed exile on the Isle of Man, joined the royalist uprising under Charles Stuart seven years later, in 1651. Meeting up with Charles's Scottish army as it forged south, the earl and his soldiers fought at Wigan Lane between Standish and Chorley, only to be defeated. The earl fled and with an unerring instinct for backing the wrong horse, again joined the Anglo-Scottish army at the disastrous Battle of Worcester, where they were outnumbered two to one by the Commonwealth troops and suffered accordingly. Fleeing back to Lancashire the earl was captured in Cheshire, and seen as being a great prize he was brought to trial at Chester and found guilty of high treason for supporting Charles Stuart and being a traitor to the Commonwealth. Despite denying any responsibility for the Bolton Massacre, he was sentenced to be brought back to Bolton and beheaded.

Accounts of Lord Derby's return to Bolton and subsequent execution are soaked in royalist pathos. On the journey home, we're told he was met and embraced by his two daughters, kneeling down with them on the roadside to pray while the girls wept 'because it was the last interview with their beloved father on earth'. When he arrived at Bolton to be executed at one o'clock, the beheading was excruciatingly delayed for two hours because the scaffold wasn't ready. The chronicler blames the delay on the good people of the town refusing to lend any assistance and crying, 'O sad day! O wofull day! Shall the good Earl of Derby dye here?' I suppose the thing to remember is that this execution was Lancashire's equivalent of the beheading of Charles I. The Stanleys were literally viceroys of Lancashire. They'd been overlords from 1485 when the earldom was created, and being instruments of king and government had enjoyed a monopoly of power. To the relatively backward and God-fearing people of Lancashire – ironically backward in no small measure due to the domination of the Stanleys – the execution of Lord Derby must have seemed like an act of outrageous sacrilege. But to others it was the necessary removal of an ancient yoke of feudal repression and the prelude to a new age of democratic enlightenment and individualism which in time was to thrust Lancashire to the forefront of the Industrial Revolution.

CHAPTER ELEVEN

EXODUS FROM THE LAND

PERVERSELY, one of my favourite times of year is the winter solstice. I put it down to the dark vein of melancholy in the Lancashire temperament, something bred into us by weather and landscape. I like to climb onto the moortops on a grey winter afternoon, past the dark cloughs where the beech trees shine black with rain and in the tangled tracery of branches the rooks complain and pigeons flap restlessly; where there are trees to remind us of our ancient upland status such as the ghostly birches or the alders whose catkins turn to trembling bronze in a rare burst of sunlight. For the sky is forever changing as the clouds merge and dissolve, but all on the same theme of grey: dove grey; slate grey; black despair grey powerful enough to dissolve even the hills themselves until you are left walking in a sea of mist where black, wet-stained walls suddenly loom and underfoot is nothing but mud and khaki-coloured moss and spikes of spiteful reeds. And as the mist breaks into ragged curtains of rain I stand at a wall with cattle left out by a callous farmer. There are beasts in calf which seem almost as wide as they are long, and I can smell their earthy, cuddy smell. And they let me stroke their flanks where the beast to be lies, to be born into mud and wet and wind and shite. And in a sudden rage I stand and shake my fist at the sky and curse that I ever stayed here and gave all the best years of my life to these God-abandoned hills, a place only fit for the sheep which seem to merge into the landscape and uncomplaining find nourishment from the mean and grudging grassland. But when the sheep raise their tousled heads and stare at me with those distant, amber eyes my thoughts turn to those ragged Celtic warriors who made these hills their home and would fight to the death to defend them. And somehow I once again feel glad and proud to belong to such a place of harsh beauty, and I am filled with resolution to love it whatever the time of year. They don't call the Pennines the backbone of England for nothing.

But on kinder days, when the wind drops, as it's supposed to do in those halcyon days around Christmas, and it turns cold and there's a light snowfall, the landscape is transformed. Every wall, track, plough line, spoil heap and mine-working in our scarred and work-torn landscape is etched black against the snow, like the negative of a photograph. And how the snow draws out the darkness of the bare winter woods, as light always creates shadows. And such a scene seems to trigger memories of similar scenes, drawing out the past from its own shadows. I remember the walk up into Alkincoats Park in Colne when I was a child and passing through the gate in the walled garden near the old hall, standing in the fields which look down into Blakey Bottoms near the old yeoman farmhouse. The sheep were scratching at the snow to get at the frozen grass beneath, and I noticed how they always left the single bent stems alone to tremble in the icy wind above the snowfield. And in the distance, Pendle Hill in the snow has taken a step forwards and is a huge white whaleback. Meanwhile down the valley beyond Burnley and the long-gone cooling towers of Huncoat power station, a crimson sun ignites the sky as it descends westwards to the sea. Such days, past and present, merge in one timeless moment.

But most evocative of all is that moment before nightfall when all the lights in the valley towns begin to flicker on. Necklaces of street lights morphing from that exotic pomegranate colour to the rich sodium yellow of the mature light, and all the other islands of light that start to glow and twinkle. And although the cold of night has begun to bite and the air has the bitter taste of cold tin, the lights of the town begin to beckon, warmly calling you home. The cold clear yelp of a fox pierces the drone of the distant traffic and high overhead vapour trails lit by the dying rays of the sun thread the sky between the emerging stars. Nature and man are so close together in many of our Lancashire towns, so intimately linked. There's none of the scary loneliness of mountain Scotland, nor the isolated exposure of the flatlands of eastern England. The countryside around is for ever close by, part of our lives, if we so choose. We are hybrid creatures, half urban and half rural, and this is not just because of our proximity to open country but because our roots are in the country. And it is the tracks and footpaths like the ones I take out of the valley and into the hills which are the links with our country roots.

Where else in England will you find so many public footpaths as those in Lancashire which link town and countryside? Today they are usually deserted. To meet anyone tramping along them is an event. Maybe you'll see the occasional madly pedalling mountain biker clad in a Darth Vader helmet, or a teeth-locked jogger, or the odd introspective sociophobe like me, forever brooding upon the past. But for me, these are ghost roads, haunted by all the souls who have tramped up and down them in the past. They were the arteries which fed the Industrial Revolution with its most vital nutrient, labour. Down

Path to the mill, Narrowgates, Barley.
PHOTOGRAPH: AUTHOR

these roads and tracks came the mill workers who for centuries had lived on the land and woven cloth on their handlooms in their farmhouses and cottages; but with the arrival of steam power and the factories, they were forced by economic necessity to abandon their farmsteads and smallholdings for the town. The paths are linear monuments to an extraordinary social change. From country dwellers working at their handlooms, able to break off to help churn some butter or chase the sheep from the vegetable patch, dig up a few potatoes for dinner or pass the time of day with a neighbour, to factory fodder, locked away amid the noise and danger of remorselessly revolving machinery, bound to a schedule no longer dictated by the age-old natural pattern of daylight and the seasons, but by the time clock and the hungry production system. These paths are the record of the route we took on the most significant journey in the history of humanity, from rural peasant dependent upon the land for his subsistence to modern wage earner who relies for his existence upon the urban industrial machine. And it was Lancashire which led the way on this journey.

Wycoller is a village east of Colne on the edge of the Brontë moorland of Yorkshire. When I was a lad it was a ghost village. We used to walk there from Colne and wander around inside the ruined cottages and farmhouses, hanging about until nightfall in the hope of seeing the headless horsemen thundering past the ruined hall and over the packhorse bridge. But that was a legend. In those days I was unaware of the real ghosts of Wycoller, the handloom weavers.

In 1820 the population of Wycoller is thought to have been around 350. By 1851 it had dropped to under 250, and by 1871 it was a mere 100, made up mostly of farmers. These simple statistics illustrate the impact of the factory system upon the domestic business of handloom weaving. The decline reflects the migration of village folk into the towns, the severing of the umbilical that had attached us to the land since our first Lancashire ancestors erected their wood henge on Bleasdale Fell. Fifty years to undo the habits of 3,000 years; a foretaste of the dramatic rapidity of modern social change.

And since the boyhood days of our ghost hunts, Wycoller has changed spectacularly again. Today's village is an exclusive little dormitory for the well off. The houses where the clumsy wooden handlooms once occupied the bedrooms are now fitted out with en-suite bathrooms, I should imagine, with Heald's duvets woven on automatic looms in Taiwan. The village is so

Packhorse bridge, Wycoller.
PHOTOGRAPH: AUTHOR

exclusive these days that as soon as you arrive at the car park you're met by a notice urging you not to bring your dog unless it's on a lead because visitors' dogs have been known to attack the local canines. Now I always thought that dogs, being territorial animals, grew more courageous the closer their proximity to their own front door and therefore shouldn't need a bylaw or whatever to protect them. So the notice either suggests that the local dogs are all of the puny lapdog variety (perhaps even distant descendants of Prince Rupert's poodles?) or else the notice is not about dogs but their owners and is an attempt to discourage those undesirable folk you sometimes see with pit bulls snarling at their heels. Whatever it meant, I locked my own pooch away in the car, it being a mongrel species of the yellow variety with bad breath and generally capable of lowering the tone of any location by its behaviour; and after wondering for a while about my own desirability as a visitor to such a fastidious place, I threw caution to the wind and set off down the path to the village.

The other unwelcome visitor to Wycoller is the motor car and of this attitude I wholeheartedly approve. The car park is some 500 yards away from the village and I wouldn't have cared if it had been five miles. (I keep calling Wycoller a village, but it's really a hamlet. One of the first things you meet when you enter is a plaque on a wall which announces: Winner of Best Kept Village Competition, Hamlet Class, 1995.) To see a village without the visual pollution of rows of motor cars lining its streets and snickets is a welcome sight these days. (I am already responding to the pervasive spirit of tidiness which is the essence of Wycoller.)

The other advantage of placing the car park out of the village is that it enables the visitor to inspect the ancient vaccary walls which line the fields to the south of the approach road. These are sandstone slabs set upright rather like rugged headstones around the edges of the fields. The vaccaries were cow farms dating back to the time when the de Lacys successfully farmed the forests of Pendle and Trawden. The slabs aren't capable of confining sheep but must have been successful at restricting the movements of less vagrant beasts like cows and oxen. They are a unique reminder of the long history of animal husbandry in the area. Today's tenants are some of the raggiest and dirtiest sheep I've ever come across: small, urchin-like creatures with long valances of tangled, muddy wool and horns like polished ammonites. They've been on the receiving end of weeks of rain and the fields are a morass. Wycoller is in a hollow, with moorland rising steeply on three sides and the river splashing noisily down the middle of the village. You can see immediately the advantage of such a damp place for the spinning and weaving of wool. I recall wandering around the village many years ago in the company of the late Stanley Cookson of Trawden, who pointed out to me the small holes worn in the stones of some of the house walls. He called them 'wuzzing' holes (I never saw the word written down, but that's how it sounded), and they were made by the wooden spindles which the handloomers used to spin against the walls in order to draw out the wool to make the thread.

If moss and lichen are barometers of dampness, Wycoller is as near as it gets to living underwater. I have never seen walls so scabbed with lichen as those around the ruined hall, and the tops of the ruined stonework drip with moss. The masonry of the hall is black and the long mullioned windows, once undoubtedly handsome, now gape with a sullen emptiness. It's the most melancholy and moody ruin, especially on days like the day I visited, with a heavy sky the colour of dull pewter. Only one crumbling stack of stones is left standing beyond the first floor, like the glum turret of a plundered castle. It's the sort of ruin they were fond of in Victorian times and would have provided a setting for a poem by Tennyson about some jilted maiden trapped forever amongst her forlorn surroundings. It's the very nadir of the dead season and the tumbled walls of the outbuildings are choked with brambles and dead bracken and briars with berries the colour of dried blood. For me, Wycoller Hall seemed full of bad memories, as if something terrible had happened here once, and I was reminded of the legend of the headless horseman who was said to be the ghost of a squire who had murdered his lady here in a fit of jealous rage.

'What a jolly meeting place it would have been to enjoy a tipple and harvest supper'

I was glad to hurry past the hall towards the warm yellow lights of the nearby visitor centre, a restored aisled barn built in the 1630s on the site of an even earlier cruck barn. The original timbers stand precariously balanced on stone supports, giving the whole internal structure a rather fragile, spindly look, with pale, wormy wood, porous as pumice. The cold rises from the flagged and cobbled floor which has the stillness of an ancient church. In fact, the timbering of the roof is identical to that of many old churches and cathedrals, so you have here a shrine to a lost way of life where the land and what you could raise from it was the basis of everyday existence for everyone. It is a stone and timber shell from which the life and meaning have long since gone, to be replaced by the lifeless paraphernalia of a museum: display cases full of flints and old clogs, a huge key to the old hall and a stuffed kestrel instead of the owl who once silently patrolled the aisles in search of rats and mice. There's fashionable modern decking on the floor and soft buttery lights up on the walls to cast a romantic, nostalgic glow over the past, which is the way of the heritage business. So I found myself dreaming of the days when the floor of the barn was used for threshing corn and the aisles were filled with the warm, cuddy breath of safely wintering beasts. And I thought of what a jolly meeting place it would have been for the villagers to enjoy their tipple and harvest suppers and dance and make merry like the rustics out of a story by Thomas Hardy; of all those seasonal and communal activities associated with village life, when people shared a common purpose in drawing a living out of the land and would have made Wycoller as warm and boisterous as a basket full of puppies; something, alas, so desperately missing from the Wycoller of today.

Leaving the barn and returning to the village, you can cross the river by the old arched packhorse bridge used by handloom weavers taking their finished cloth to the old Piece Hall in Colne. The bridge is probably the most painted scene in the whole of Lancashire, affectionately adorning hundreds of living-room walls. But then Wycoller occupies a special place in the hearts of local people, either because it was a destination of so many childhood strolls or, more intangibly, because many Lancastrians from this corner of the county are responding to those invisible roots which once anchored their forebears to the land or the slow toil of the handloom. But today's village, with its tastefully renovated houses, sandblasted to a pristine perfection, carefully maintained walls and tidy courtyards, has itself something of the look of a rather lifeless watercolour. I'm sorry if I seem to be going on, and I'm sure the people who live there are very proud of their houses and village, but I'm reaching after something that makes me very uneasy about rural living as we experience it today. As I wandered up and down the tiny main street thinking about it, until some of the curtains started to twitch, a man came out of his house and began fussing around his motor car. It had a huge union jack painted on the roof and it occurred to me that villages such as Wycoller are at the heart of how we still like to see ourselves as English people. We become successful and move out of the town and into the country. But we have no relationship with the countryside any more. Nor do we have any real relationship with

Tithe barn with
visitor centre.

PHOTOGRAPH: AUTHOR

other people in the village. The surrounding land or the common activity of handloom weaving no longer sustain people. There are no shops (apart from the obvious tourist magnet of a gift shop) upon which village people depend. There's no pub, vicar, blacksmith, medicine woman or whatever to carry out some sort of role which draws people together. Everyone lives in isolation; every house has that 'Hands off! Englishman's castle' feel about it. All the subtle bonds which united people in the past and made a community have disappeared. Today the only thing which connects people who live in Wycoller – along with many of the villages of Bowland and the Ribble valley, and you'll be able to add your own examples – is the ability to afford to live where they do. In other words, money. In the past we might have shared the same fields or teams of oxen, or room on the threshing floor, or knees-up in the aisled barn, but today the only thing the villagers share is the same exclusive postcode and, as you observe each television aerial poking up above its well-appointed chimney pot, the dubious shared benefits of mass communications, which, with their emphasis on global entertainment and marketing, do nothing whatsoever to foster a sense of local belonging. There, that's what I wanted to get off my chest about Wycoller.

But there's also something else at work in Wycoller helping to breathe life in to the socially moribund English village and keeping it in its fossilised state of artificial perfection. I mentioned the Best Kept Village Award. Well, that was issued by an organisation calling itself 'The Community Council of Lancashire'. Inside the restored aisled barn, the lavish investment in toughened glass, hardwood decking and display cabinets was funded by another organisation I'd never heard of called 'The Lancashire Environment Fund', along with the 'Lancashire Tourism Partnership' and 'The Heritage Trust for the North West'. And step outside and it's hard not to bump into a van or pickup belonging to the Lancashire County Council Countryside Service, with a warden fetchingly attired in Lincoln green jumper and woolly hat tending a Millennium tree or numbered bird box, or else hanging around looking at his watch in a study centre set out with stuffed badgers and foxes frozen in mid-snarl.

For these are the people whose job it is to maintain Wycoller's life support machine. And the organisations which employ them, their purses heavy with public money, are responsible for creating this rather precious and artificial concept of a country park, which is what Wycoller has become. In the face of the massive defection from the country into the town begun by our handloom weaving forefathers, the country park is a modern rearguard action to try to bring people back again, if only for the duration of an afternoon. Their neatly prescribed walks, fact-filled visitor centres and schemes to resuscitate ancient rural crafts are all an attempt to recreate a lost Arcadia in a neatly packaged and marketed experience. In the plate-glass panelled, centrally heated information office incongruously located in the corner of the ancient aisled barn, the shelves groan with pamphlets and publications. Here I discovered that Wycoller was to become the focal point of a project involving brick-carving, lantern-making, shadow-puppetry and wood-sculpting. Willow-weavers would construct a giant willow tunnel and sculptural figure. Droves of artists would descend to demonstrate their crafts, including sculptors, puppeteers, performance poets, environmental artists, story-tellers and face-painters.

Now this is all fine by me. I'm no Philistine, I hope, and the more creative we all become, the better. I'm happy that children will become involved in walking Wycoller's paths and 'responding creatively to its history, people and environment', even if the phrase sounds a rather empty one that's been included because it looks good in a brochure. Anything's better than seeing them stuck in front of a computer console playing 'Psychopath Killer III', or intimidating grandmas outside the post office. But I'm not so happy about cohorts of 'artists' I've never heard of descending upon places we locals know and love and exploiting it for their own self-serving ends. And I'm certainly not happy about the butter of money and resources being spread so thickly in one place when others are ignored. Wycoller and places like it don't need sculptures stuck around the place or poets trilling from the trees when it has its own eloquent ruined hall and marvellous bridges. Wouldn't the cultural deserts of consumerism that many of our town centres have become

Aliens land above Wycoller.
PHOTOGRAPH: AUTHOR

benefit from some similar attention? A string quartet outside McDonald's on a Saturday afternoon? It's no dafter than a willow-weaving workshop at Wycoller. It is a measure of the distance we have travelled away from real nature and the countryside that people should need to invent such bogus rustic activities; that we should all have to traipse around a country walk with a guide dressed like an extra from Robin Hood waving a countryside code, or listen to boring demonstrations of how to make corn dollies by someone wearing a fustian smock in a craft centre; or suffer condescending notices about only taking our dogs for a walk if they're muzzled. As if we were not allowed to escape from our over-organised and over-regulated lives for a while and just go out and explore our own bit of countryside when and where the spirit leads us without the countryside commissariat interfering, for all the worthiness of its intentions.

> 'I feel strangely nervous and begin to wish I'd brought a torch'

And finally, I wonder about the genteel silence which seems to hang over the real inhabitants of Wycoller: the solicitors and company directors and people like the person who had parked his Aston Martin next to the packhorse bridge when I last visited. Where do they fit into the fauna and flora of the country park? When the visitors arrive for their edifying countryside experience, I suspect they feel like an exotic species of goldfish, shifting around in the shadows behind the mullioned windows amongst the ghosts of the handloom weavers.

I decided to take the footpath from Wycoller towards Colne, the one-way journey of those handloom weavers 150 years ago. Or perhaps there was an interregnum when they continued to live in Wycoller while making the daily journey on foot to the mills of the town. I walk a soggy path, dodging the puddles of mud. It's something called the Pendle Way and is clearly only intended to be walked in summer, a dry one at that. The signposts are marked with a witch on a broomstick and the path is truly accursed, blighted by being through low-lying land next to the river. It's already starting to get dark and the wind-torn thorn trees that dot the landscape are beginning to look like props from Macbeth. I feel strangely nervous and begin to wish I'd brought a torch. A candle in a jar would have done, which I'm told the weavers would have carried, though with a nagging wind swirling across the fields and a tendency for the wind in these parts to drop straight down out of the sky, how they managed to keep it alight I can't imagine. I'd recently read a ghost story by M. R. James about a lone man in an empty landscape being pursued by some dreadful entity, and in the twilight I could hear the words of the story whispering in my brain: 'Who is this who is coming?'

The mid-nineteenth century, when the first mill workers began to make this journey, is but a stepping stone away from those darker times when the peddler John Law imagined himself struck down by the witch Alizon Device in a field somewhere near here. Street lighting hadn't arrived, and the dark forces which haunted the medieval world and found expression in some of the grotesque carvings of the churches still fretted away at the imagination. I was relieved to see the lights of Laneshaw Bridge beckoning and for my mind to be kept busy dodging the quagmires.

But now the river has eroded the path and I must skirt round a flooded field before I can find my way back to the path and a notice which belatedly announces 'Risk of River Bank Collapse'. It's funny how public notices invariably tell you what you've already found out by bitter experience, for example, once you've been gored by the bull. I imagine sadistic officials hidden away in offices gloating over our misfortune while congratulating themselves that they'll never be sued on account of their entirely ineffectual notices. And just as I arrive within a stone's throw of the road, I manage to slither face down a muddy bank and so emerge into civilisation looking remarkably like an African mud man. But nobody seems to notice when I enter the pub. Christmas celebrations are in full swing and there are lots of cheery, beery faces lit by candlelight and the glow of tinsel. Laughter explodes around me like Mills bombs. Perhaps they've seen the mud and think I'm a mummer come to join them. One old-timer still wearing his flat cap in preference to a paper one out of a cracker is clutching half a pint of stout and a mince pie and looks thoroughly out of place amongst the glittering fruit machines and pop music, surrounded by young men with spiky gelled hair and loud voices who swear as naturally as the rest of us breathe. I'm back in the modern world and the handloom might as well be in a museum along with the square wheel.

To see a handloom and get a picture of what it must have been like to share your bedroom with one I had to go to a museum. Not a Lancashire one, I'm ashamed to say, but a museum in the West Riding of Yorkshire where they're thoughtful enough to keep them open over most of Christmas to prevent us becoming brain-dead from a surfeit of Trivial Pursuit and Miss Marple. At least, that's the case at Cliffe Castle in Keighley, a short car journey over The Moss from Laneshaw Bridge. At the risk of being stripped of my Lancashire citizenship, I confess to a great liking for Cliffe Castle Museum. Its collection of rocks and minerals is one of the finest I've seen in any provincial museum. But I was looking for Timmy Feather. Timmy was the last handloom weaver in the region to continue the craft until his death in 1910. It takes a rare breed of cussedness to persist, in defiance of a century of Industrial Revolution, right into the twentieth century. This appeals to me not only because I'm the last of the Luddites and would happily go around smashing up four-wheel drives and stamping on mobile phones if I wasn't afraid of being locked away for it, but also because defiance was a quality which enabled our grandparents to survive the ups and downs of the textile industry, to say

'It's funny how public notices invariably tell you what you've already found out by bitter experience'

nothing of the vicissitudes of the northern climate, and still come up with a grin on their faces, like Ken Dodd collecting a pay cheque.

Timmy Feather was born in 1825 and lived at Stanbury, which, as the crow flies or a squelchy treck over Crow Hill by Boulsworth takes you, is not so far from Wycoller. So for his general cussedness and his proximity to our county I'd like to nominate Timmy Feather as an honorary Lancastrian. There's a photograph of him seated at his spindle-back chair, that resolute grin on his face ('Progress? What progress?'). He's smoking his pipe and his skin has that dark, leather look that people had before they bothered much with soap. He's wearing a coat as ragged and greasy as an old peg rug. In another picture he's got his bowler hat on while he doggedly winds his own bobbins. But behind the photos, in all its glory, stands his handloom. It's as big and square as an old printing press and if you installed one in a bedroom today it would take up the space of four walk-in showers. Slung high up on the wooden frame, black as a bat, is Timmy's hat stuck on a makeshift peg, and down by the side is his walking stick, which confirmed my theory that handloomers were much given to breaking off their work and popping outside to wander about

Cottages at Downham.

a bit and feed the hens. It proves that the greatest privation to the ordinary man and woman through the introduction of the factory system was the loss of their freedom, something which, in my opinion, even today's workers can never be adequately compensated for.

I'd always had the impression that handloom weavers stood at their looms like they had to in the mills. But no, there's a stool in front, although it's very low down and above it is a narrow leather hammock which is stretched from one side of the frame to the other. Another photograph showing Timmy at work reveals that he sat on the hammock and the stool beneath was for his feet. There he is, perched over his loom, his knees bent almost to his chest, a snood of white whiskers round his face, looking all shrunken like some sort of industrious dwarf in a fairy story. The warps hang down from wooden slats like the strings of a puppeteer and underneath are treadles for moving them up and down. I could detect no means of moving the shuttle across the loom except by hand and every part, including the cogs which rotated the beam of finished cloth, was made of wood. I could imagine those mechanically minded people of Bolton and the like itching to get their hands on such an antediluvian piece of equipment to improve it, which is, of course, just what they did in Bury when John Kay invented his 'flying' shuttle. I'd read that the handloomers produced a fine-quality worsted that was much sought after, but the stuff coming off Timmy's loom looked more like sackcloth. But this is only to be expected when you saw the raw material Timmy had to work with: a barrel of very grimy, greasy-looking wool standing next to his spinning wheel. From what I saw at Cliffe Castle, handloom weaving appeared to be a slow, grim and dusty business, as far removed from the Lady of Shalott as Wigan Pier is from the Savoy Hotel.

This insight into the domestic conditions of the handloom workers inclined me less to the view, inspired by my own technophobia, that the original opponents of the factory system who smashed looms and pulled the plugs from the new-fangled steam boilers were rural reactionaries resisting the tyranny of the machine age. More likely, they were simply men and women who had enjoyed the freedom of their own home and plot as a means of livelihood ever since Adam had delved and Eve had spun, rebelling against the forced migration into an alien and unnatural setting of factory and urban slum.

But Luddites apart, where did the people who welcomed the new factory system and came to swell the numbers in the Lancashire towns come from, apart from Wycoller? Titus Thornber, whose family grew to become mill-owners, records that his grandfather set out from Rimington on the edge of the Ribble valley to make a new life in Burnley. I've come across people who told me their families originated from high in the Yorkshire dales, and a study of surnames which are common to both places will confirm this. But mill-town Lancashire took new blood from much further afield, including the south of England, which always makes me wary of those who vociferously claim their northern pedigree without delving very far into their family background. My own late mother told me about how her grandfather, George Henry Smith – yes, we had Smiths on both sides of the family, confirming my profoundly plebeian origins – came from Suffolk with his wife to work in the wool mills of Bradford. I've never traced their exact origins myself, but do possess a most unusual and poignant memento which points in that direction. It's a small pot, like a christening cup, but commemorating a much more melancholy event. Written in gold lettering on the side are the words: 'Henry Smith of Alkborough. Born July 13th 1856. Died June 24th 1857'. I once journeyed to Alkborough, which is a small windswept village on the south side of the Humber estuary in North Lincolnshire, but could find no record of any family burial in the churchyard. Was the simple inscribed cup all the family could afford? I wrote to the North Lincolnshire Register Office and received a copy of the child's birth certificate. His father was a George Smith, described as an agricultural labourer, and his mother was Mary, who must have been illiterate because she could not sign her name on the certificate but only mark it with a cross. I don't know whether or not the dead infant was the brother of my mother's grandfather, another child of George and Mary who luckily survived to pass on some of that genetic material which lives on in me, that precious protoplasm which allows history to live on in all of us and the very contemplation of which can fill us with a sense of amazement at the mystery and continuity of human life. But what were the Smiths doing in Alkborough? The village is famous for its maze, believed to have been made by monks in the twelfth century, and it's apt that I should find myself lost in speculation. Were they journeying northwards looking for work, and did Alkborough provide George Smith with employment as a farm labourer for a while before that inevitable journey into the mills of northern England?

'That precious protoplasm which allows history to live on in all of us'

What is certain is that this sort of emigration was widespread throughout the nineteenth century, and rural Suffolk in particular provided the labour which the expanding mill towns were short of. Over 100 Enclosure Acts between 1770 and 1880 deprived so many families of the means of support in rural areas, and a slump in corn prices after the Napoleonic wars led to further hardship. After the Poor Law Amendment Act was passed in 1834, half of the population of Suffolk was receiving relief of some kind. And just like the villagers of Wycoller, many of the farming families of Suffolk relied upon the domestic textile industry of combing and spinning wool which was hit heavily by advances in mechanisation. So by the time of the 1851 census, 50,000 people born in Suffolk were living elsewhere. In fact, between 1835 and 1837, a migration scheme was in operation between Suffolk and the mill towns of Lancashire and Yorkshire where people were encouraged to move. Families journeyed to London and then travelled northwards by canal boat in a journey which took about five days.

I'm indebted to the work of Sandie Geddes who, with the help of members of Bacup Natural History Society, charts the movement of one family from Suffolk to Bacup as part of a college thesis and in so doing compares the life they left behind in the Suffolk countryside with their new life in a burgeoning Lancashire mill town. The picture of country living which emerges is one of depressing poverty under feudal landlords in tied cottages from which eviction was a constant threat. Despite a cottage garden or patch of land on which the family could cultivate vegetables, their existence was far from idyllic. Overcrowding, open drains and cesspits and drinking water which was often polluted produced conditions that were little better than rural slums. Rudimentary schooling for the children would be provided by a charity school but would always take second place to long hours from dawn till dusk helping out on the land. But one of the greatest evils of land working was the gang system where masters and farmers would agree a price for harvesting a crop and then employ the cheapest labour, often women and children, some younger than eight years old, working as many as 14 hours a day for starvation wages. (It is both astonishing and shameful to me that the gang system is still in operation today, and that gang masters are still growing rich through the exploitation of migrant workers paid wages of barely subsistence level to fill supermarket shelves for the rest of us.)

In 1836, the year in which the family moved from Suffolk, Bacup was rapidly expanding as a mill town. Mill workers would be expected to work 12 hours a day and nine hours on Saturday. Factory work was hazardous, especially for the children in constant danger from unfenced machinery. A contemporary account describes a child day-dreaming, as children do, or else unable to concentrate through lack of sleep, and straying too close to the flying machinery:

A coil of strap fastened the boy's arm to the shaft, and round he went. His leg was cut off and fell into the room, his arm was broken in three or four places, his ankle was broken, his head was battered; he was not released alive.

Pollution from flying cotton fluff – or dawn, as the mill workers of my childhood called it – was a health hazard and cause of chronic lung disease. By 1849 Bacup had 29 steam engines as well as foundries, dyeing establishments and a gas works, all further sources of health-damaging pollution and a world away from the fresh air and wide open skies of the Suffolk land-worker. Living conditions were overcrowded. The infant river Irwell which flows through the town was an open sewer, often overflowing into the cellar dwellings that lined its banks. Disease was rife and infant mortality high. Food couldn't be grown, so the workers had to rely upon shops selling produce that was often of a poor quality and sometimes

'It is both astonishing and shameful that the gang system is still in operation today'

Full-blown industrialisation.

adulterated to make unscrupulous shopkeepers more profit. The employment of children under the age of nine was prohibited and part-time schooling for the 9–13 year-olds was enforced, though after 13 there was nothing to stop children working as many as 69 hours a week. It wasn't until 1847 that the Ten Hour Act was introduced. Astonishingly, some of the many who opposed this humane restriction of working hours argued that people were better off working longer hours because conditions in the factories were better than those in their own homes!

The conclusion of this comparison between town and country seems to be that life could be equally grim in either place. Disease, starvation and the workhouse was the universal lot of the nineteenth-century worker and his family.

CHAPTER TWELVE

HORRORS OF INDUSTRIAL MANCHESTER

THE GREATEST SYMBOL of industrial expansion in the nineteenth century was Manchester, along with its satellites of Stockport, Salford and Oldham. In the first four decades of the nineteenth century Manchester's population tripled, to almost a quarter of a million. What today, viewed from the Roman causeway on Blackstone Edge, is a dreary urban sprawl stretching as far as the eye can see (or the mist will allow), before 1800 was a leafy vale sprinkled with a few self-contained communities. Even in the 1840s, when Mrs Gaskell wrote *Mary Barton: A Tale of Manchester Life*, the novel begins with the family strolling through rural fields only half an hour's walk away from the town, where 'may be seen the country business of haymaking, ploughing, etc.', and 'the artisan deafened with the noise of tongues and engines may come to listen awhile to the delicious sounds of rural life: the lowing of cattle, the milk-maids' call, the clatter and cackle of poultry in the old farm-yards'. And in contrast to the grim scenes of urban hardship which are to unfold, Mrs Gaskell goes on to describe the idyllic picture of farmhouse porches covered in roses, and gardens crowded with herbs and flowers. It is a revealing historical and sociological insight made through the pages of fiction about the new citizens of industrial Lancashire. They are still peasants at heart, returning to their rustic roots for spiritual nourishment in the short time they are free from the suffocating demands of their industrial masters.

Dr Aikin's tome *A Description of the Country from 30 to 40 miles Round Manchester*, published in 1795, has etchings showing idyllic scenes of wooded vales and meandering rivers with horses and cattle grazing peacefully and sportsmen out shooting. One view of Manchester published in 1793 shows a foreground of grazing cattle and silver birches with a winding river, its banks thick with trees and hedgerows. In the distance is Manchester under a clear sky with spires and church towers instead of mill chimneys, giving no clue to the Plutonian transformation which was already taking place there.

Dr Aikin then goes on to explore the surrounding suburbs. 'The air of Prestwich is pure and salubrious,' he trills, and to prove it he cites the ages of the rector and his staff. Dr Goodwin is 70. The curate Mr Scholes is 78. The churchwarden Ralph Guest is 85, and Mary Berry the sexton's wife is 86. There doesn't seem to be a lot of work for her husband to do in this rural haven which is producing the milk and butter for Manchester. In fact, much as we're taught to think that it was the damp climate and resources of water and coal which prompted the astonishing upsurge in the textile industry in Lancashire, it had as much to do with the high numbers and relative healthiness of the surrounding population that was able to fill the demand for labour in the new factories. Sturdy, well-fed peasants. How that was all to alter.

> 'Sturdy, well-fed peasants from the countryside around Manchester were perfect mill labour'

Further afield, Dr Aikin describes Oldham as 'pleasantly situated on a high eminence commanding an extensive and delightful prospect'. But he's soon back in Manchester and observing the living conditions of the workers with the appalled eye of a medical practitioner. Manchester, he records, 'unfortunately vies with or exceeds the metropolis [London] in the closeness with which the poor are crowded in offensive, dark, damp and incommodious habitations'. While merchants of fortune inhabit their elegant drawing rooms in 'spacious, excellent and large houses', he observes, 'in a house in Bootle Street most of the inhabitants are paralytic in consequence of their situation in a blind alley which excludes them from light and air. Consumption, distortions and idiocy are common in such recesses.' Elsewhere, he writes, 'I am persuaded that mischief frequently arises from a practice common in many narrow back streets of leaving the vaults of the privies open. I have often observed that fevers prevail most in houses exposed to the effluvia of dunghills in such situations.' He goes on:

> In Blakeley Street, under no. 4, is a range of cellars let out to lodgers which threaten to become a nursery of diseases. They consist of 4 rooms communicating with each other of which the two centre rooms are completely dark; the fourth is very ill-lighted and chiefly ventilated through the others. They contain from 4 to 5 beds in each and already are extremely dirty … The lodging houses near the extremities of the town produce many fevers not only from want of cleanliness of the air but by receiving the most offensive objects into beds which never seem to undergo any attempts towards cleaning them from their first purchase

till they rot under their tenants ... In some other houses in the same nest I have known a whole swarm of lodgers exposed to infection by the introduction of a fever patient.

And with a notion of immunology that must have been gathered rather from experience than any medical knowledge of the time, he goes on:

It must be observed that persons newly arrived from the country are most liable to suffer from these causes ... The horror of these houses cannot easily be described; a lodger fresh from the country often lies down in a bed filled with infection by its last tenant or from which the corpse of a victim to fever has only been removed a few hours before.

Another evil is exposed by Dr Aikin in his account of a visit to Eccles, another manufacturing town expanding rapidly at the end of the eighteenth century. This is the importing of children from other parts of the country as cheap labour for the cotton mills. He reveals:

Children of very tender age are employed, many of them collected from the workhouses in London and Westminster and transported in crowds as apprentices to masters resident many hundred miles distant where they serve unknown, unprotected and forgotten by those to whose care nature or the laws had consigned them. These children are usually too long confined to work in close rooms, often during the whole night: the air they breathe from the oil etc employed in the machinery and other circumstances is injurious; little regard is paid to their cleanliness and frequent changes from a warm and dense to a cold and thin atmosphere are predisposing causes to sickness and disability and particularly to the epidemic fever so generally to be met with in these factories ... the want of religious instruction and example and the numerous and indiscriminate associations in these buildings are very unfavourable to their future conduct in life.

But to savour the full horrors of industrial Manchester we must move forward another 50 years into the 1840s, to the accounts of the slum conditions uncovered by Friedrich Engels. Aikin was a medical man with the conscience of a social reformer. He was like James Kay who was to follow him in exposing the evils of early industrialisation and who married into the Shuttleworth family of Gawthorpe Hall. But Engels was a different cup of tea altogether. What he witnessed in Manchester was the iron which would be beaten into the white hot sword of revolution. What was happening in Manchester during the 'hungry forties' was to form the basis, through his collaboration with Karl Marx, of the most powerful, and seen by many as the most dangerous, political creed of all time: *The Communist Manifesto*.

When Friedrich Engels wrote *The Condition of the Working Class in England* he was only 24 and it is full of the barely contained, impassioned indignation of youth. He piles up epithets of disgust into his descriptions, much as the refuse, filth, debris and offal accumulated around the dwellings of the workers. The most notorious feature of Manchester's housing was the courts. When the Bartons return from their country stroll to their home in the town it is to one such of these courts. Mrs Gaskell, who lived in Manchester and had first-hand experience of the conditions for her fiction, is content to describe the courts as merely having 'a gutter through the middle to carry off household slops, washing suds, etc.'. Engels invests that final 'etc.' with the true stench of human misery. He who turns into the courts, he says, 'gets into a filthy and disgusting grime, the equal of which is not to be found … the most horrible dwellings which I have yet beheld. In one of these courts there stands directly at the entrance, at the end of the covered passage, a privy without a door, so dirty that the inhabitants can pass into and out of the courts only by passing through foul pools of stagnant urine and excrement'.* Nearby tanneries fill the neighbourhood with the 'stench of animal putrefaction'. The courts he describes ran down to the River Irk by Ducie Bridge. The Irk sounds positively Hadean, its banks full of 'a long string of the most disgusting, blackish-green slime-pools … from the depths of which bubbles of miasmatic gas constantly arise to give forth a stench unendurable even on the bridge 40 or 50 feet above the surface of the stream'. He goes on:

Above the bridge are tanneries, bonemills and gasworks from which all drains and refuse find their way into the Irk, which receives further the contents of all the neighbouring sewers and privies. It may be easily imagined, therefore, what sort of residue the stream deposits. Below the bridge you look upon the piles of debris, the refuse, filth, and offal from the courts on the steep left bank; here each house is packed close behind its neighbour and a piece of each is visible, all black, smoky, crumbling, ancient, with broken panes and window-frames.

Engels wanders from one court to another until he discovers one court whose horrors have been exposed by the development of the railway to Leeds:

Passing along a rough bank, among stakes and washing-lines, one penetrates into this chaos of small one-storeyed, one-roomed huts, in most of which there is no artificial floor; kitchens, living- and sleeping-room all in one. In such a hole, scarcely 5 feet long by 6 broad, I found two beds – and such bedsteads and beds! – which, with a staircase and chimney place, exactly fitted the room. In several others I found absolutely nothing, while the door stood open, and the inhabitants leaned against it. Everywhere before the doors refuse and offal; that any sort of pavement lay underneath could not be seen but only felt here and there, with the feet. This whole collection of cattle-sheds for human beings was surrounded on two sides by houses and a factory, and on the third by the river, and besides the narrow stair up the bank, a narrow

---

*   All quotes are from the Oxford edition of Engels' book.

doorway alone led into another almost equally ill-built, ill-kept labyrinth of dwellings.

The courts were not only home to human beings but were over-run by pigs. Apparently the local pork-raisers rented the courts and built pig-pens there so that the occupants could throw out all their refuse to fatten the pigs. This is an idea of such staggering and perverse ingenuity that I am surprised that some of our local authorities, which seem to find so much difficulty these days in maintaining a regular refuse collection service, haven't reintroduced the practice.

Even worse than the conditions around the Irk – if that can be imagined – were the conditions in Little Ireland. Little Ireland was an enclave of Irish immigrant workers living in a curve of the River Medlock south-west of Oxford Road. According to Engels they numbered about 4,000, all living in 200 back-to-back cottages. He writes:

> A horde of ragged women and children swarm about here, as filthy as the swine that thrive upon the garbage heaps and in the puddles ... The race that lives in these ruinous cottages, behind broken windows mended with oilskin, sprung doors and rotten door-posts, or in the dark, wet cellars in measureless filth and stench ... this race must really have reached the lowest stage of humanity ... But what must one think when one hears that in each of these pens, containing at most two rooms, a garret and perhaps a cellar, on the average twenty human beings live; that in the whole region, for each 120 persons, one usually inaccessible privy is provided ...

Engels' accounts of the dire living conditions of the Manchester labourers and their families, like those of Dr Aikin earlier, make much of the stench and the lack of ventilation in their surroundings. This is because medical opinion at the time believed that disease was spread by miasmas. The great killer diseases of Victorian times were cholera and typhoid. They didn't realise that these were not air-borne diseases at all, but a result of the pollution by sewage of the drinking water. No amount of whitewashing walls and installing windows that opened, which Dr Aikin was keen to recommend, would have the slightest effect until the arrival of a clean public water supply. But by and large the authorities were slow to do anything that might curb the great engine of wealth and empire which manufacturing Manchester was becoming by restricting the influx of migrant labour into jerry-built and insanitary accommodation. Rather they preferred to blame the poor for their own misfortunes. As the *Economist* of the 1840s thundered, 'Suffering and Evil are Nature's admonitions; they cannot be got rid of.'

I went to Manchester in search of the modern-day Irk, that 'narrow, coal-black, foul-smelling stream, full of debris and refuse'. Is there anything about the place that gives a hint as to what was once there? A chink, perhaps, in the thin membrane of time that might offer a further insight into that landscape

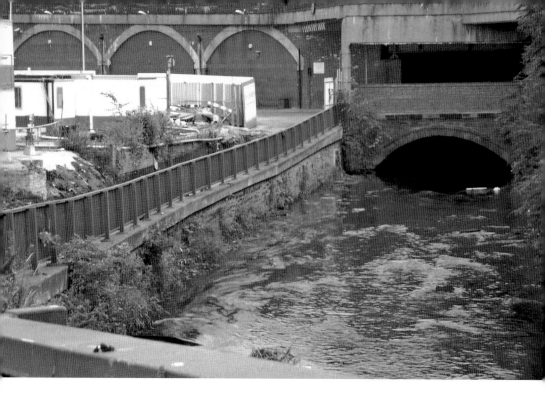

The Irk today, Manchester
PHOTOGRAPH: AUTHOR

of despair? A lingering whiff of that miasma of human misery? If you think this is a rather unhealthy reason to visit Manchester, I offer this defence, a phrase that rings in my brain when we would dissociate ourselves from the past and the people who have gone before: we stand on their shoulders. Their efforts, their suffering, have helped to make us what we are. Social reform and modern welfare grew out of the bitter experiences of our ancestors, and their sweat and efforts underpin the affluence we enjoy today. They deserve our belated obsequies.

It was a gloomy late January day when I set out to look for the river Irk, just the day to exhume a place with such a grim history. Approaching the city from the north I'm struck by the change that two centuries have wrought on that idyllic landscape of Aikin's etchings and the Bartons' rambles. Those pastoral scenes of rustic shepherds and bosky fields have decayed into a no-man's land of drab scrubland. I'm talking about the areas between towns such as Bury, Whitefield, Middleton, Prestwich and Chadderton, and Manchester's other northern satellites, whose tentacles spread and knot into the densest conurbation in the country outside the capital. They are the scant white bits on the OS map between the ugly brown stains of rampant urban growth. Only a few names hint at some long-distant pastoral existence: Whittle Brook, Stock Nook, Hares Hill Farm. The modern reality is as far removed from anything rustic as a hand-plough is from a JCB. The land through which I pass is trapped between the jaws of two motorways, the M66 and the M62, and it looks as if it has been chewed until all the green goodness has been squeezed out of it. Every tree wears a tattered head-dress of shredded polythene and like some bitter urban parody of spring, bin bags bloom from every bush. You drive past ugly red-brick semis stuck in fields, trading estates and DIY stores, all the outposts of urban consumerism which erode our countryside and seem beloved of rate-grabbing local authority planners. Mobile phone masts and a crude gravel hopper assault the sky. The khaki-coloured land, spiked with withered docks and thistles, has been worked to death, exploited for everything it's worth, until the only thing left is the final indignity of digging it up to use as a dump, landfill for the detritus of the city. Like an abused child it has grown surly and withdrawn until it gives nothing back to the passing eye or soul. It is crying out to be afforested, turned into something green and revitalised, something where nature can begin again. But instead it is just left, tossed away like the plastic bags. It is neither town nor country but, like so much of the land in Britain today, a limbo through which people pass, hurry as fast as they can in their cars from home to work, from home to the shops.

For many people it is no longer the sustaining force it was for the Bartons and those other factory workers, a place where spiritual batteries can be charged, a place to return to reaffirm their roots in the land. No wonder we fill our cars with distractions, with gadgets and onboard entertainment so that we can sit cocooned and not have to look out on this travesty of landscape, this East of Eden, this purgatory of indifference and neglect, this visual Hell. I feel sorry for everyone who has to travel every day through a landscape like this with nothing to lift their spirits except the prospect of the journey's end. And I fear that this is the Lancashire which so many strangers see when they travel here and will judge us by, and I am sad and ashamed for us.

Once inside the city centre I found the notorious River Irk, just off the bottom of Cheetham Hill Road, next to the railway lines leading into Victoria Station. It is still trying to live up to its reputation. It is a dismal, motionless, khaki slick barely more than 15 feet wide, draped on one side with rank undergrowth and on the other with the slobbering brickwork of the railway viaduct. It is a particular kind of modern squalor which litters the ground beneath the bare bushes: Styrofoam cartons drooling the discarded remains of greasy takeaways and tabloid newspapers filled with pink and smiling topless models. Under the railway arches, dozens of businesses, some behind glass grown opaque with dirt and age where shattered panes create an atlas of shadowy shapes. And

'Social reform and modern welfare grew out of the bitter experiences of our ancestors, and their sweat and efforts underpin the affluence we are enjoying today'

there, beneath, is the river, not motionless after all, but sliding sluggishly, furtively, towards the heart of the city, slipping around sacks of refuse that have split and disgorged their innards into the water, while below the surface lurk dark, amorphous shapes, the nightmare past resolutely refusing to visit the light. And at the far end of a long stretch beside the railway, the river finally disappears into the blackest of tunnels from whose shadows, like a chained beast, come the growling sounds of trains passing overhead.

So the Irk becomes the symbol of Manchester's dark history as it slips into the bowels of the city, dark conduits of suffering and shame forever hidden, as high above, the new Manchester reinvents itself in a glamour of glass and futuristic shapes. All this area just north of the city centre is one glorified building site. As I stand by the banks of the obscene Irk, behind me a vast crane swings a girder into place. A notice on the growing apartment building proclaims, 'An urban oasis. A fresh approach to city living in Manchester.' How those court-dwellers of the 1840s would have gaped with wonder at this brave new world. After the fallow years of Victorian grime and soot which was still the city when I was a child in the 1950s, Manchester has become reborn as a symbol of international enterprise and vitality. Whether this renaissance will have its darker side like that chronicled so vividly by Aikin and Engels remains to be seen.

Manchester reinvents itself.

CHAPTER THIRTEEN

THE YEARS OF UNREST

THE UNREST which grew among the working population of Lancashire during the first half of the nineteenth century cannot be explained simply by the dreadful living conditions suffered by the immigrants to towns like Manchester. We've already been given an idea of the kind of poverty left behind by the families who came north from rural Suffolk, and the conditions in Ireland that brought so many of those countrymen over to work here can well be imagined. The growing factory system treated the workers as though they themselves were machines. The term 'hands' was used by the manufacturers and was an indication of the way human beings were being reduced to the sole commodity for which the new system valued them. There was no skill, or else why were so many of the factory owners happy to employ pauper children in their mills? There was no pride in any craftsmanship, just a gluttonous market that swallowed what was produced by the yard, by the mile, and dispatched it across the world where it was never seen again. Compare this to a medieval mason whose work was on display in his parish church, or the village blacksmith who had to answer to his neighbour if the wheels of the cart he had made fell off. Under the new system the only concern of the worker was to earn money. All the skills and subtle bonds which had made him a valued part of the community were replaced by the power of money. The possession of money became the sole criterion by which success was judged. It is an all too sad but familiar picture which we recognise in our society to this day.

But it would be wrong to suggest that unrest was confined to the factory worker alone. Those who stuck to their handloom had seen their earnings drop from around 33s. a week in 1795 to only 9s. in 1819. It was not just the influx of cheap factory-made goods which forced their earnings down, but also the fact that the number of weavers in the industry had soared as workers were driven out of processes like spinning (which had been the most time-consuming operation and which was the first to be mechanised). Richard Arkwright, sometime of Preston and of Cromford in Derbyshire, became the largest cotton spinner in England, using steam power to drive his new water-frames which could produce a massive increase in the amount of cotton yarn compared to traditional spinning methods. And Samuel Crompton of Bolton had refined the production of fine yarn with the invention of his spinning mule. Meanwhile, in the factories the glut of workers, whether from the bogs of Ireland or the workhouses of London, gave the manufacturers the whip hand when it came to setting wages, and until 1824, the Combination Laws made all forms of trades unionism illegal. The government was run by the moneyed and land-owning classes and was firmly on the side of the mill owners and not the creators of their wealth. To change the government, the working classes would need the vote, which they didn't have. Across the Channel in France the ordinary citizens had taken matters into their own hands and the result had been the rumble of tumbrils and the swish of the Guillotine. So the government here began to look nervously over its shoulder and to tighten its grip on the reins of power. Here in Lancashire it led to the most savagely repressive measure this country had known against its own kind since the Civil War. It became known as the Peterloo Massacre.

On the afternoon of Monday 16 August 1819, the Manchester Yeomanry Cavalry, a group of amateur soldiers set up for the defence of the town, whose officers were drawn from the local cotton manufacturers and merchants and whose greatest claim to military fame seems to have been the ostentation of their sky-blue jackets and a reputation for brutality against ordinary citizens, drew their sabres and charged upon a large gathering of workers crammed into St Peter's Field in the centre of Manchester. Estimates of the number of workers vary from between 30,000 to 150,000. They had assembled to hear the famous orator, Henry Hunt, speak about the radical reform of Parliament. How necessary this reform was you can gather from the fact that at the time, Manchester, Salford, Bolton, Rochdale, Ashton, Oldham, Stockport and Blackburn couldn't muster a single MP between them, whereas some places in the squire-infested shires of southern England managed to return MPs, usually themselves or their cronies, without having any constituents for them to represent, places famously known as 'rotten boroughs'. In addition to the Manchester yeoman storm-troopers, the local magistrates, drawn from the local bastions of wealth and privilege, the squirearchy and the Church, had a further six troops of cavalry and seven companies of infantry, as well as an army of special constables, standing by. An equally nervous government in London had declared the meeting to be illegal. Nevertheless, it was a hot summer's day and workers from all over the area, men and women alike, had dressed in their Sunday best, unfurled their coloured banners, and in a carnival atmosphere marched upon Manchester to hear their hopes for a fairer world blessed by some of the leading radicals of the day.

The cavalrymen, described as 'tyrants on horseback', lunged and slashed with their swords at the defenceless crowd. Almost immediately a woman was trampled to death by one of the horses. In a fug of heat, dust and blind terror, blood was added to the sweat and tears of the upstart working classes who were making Manchester rich and Britain Great. In the indiscriminate carnage that ensued, 17 people were killed or died of their wounds, including a woman of 71, Alice Kearsley, and over 650 were injured, some of them shot. A day out in the sun for a group of pauper peasants and factory slaves had turned into the most grotesque abuse of political power by the ruling classes in recent history.

Considering its importance in this country's struggle for democracy Peterloo remains largely ignored by the modern city of Manchester. St Peter's Field is certainly no longer a field. What had been an open space a little over 150 yards square used for public gatherings is now heavily built upon. I know from a description I'd read that one side of the square was formed by Mount Street and another by the old Quaker burial yard, so I set off to exhume whatever I could of the scene of the massacre. Distracted by my task I nearly got run over by an impatient motorist in a street behind the town hall square. Modern-day Manchester is a self-absorbed hotbed of consumerism with little time for dawdlers and dreamers. No one I asked seemed to have heard of Peterloo. Had a collective amnesia seized the city over this appalling betrayal of its ordinary citizens? I wandered into the great round Central Library, a place in whose theatre we sat as schoolchildren, transfixed by our first experience of live Shakespeare, a revelation after the dry reading-round-the-class of set GCE plays. A kindly reference librarian looked puzzled at my request, but soon had a booklet out announcing that there was a blue plaque commemorating Peterloo somewhere by the Free Trade Hall on Peter Street.

'Manchester produced radical reformers who campaigned for the improvement of working lives'

The Palladian façade of the Free Trade Hall is still one of the most impressive sights in Manchester. The carvings above the blind pillars high above the road depict the bounty of free trade. Each shows a classical female figure surrounded by the spoils and tools of commerce. One, with a lion behind her, is clutching a great elephant tusk, with an amphora by her side, around which spill exotic fruits. Another stands in front of a noble-browed sheep with bales of wool and cotton about her. A third is surrounded by riveted steam engines and cogwheels, while yet another rows a boat. Although Victorian, this still firmly defines Manchester for me. Absent are the muses of art, literature and science which embellish so many of our Victorian halls and buildings. Here, everything is resolutely commercial. It's all about the creation of wealth through unrestricted trade, and this is the real heart and soul of Manchester: mercantile (I forebear to say mercenary). It was the cotton manufacturers who made her rich. People like John Thornton of Mrs Gaskell's *North and South*: brusque, seemingly ruthless and entirely unsentimental capitalists. But, of course, he's more than that, otherwise he wouldn't be deserving of the book's heroine, Margaret Hale. He's keen to improve his mind and to study the classics under Margaret's father, and his sympathy for the suffering of his workers slowly emerges. And similarly, Manchester wasn't all unscrupulous mill owners throwing up badly built, cholera-infested tenements in pursuit of their own naked greed. There was more to the city in Victorian times than free trade. It produced the radical reformers – including the *Manchester Guardian* newspaper – who campaigned for the improvement of working lives. It had an intellectual life in the free libraries, Owen's College, the forerunner of the university, and the plethora of literary, philosophical and historical societies, not least the Lancashire and Cheshire Antiquarian Society who had their headquarters in Manchester and whose members we met at the beginning of this book speculating about the origins of the Bleasdale Circle. It's just that commerce was the motor of Manchester's astonishing growth, its prime mover, and in many ways, after the doldrums of the last half-century, things have come full circle.

It is shocking to realise that today the Free Trade Hall is indeed only a façade. Stand back and you see, climbing high into the grey sky behind it, a hotel. I counted 13 storeys of glass and concrete rising incongruously out of what was once the home of the Hallé orchestra. Culture brutally pushed out of the way by commerce. As I stand outside today, instead of seeing queues of concert-goers I watch the weekend visitors arrive with their expensive leather overnight bags. They all seem to be youthful, abandoning their black

The impressive facade of the Free Trade Hall.
PHOTOGRAPH: AUTHOR

limousines on the double yellow lines outside and swaggering into the hotel foyer full of the confidence which money can buy. This is what free trade has thrown up today: a market for the rich and trendy young consumer. They dress like urban warriors planning their assault on the fleshpots of the city: the clothes shops, restaurants and night-clubs. In keeping with an old textile town, the women have a ragged sheep look. They wear long suede coats trimmed with wool and fur and hairy boots. The rest of their clothes are layered like casual piles of sweaters. Their hair looks as though it needs the help of a good carding machine. To me the men don't look a lot different. Sexual differences are obscured in the interests of maximising fashion sales. To me, hopelessly out of date and unfashionable, they are the opposite of well groomed. They are tousled. They are Raquel Welch and her mate in *One Million Years BC*. But instead of throwing stones they'll be tossing around credit cards.

Above the hotel foyer is an old stone carving of a mill girl next to a bale of cloth with the square mill beside her. She and a million like her made Manchester possible. She seems to stare bemused into the future. Through the hotel window a girl is spraying the glass behind which stands a plaque commemorating a meeting here in October 1905 when Christabel Pankhurst tried to ask whether the incoming Liberal government would give votes to women, and she, along with Annie Kenney of Saddleworth, was thrown out for her impudence. For daring to resume their protest outside they were thrown into Strangeways gaol and the suffragette movement was born. History everywhere, but through a glass dimly, all these struggles against inequality and injustice which are long forgotten in the modern scamper for affluence. And here at last, the blue plaque commemorating Peterloo. Its wording makes me want to shout out in dismay:

> The site of St Peter's Fields where on 16th of August 1819 Henry Hunt, radical orator, addressed an assembly of around 60,000 people. Their subsequent dispersal by the military is remembered as Peterloo.

What! No word of the 11 dead, the hundreds injured? No mention of a massacre? All deftly air-brushed out of history. Whoever worded this plaque clearly didn't want today's carefree consumers to be put off by any graphic reminders of official brutality.*

And for those who savour irony, across the street, right in the middle of what was once St Peter's Field, is an Army Recruitment Office. And just in case we don't get it, behind this in Bootle Street, albeit established in 1934, you'll find the city police headquarters. And there's me thinking Manchester had forgotten its Peterloo!

St Peter's Field is such a symbolic place in the history of our struggle for democracy that I wonder why they couldn't have left the space open and made

---

* Since writing this, a new plaque has appeared acknowledging, after 188 years, the killing of 11 people and four more who died later.

a little park – Manchester city centre is sorely in need of them – a public open space or memorial garden where people, tired of their quest for consumer trinkets, could walk and maybe reflect upon this wonderful age of freedom and how hard won it was by our Lancashire forebears. There's still chance, while Manchester is rebuilding itself. Surely they could make do with one less office block or apartment building. They could start by knocking down the club that offers 'Eating, Drinking and Cavorting' with drinks all night on Monday for just £1. (Am I beginning to sound like Oliver Cromwell?) The only open space left today is the tiny burial yard behind the Friends' Meeting House in Mount Street. But it's been tarmacked over and turned into a private car park, even though over 600 lie buried there. A single row of stunted bushes marks it off from the busy streets, where in the cold sleet of a wet Manchester afternoon a solitary white blossom tree is coming bravely into flower.

What were the consequences of the Peterloo Massacre? The radical ringleaders of the meeting were rounded up and imprisoned, while the sabre-waving bully boys of the amateur cavalry were praised for their bravery by the powers that be. Parliament then enacted the most draconian laws to repress freedom of protest. As the cotton trade picked up again, workers returned quietly to their factories, and popular support for radical reform slid into decline, while Peterloo disappeared into the history books for people like me to resurrect occasionally and, after my knuckles have ceased to whiten as I write about it, to reflect more calmly upon whether or not there is any remaining legacy of radicalism here in Lancashire. Did Peterloo leave any lasting scars on the collective psyche of Lancashire people to make us more bitter or bolshie against authority or class exploitation or the unscrupulous use of privilege and power? Or was it all water, albeit mixed with blood, under the bridge of history?

If Peterloo did leave scars they never showed. I think by nature we Lancastrians are rather conservative. The authoritarianism our great grandparents got used to in the nineteenth century was the authority of the mill, and the new mill owners were tolerated because they often came from the ranks of the weavers themselves. I'll not forget speaking to a group of retired mill workers who had experienced life in the cotton mills of the pre-war period, when owners stood at the factory gates with a watch in their hand at seven o'clock in the morning and the gates were locked on latecomers; where faults in cloth were fined, and the looms ran right up until the hooter went on Christmas Eve. I asked whether they resented the bosses' almost inhuman strictness, and none of them did. 'We'd have done the same if we'd have been in their shoes,' said one. When the boss himself had been through the mill, though he may now have arrived at work in a chauffeur-driven car and lived in a big house with servants well upwind from the factory smoke, there was a mutual respect born out of common roots, something that never existed between the country squire and his peasant ploughman. If there was any bitterness or resentment, it found expression in an undercurrent of stoical cynicism, in a debunking sense of humour, rather than outward rebellion. Take the case of the tacklers or overlookers, the self-appointed despots of the mill and the most immediate figures of power and authority in the weaving shed, because their decision as to whether or not to come right away to repair a broken or malfunctioning loom was economic life or death to a weaver on piecework. The weavers' means of retaliation were the tacklers' tales, stories put about which subverted the tacklers' authority by investing them with almost idiot status. The stories carry the barbed edge of much Lancashire humour which survives in many of our native comedians today.

There also began to develop among the weaving community – and this can be said of other industries, such as coal mining – a powerful sense of solidarity, of all being together in the same boat which, even if it didn't find expression in active revolt, made hardship more bearable because it was shared. This was the social glue which united so many Lancashire industrial communities, and I'm sure it became every bit as strong as in the old village communities before the Industrial Revolution. But woe betide you if you didn't fit in, if you adopted airs and graces seen by others to be above your station,

An illustration from *A View of the Lancashire Dialect*, containing the Adventures and Misfortunes of a Lancashire Clown by Tim Bobbin, published in 1750.

or, worse, were caught sucking up to the bosses. Then, the most effective and hurtful weapon of the group came into operation, that of exclusion.

The use of ridicule to get your own back on authority is an old weapon in the Lancastrian's armoury of class revolt. I was familiar with Tim Bobbin as a pub name, but it wasn't until I read Dr Aikin's book on Manchester and its environs, published in 1795, that I found out who he was. According to Dr Aikin, Tim Bobbin was a Lancashire clown whose dialect poems made fun of all the 'silly credulous boobies amongst the gentlemen' of his neighbourhood, one of the most celebrated of which, *The Blackbird*, ridiculed a Lancashire justice, no less. (It was the bumbling magistrates who had been responsible for unleashing the might of the military on the people at Peterloo.) Tim Bobbin was the fictional invention of one John Collier, born near Warrington and the son of a clergyman. He began life as a handloom weaver, but finding little expression for his 'volatile spirits and eccentric genius' in this employment, he became an itinerant schoolmaster until he finally settled in a post at Milnrow, near Rochdale. He taught himself music and drawing, playing the hautboy and common flute, and indulging his talent for drawing which soon developed into caricatures, 'copying Dame Nature in some of her humorous deformities and grotesque sportings with the human race ... such as were best to excite risibility.' As soon as these pictures were completed, he would carry them to the inns of Rochdale and Littleborough and sell them. His work was soon in great demand by the merchants of Liverpool who saw to it that they were spread as far and wide as the West Indies and America. The money he earned soon went 'merrily in a cheerful glass with a joyous companion'. So no wonder they called pubs after him.

Collier seems to have been the inventor of the Lancashire dialect poem, that peculiarly local form of versification you either love or hate. (Perhaps this is a test of a true Lancastrian, where hatred is a measure of alien middle-class aspirations?) Apparently, wherever Collier went he collected words, or 'all the awkward, vulgar, obsolete words and local expressions which ever occurred to him in conversation amongst the lower classes'. From these he developed his Lancashire dialect, in which were recounted the adventures of his character Tim Bobbin. These became in such demand that he was regularly summoned to the inns to recite them. So, if magistrates and the local gentry and maybe tyrannical mill owners were the subject of his satires, this is no doubt how the lower orders were able to harmlessly let off revolutionary steam. I imagine these scenes of clandestine rebellion behind the closed doors of the pub; red-faced revolutionaries beating their tankards on the tables and guffawing loudly at their so-called betters who had such unfair control over their lives, before staggering home and toppling into the beds, to wake up next morning to a world that hadn't changed but appeared somewhat more tolerable – after the headaches had worn off.

After Peterloo, overt revolt broke out once more in Lancashire in the Chartist riots between 1834 and 1840. In Mrs Gaskell's *Mary Barton* John Barton is chosen to be a workers' delegate to deliver their petition to

Parliament. As one of his fellow workers urges: 'Do ask 'em to make th' masters break th' machines. There's never been good times sin' spinning-jennies came up.' Although the Chartists' leaders were agitating principally for parliamentary reform, for the vast majority of workers it was the misery of unemployment and poverty brought about by the new factory system that was the problem. And discontent wasn't just confined to larger towns like Manchester.

In 1826 angry handloom weavers rioted and broke up power looms in Burnley, Blackburn and Accrington. The diary of one handloom weaver shows his wage falling to 4s. a week. When he became unemployed he received a dole of 6lbs of meal a week. When he was in work the family had been used to 27lbs a week. Those who were employed in the factories were on skeleton wages because the factory owners left the difference between the wages they paid and the cost of subsistence to be made up out of the poor rate. To meet the soaring cost of poor relief there was even a relief fund set up in London. Marsden, in Nelson, received £45 in 1826: £20 went on clogs for paupers, £15 for clothing females and £10 for clothing workhouse paupers. One handloom weaver earned only 3d. a week. With his extra 1s. 6d. poor relief he had to find food, firings, candles, clothing and rent. (Oatmeal cost a penny h'penny a pound.) In 1831 a letter read out in the House of Commons from a church minister describing local conditions revealed families of '6, 7 and 8 with one bed and a lap or two of straw. Nauseous smells and a miserable aspect. Half a pound of mutton fat serving 5 meals for 5 people and a family. Little children in a cradle with only straw to lie on and covered with a cotton fent.'

Contemporary accounts of the cottages of handloom weavers by the Rev. W. Cooke Taylor reveal boxes for tables and stones for chairs. Breakfast consisted of oatmeal and water, dinner of flour and water with a little skimmed milk on alternate days, and for tea, more meal and water. Children, he records, often ate vegetable refuse picked up on the market. In Burnley a visitor found 'groups of idlers in the streets, their faces haggard with famine and their eyes rolling with that fierce and uneasy expression which I have noticed in maniacs'.

In Colne the scab of suffering and discontent of the handloom weavers finally broke. And the consequences are recorded upon a gravestone in the town's cemetery. It reads:

> Here lieth all that is mortal of Martha, wife of Tom Halstead of Colne, departed this life Dec 18th 1829 aged 60 years.
> And Joseph their son who was barbarously murdered in the 44th year of his age while engaged in his duty as a special constable during the riot which took place in this town on the evening of 10th of August 1840, leaving 4 orphan children to lament their loss.

History blames the Chartists for the riot. A few political agitators might have applied the match, but the powder was dry and ready to explode. An account of events described the crowd of men 'with a sullen and determined look' moving towards the town centre. They had armed themselves with spiked railings from a churchyard. News spread and the two nearest magistrates swore in 70 constables before repairing, judiciously, to the security of a room at the King's Head. When the mob reached the town, a lamppost was smashed. The Riot Act was read, but had no effect. The inevitable clash took place in Cross Street where a shower of paving stones hurled from the rooftops greeted the arrival of the police. The battle was cut short by the tolling of the church bells which the rioters thought was a signal for the arrival of the militia from Burnley and they dispersed.

But Joseph Halstead stayed put. Whether or not he'd come into contact with one of the missiles hurled from a roof, I don't know. But he was as dead as a paving stone.

They found and tried a man called Richard Boothman for his murder and he was condemned to death. But he was eventually reprieved and sentenced to life imprisonment in Van Diemen's Land, which is a chilling way of saying he was transported to Australia, or Tasmania, if you want to split hairs; whatever, it was rather a long way from Colne. The consensus among local historians seems to be that the incident in which Joseph Halstead met his death was Colne's hour of shame. His gravestone is the very first you meet when you enter the cemetery. I'll swear that it's been moved from where I last saw it, either as a warning to today's townsfolk to steer clear of seditious doings or else because an element in the town still haven't lost their fondness for heaving around heavy stones. (I notice that quite a few of the gravestones seem to have been pushed over and broken.) But while I would wish on no man the fate of being brained by a paving stone, I can't help but note that Joseph Halstead was described as being a cotton manufacturer. Was he one of those mill owners who took advantage of the system of poor relief in order to pay his workers well below subsistence level? Who contravened the new Factory Acts and had men working as long as 18 hours a day and children as many as 12 hours? Or did his mill contain machinery that wasn't properly protected and over-tired children were expected to clean while it ran because to stop it lost the manufacturer money? Was Joseph Halstead perhaps singled out as a representative of a callous new factory system which put personal profit and individual greed before all else? I don't know. I might be doing him an injustice, and perhaps he was a lovely man. Until old bones can get up and speak, we'll never know.

But I do know that this period marks a low point in the history of Lancashire's working people, from which things could only move upwards. The painful metamorphosis from independent peasant farmer, however poor, who had enjoyed the freedom of the land and his own cottage labours, into the town-dwelling factory worker tied to a time-clock and dependent solely on a pay-packet, was almost complete. And Lancashire's unique identity as a manufacturing giant, the engine of Victorian wealth and Empire, was about to emerge.

CHAPTER FOURTEEN

THE VICTORIANS: LANCASHIRE'S GOLDEN AGE

ONE OF THE GREAT ADVANTAGES which the industrial towns offered over the countryside was the opportunity for self-betterment. And one of the most remarkable local examples of this can be found a little more than a mile away from the handloom weavers' ghost village of Wycoller.

I've moved west in the direction of the Calder valley to Winewall, which is high enough to command a fine view of Pendle Hill rising with stubborn solidity above the rooftops of Colne a mile away. Today Pendle is silvered with snow and spotlighted by the morning sun as it beams through the broken cloud. I can only think that we must believe that the dead are fond of fine views because I'm standing in the graveyard of the old Inghamite church, and for such a little chapel of a relatively insignificant offshoot of Methodism, the graveyard is crowded with headstones. They climb up behind the square grey chapel right to the top of the hill where, if the dead truly can turn in their graves like we say, they could look south towards the flanks of Boulsworth Hill as well. The place is full of good old Lancashire names. There are Pickleses, Hindles and Halsteads, Horsfalls and Hargreaveses, all standing side by side in mildewed solemnity. But for sheer numbers, none can rival the Hartleys. There are hordes of Hartleys buried here, a surname so beloved they even use it as a Christian name. So as well as a Hargreaves Hartley from Haworth (let's hope he could pronounce his aitches), there's a Hartley Pryce and a Hartley Edmundson buried here. Where would Lancashire be without its Hartleys? I can think of the Wallace Hartley, who was brave – or daft – enough to go on conducting his band while the *Titanic* sank around him,

and the Hartleys who were into jam in a big way. But there must be many more among the unsung rank and file of Lancastrians. But my favourite name here is Hiram Pickles. I like to think he may have been a textile manufacturer with a reputation for sacking his workers. Hire 'em and Fire 'em Pickles. For anyone interested in writing fiction, graveyards are a rich source of names for characters. I've squirreled away Miles Hardcastle who was buried here in 1876. I'm surprised we've never heard more of him. With a name like that you'd think he'd have been destined for great things. If not, I'd settle for him turning up as a suave seducer in a Victorian melodrama: 'Mother, our Sissy's bin seeing that Miles Hardcastle again!'

But in the real Victorian world the heroes were the men of commerce and industry, and right at the bottom of the churchyard, close to the cottages on the roadside, lies one such person. He's James Nelson, and Jimmy Nelson, as he was known fondly to his workers, is the reason why I'm here. His is the story of how an ordinary man, born into the misery and turmoil of the early years of the Industrial Revolution, rose to become one of the architects of our spectacularly successful textiles industry.

Jimmy Nelson was born here in Winewall in one of the cottages below the Inghamite chapel graveyard in 1832. His dad was a handloom weaver, and Jimmy was taught the trade. With his dad he journeyed the 21 miles to Halifax cloth hall to sell his finished pieces, setting off at five in the morning and not returning home until ten o'clock at night. Around the time of the Chartist riots in Colne, when Joseph Halstead lost his fight with a flagstone, Jimmy went to work in a factory in the town. He got a job as a weaver on power looms at 1s. 6d. a week. In 1843, after the repeal of the Corn Laws, wider markets became available to the cotton cloth producers. Population figures for Nelson (it's a strange coincidence that Jimmy and the town he helped to put on the map should share the same name) show that in 1801 it contained a mere 2,300 people. By 1901 there were 40,000, rising to 47,500 in 1911. Expansion like this was due entirely to men like Jimmy Nelson. By 1867 he'd worked his way up from weaver to mill manager. When the mill closed down in 1881 and James was 50, he financed his son and son-in-law in a family business on their own. James was tied by contract to his old employer and couldn't join them until 1884. They rented a mill in Brook Street in Nelson

A remnant of Valley Mills.
PHOTOGRAPH: AUTHOR

on the old 'room and power' system. This was a good way to start in textiles without a crippling financial outlay. You rented space in a mill with steam power provided. Jimmy and his son Amos began with 160 looms. By 1895 they had their own mill, Valley Mills on Southfield Street, and in the next decade were running 3,000 looms in two vast weaving sheds and were employing 2,000 people. At their height they were weaving 400,000 yards of cloth a week, a long way from 30 yards on a handloom. The years 1880 to 1913 were a golden age of prosperity in the Lancashire weaving industry. Every year 8,000 million yards of finished cloth were produced, ⅞ths of which was sold abroad. They used to say that Lancashire wove enough cloth before breakfast to fill the home market and the rest of the day was for export.

I had to visit the site of this once great crucible of wealth production, the mills which, with the raw heat and power of steam engines, the roar of thousands of looms and the singular patience and skill of so many Lancastrian workers, wove the subtlest of cloth and gave rise to the truism, 'Britain's bread hangs by Lancashire thread'.

Today, Valley Mills in Nelson holds scant clues to the mighty place it once was. The two giant weaving sheds have been razed, and in their place are the anonymous grey prefabricated sheds of a modern engineering works. Air-conditioning ducts and extractor fans hum quietly away where once the clatter of looms deafened. The hiss and roar of steam have been replaced by the silent electron, and the river, which once dictated the location of the weaving mill, has been tamed into underground culverts and compressed between concrete goits. Instead of the mountains of empty weft baskets piled up in the yard, which as a child I remember outside every mill, there are now stockpiles of stainless steel pipes and skips full of shining swarf. Beside the river, which still manages to dance and sing in its concrete prison, they've done some landscaping, a narrow sward of green scattered with shrubs which have been savagely pruned to the ground and heavily mulched with woodchips. A blue tit pipes metallically from the branches of a sycamore tree, while a squirrel plunges headlong down the trunk to scrabble around in the earth for something he buried last year in the season of plenty. Life goes on despite the enormity of social change. I only once came along here when I was at school in Nelson and I remember how, when the shed doors were opened into the street, the blast of the looms almost knocked you over. Now the same street is silent. I pass two houses in close proximity, both with warnings in the window: 'Beware of the Dog. Enter at your own risk!' and 'Beware of the Dog. It will bite!'

Despite the apparent tranquillity of these back streets, a sense of perceived threat hangs over them, as it does over so much of modern life. I am reminded of the endlessly repeated memory of those who talk about the old days: 'We allus left us front doors unlocked.' It is the mantra of a lost age of innocence. Old ladies pass by, struggling home with shopping from the town centre. It's still only ten in the morning, but old habits die hard and those who once worked in the mills still rise early. The terraced streets all have rustic names.

Trash defies the greening of Milltown.
PHOTOGRAPH: AUTHOR

There's Ash Street, Holly Street, Larch Street and Fir Street. I once courted a girl from Fir Street, and when we returned home from the cinema on a Saturday night I learned how to kiss up against the stone gable of her street. The Arcadian innocence of the street names belies their origins as cheap and utilitarian housing for the mill workers who flooded into Nelson around the end of the nineteenth century. This location of homes and workplace next to each other is no longer acceptable. Today the boundary which separates the factory from the street has been planted with shrubs. Dogwood stems burn brightly behind a wickedly spiked galvanised security fence. Brook Street today is the home of Farmhouse Biscuits, a name redolent of rustic tradition but ironically still partially housed in the remains of an old weaving shed. (Is this where the Nelsons began?) The attempt to transport bits of the country into the town in the form of shrubs and small trees doesn't work. The town, in the shape of our own untidiness, fights back, and we end up with the binbag blossoms of the motorways. No wonder that, by and large, the derelict mills of our industrial past attract the fag end of the modern economy: the scrap

A Jimmy Nelson street.

works, the car repair yards and the here-today-and-gone-tomorrow discount furniture warehouse. Meanwhile, people have to live here, look out every day from their kitchen windows or wake up every morning to someone shifting pallets with a fork-lift truck or bashing dents out of a pranged motor car; and no amount of dogwood hedges will make that sort of neighbour any more acceptable. No wonder places such as this become the ghettos of the poor and underprivileged who can't afford to live anywhere else. Great areas of urban Lancashire are like this today, and to the outside observer define our region. It's the price we've had to pay for being at the forefront of the Industrial Revolution and making Britain rich. If, like putting dye down a drain, you could trace the whereabouts of today's invested wealth generated by our mill towns, they should tax it and use the proceeds to get rid of these houses and build new, agreeable ones away from the mills. I'm sure there are people around who are still doing very nicely out of the labour of Lancashire mill folk and I'll bet they could well afford it. Call it a retrospective environment tax, if you like. It would go down like a lead balloon in share-holding, stake-holding Britain.

Jimmy Nelson was just like any other nineteenth-century capitalist in building houses for the workers so close to the mills. You can still see the rows Jimmy built clinging to the valley side just above the site of the mill. Not hugging the contours like the hill villages of Italy or even Hebden Bridge, but plunging breakneck down the slope. (It's cheaper to provide the services that way, you don't have to dig as many holes.) Straight out of bed and into the mill. No excuse for being late. It's that inclination again of the Victorian mill owners to treat their workers as part of the machinery. But it would be unfair to accuse Jimmy Nelson of treating his workers as mere operatives. Climb up past his houses onto the hilltop and you can begin to see how he and his son, Amos, catered for their social and recreational needs. Gaunt and imposing on the skyline is what remains of Jimmy Nelson's social club. With its distinctive lantern tower, it served as an advertisement for just how enlightened the Nelsons were. Outside I walked across an expanse of overgrown grass that was once tennis courts: room for at least a dozen, I would have thought. And there was a bowling green, now spiked with withered docks and littered with broken glass, but with a handsome arched seating area to retire to if the weather took a turn for the worse. I spoke to David, who had lived in the mill manager's old house nearby for 40 years and remembers the mill running football and cricket teams. (The Nelsons sold the mill to Courtaulds in the 1960s and in 1981 Valley Mills closed.) He told me how the social club had been famous for its ballroom which has a sprung floor that came from Blackpool Tower. (I think I've heard that story before of another ballroom, so I wonder if it's apocryphal. I mean, just how many ballroom floors did they go through in Blackpool?) Up to five years ago there was line dancing in the building. But after a chequered recent history as a club – there was dark talk of a murder here not so long ago – David told me that the building was now in the hands of the receivers. 'It's got to come down. There's all fungus inside and the parker [*sic*] floor has started to come up. It's in danger of collapsing.'

To stand above Valley Mills beside the decaying social club with its boarded-up windows and starlings roosting in the lantern tower is to witness a sad decline. The club, with its tennis courts and cricket fields, is not just a symbol of a lost era of prosperity and industrial greatness but of the strong social ties that held the mill workers together. Today, you can look out past the acres of despondent allotments and hen pens full of mouldering caravans and dismembered pantechnicons at the town that was synonymous with the Nelson name. The rows of grey-roofed regimented houses still dominate and define the landscape. But with the mills closed, the bonds which linked people in a common purpose are gone and the rows of terraces begin to look more and more incongruous. I recall visiting some of the old pit villages of County Durham after they'd landscaped the pits away and all that was left were the rows of houses with no apparent reason for them being there any more. Nelson is starting to become like that. New estates are being built on the hillside where I stand, more random and individual, more spacious than the old terraces. And they're turning their backs on the town as they move towards the greener sites away from the valleys and the dead carcass of the old industry. But they're for the better off. So, just as poverty and need brought people from the countryside to these valleys to work in the mills, now affluence is taking us away. So what will become of all these Victorian terraces? One day soon they'll have to knock old Nelson down and start again. And Colne, and Burnley, and the greater part of industrial Lancashire. We can't all move into the country; there's precious little of it left in Lancashire as it is. It is a wonderful opportunity for visionary planners to start again with these cosy old valleys by building new houses that are as distinctive as the old but modernise the way we live without destroying the old sense of community. I wish I could see it happening already, but a lot of our new houses are no different from anywhere else in Britain. We are losing our individuality. This is something I'll be looking at in the final chapter of this book.

Meanwhile, Jimmy Nelson, when he died at the age of 79 in 1912, was content to return home to where he began in Winewall, to a tiny corner of the Inghamite chapel graveyard. I think he must have wanted to be as near as possible to the cottage where he was born, no more than a couple of hundred yards away. Two hundred yards from start to finish, from poverty and a handloom to a giant factory with 3,000 automated looms, from cottage economy to the pinnacle of this country's industrial power. Such a lot for such a short journey.

Jimmy Nelson's son, Amos, was much happier to forget his humble origins. Out of the success of Valley Mills, in 1920 he bought Gledstone Hall near West Marton, over the border in Yorkshire. Then, on a boat trip to India with his wife, he met the celebrated architect, Edwin Lutyens. Lutyens was off to design a palace for the Viceroy of India, so he had big ideas. He also knew how to spend his clients' money. He persuaded Amos to knock down the old hall and have him design him a brand new one. The result was a neo-classical mansion, with gardens designed by his friend Gertrude Jekyll. It was built between 1923 and 1927 and 200 workmen were employed. It cost Amos a fortune and nearly bankrupted him. He had to cash in his investments to pay for it. I could find no record of what his workers from Southfield Street in Nelson thought of the project. It would be a long way to march if there were ever 'trouble down at t' mill', and they wanted to put a few of his many windows in. The hall has recently been bought by the artist Margaret Francis, originally from St Helens, and the workmen are back

'It is a wonderful opportunity for visionary planners to start again with these cosy old valleys by building new houses that are as distinctive as the old'

turning it into an exhibition centre that will open to the public. She let me wander about outside to get some sort of impression from the building of the kind of person Sir Amos had become. He'd had his own crest designed with the motto *Perseverantia et Labore*, which could be taken as his own personal creed or the watchword for what he expected from his workforce to keep his money coming in. There's a cold grandeur about the place viewed from the north-facing front with its huge pillared portico and sombre collection of stone urns, relieved only by the steep-pitched rustic roof of small moss-encrusted tiles, one of Lutyens' trademarks. There's a stone bell-tower to one side and a bronze naked Cleopatra on a wall above the kitchen. The wrought-iron gates look rustily out on the rolling, grassy dale of Craven where sheep stare back unimpressed, as sheep do. It's a landscape far removed from the noise and grime and teeming congestion of Valley Mills where the Nelsons kept their golden goose. On the gates is their coat of arms, which shows both the Lancashire and Yorkshire rose. But if Sir Amos thought he was bringing the two together by living here, I think he failed. The daily journey to the mill and back in the chauffeur-driven car was a quantum leap between two universes. The gulf must have been amplified by the hall's interior, designed through the influence of the arts and crafts movement of William Morris. At the back, the house resembles nothing so much as a French château, with its array of green shuttered windows.

There's a severe formality about the Jekyll gardens with their long rectilinear lawns and beds and a sunken lake which captures the chrome reflections of the sky in its muddy water. The stonework at the back of the hall is all so precisely dressed with punctilious punchmarks, and in the roof there are no valley gutterings to interrupt the meticulous jigsaw of tiny tiles. As a result the tiles here have started to break up and, as a student of leaking roofs, I smell trouble. But what do you expect if you get a southerner to design your house up here? And, as if to emphasise the unnatural feel of this stylised import into these parts, the house and its gardens impart an uncomfortable, echoey feel to the sounds of the natural world around: the sudden hollow explosion of a male pheasant and the petulant clamour of rooks locked in some nearby wood. Perhaps Nature still feels the incongruity of the presence of a hard-headed Lancashire textile magnate in such a rarefied setting.

Personal fortunes like the Nelsons' were being amassed throughout Lancashire in the late Victorian era and it can be surprising to discover just where these riches were being made. In his book *Men of Property*, W. D. Rubinstein lists the numbers of textile millionaires throughout the country. He also lists the half-millionaires. Now in today's age of super-rich billionaires, half-a-million may not seem much. But when you consider that two of the top three richest men at the end of the nineteenth century were leaving fortunes in the region of £3 million, half-a-million begins to sound more impressive (Rates of pay for weavers in the 1890s were around £1 a week.) Of the 40 half-millionaires who made their money in cotton, no fewer than 12 of them came from Oldham which, according to Rubinstein, represented 'as high a ration of population wealth as in virtually any town or industry in England'. Just what it was about Oldham which was so conducive to fortune-making would furnish a very interesting study by someone of a more scholarly disposition than mine. I can only speculate that, since the figures are drawn from probate records and represent the money people left after they died, in Oldham they didn't subscribe to the popular Lancashire belief that 'there's na pockets in shrouds', and that they enjoyed reading the local newspaper from the grave in the days when wills were published. But for every rich cotton manufacturer who left half-a-million I bet there were half-a-dozen more who spent it. You only need to look at the grand Victorian mansions they left behind, in the leafier outskirts of our towns well upwind from the smoke and smell of their mills, or even further away up in the Lake District, to recognise that this was indeed a golden age for Lancashire cotton.

CHAPTER FIFTEEN

THE VICTORIANS:
A MELANCHOLY EPISODE

I HOPE you will not think me too morbid if I visit another cemetery so soon after Winewall. The Victorians do seem rather to have relished death, and were not afraid to let their sentiments show, especially in the ostentatious memorials they were fond of erecting in their graveyards. But then death was an ever-present part of life. Infant mortality was still the scourge of Victorian England: smallpox, scarlet fever, diphtheria, tuberculosis, Asiatic cholera, the list of fatal diseases makes us sound like a third-world country rather than at the forefront of material progress. But there were still bad water and overcrowding, and the filthiness of the air from burning prodigious amounts of coal in both factories and homes took its toll. In 1860 the death rate for Lancashire was 25 per cent above the national average, and a stroll through any of the old chapel churchyards – if they haven't been turned into supermarket car parks – will provide ample evidence of how busy the Fell Sergeant must have been, especially among the young. I recall a visit to the Haggate Baptist church near Burnley where William and Nanny Jackson lie buried with all seven of their children, none of whom lived beyond the age of 18. Apart from the thought that as parents ourselves we can't fail to be touched by so many cherished young ones being taken away, the very anonymity of these Nellies and Marthas, Willies and Josephs, is particularly poignant. We know nothing about them and never will, and it's easy to turn away, like time itself, and move on. But sometimes the tragedy of these wasted lives was big and shocking enough to make an indelible mark upon the whole community. One such was in Nelson, and the inscription can be found on a large memorial stone in the town's cemetery off Walton Lane. It reads:

In loving memory of:
Helen Clegg, aged 21 years
Frances Crossley, aged 21 years
Nancy Pickles, aged 20 years
Mary Alice Reed, aged 21 years
Mary Jane Smith, aged 21 years.

Five young ladies, all unmarried, who as Sunday school teachers at the Wesleyan church in Carr Road seem to have led exemplary and blameless lives. Five cotton weavers, brought up in this dark, damp and insanitary valley, yet whose deaths owed nothing to soot or streptococcus. Instead, they lost their lives in a pleasure boat accident on Derwentwater on 12 August 1898.

The cotton trade was at its height, wages were good, and people were enjoying a level of affluence which enabled them to dress smartly and even take holidays. The tragedy happened on Nelson Feast when, for just one week in the year the looms stopped, the fires were put out, the black smog from the chimneys cleared and the mills opened their doors to fresh air and sunlight as the whole town went on holiday and took to the hills or the seaside. I'd say that it was pure *Water Babies* if the words weren't so horribly ironic.

Helena, Frances, Nancy, Mary Alice and Mary Jane had all gone to Keswick as pious young members of the National Home Reading Union Holiday Association. They were all Sunday school workers and teachers and they were intimate friends, especially Helena Clegg and Frances Crossley who were inseparable and whose ages differed by just two days. On the last full day of their holiday, the Friday, they had decided on a boat trip on Derwentwater from Portinscale south to Borrowdale. It's about three miles. The boat was a rowing boat, a big one. It was 20 feet long and 4 feet wide. But it was only 17 inches deep in the centre. There were eight of them and it was only a six-seater boat, but the boatman said it would be all right and it would take eight. They were joined by three men. A Mr James of Swinton and Mr Lane of Newton-le-Willows, who each took a pair of oars, and Mr Ratcliffe, a much older man, who sat in the bow while the girls sat in the body of the boat towards the stern.

> 'The cotton trade was at its height, people were enjoying a level of affluence which enabled them to dress smartly and take holidays'

They set out about nine o'clock in the morning. According to the writer from the *Nelson and Colne Express and Advertiser*, 'There was nothing in the appearance of the sky to indicate in the slightest degree that the trip was unsafe'. And to underline the point, he launched into a passage of the most florid and fantastic prose: 'The green umbracious foliage which skirted the lake was scarcely ruffled. Overhead the skies were of Cerulean hue, and Old Sol, apparently in the most amiable mood, was steadily climbing to the zenith.'

A more reliable source – a reporter from another newspaper who had bothered to interview a girl who had set out in another boat – struck a more chilling note. 'It was a fine start,' she said, 'but a quarter of a mile out from Keswick we felt a gale of wind coming down from Borrowdale. This was ominous, for we had heard and read that when the wind blows down from Borrowdale, Derwentwater is not fit to boat upon.'

Nevertheless, from his office in smoky Nelson our *Express* reporter continues to indulge his poetic licence: 'Merry peels of laughter rang out in intervals over the water at some quaint jest or merry notion.' In reality, things were very soon somewhat different.

It had been impossible to see how rough the lake was when they set out because of the islands, and they soon became alarmed at just how choppy it was. One of the oarsmen had the sense to make for the leeward of St Herbert's Island. But it was at this point that Fate struck. Because they were shipping in water at the bow end and he was getting wet, Mr Ratcliffe, a locomotive foreman from Bradford, decided to move further back into the boat. This meant more weight towards the stern. Then, one of the girls, who, according to the oarsman 'were behaving splendidly at the time and were perfectly quiet', shouted, 'Heigh! Stop!' Her luncheon satchel had fallen overboard and was floating away. The oarsman, Mr James, went on: 'I stopped rowing and was just about to back water to get it' (no more forward momentum, so the boat would sink even further into the water – and it's only seventeen inches deep, remember!), when someone cried, "The boat is filling!" It came in bodily from the stern and the stern was sinking rapidly down. It was coming in with a rush. The boat was rapidly sinking and the girls were in the water.'

Mr James and Mr Lane struggled to remove the oars and throw them to the girls:

I was still standing in the boat up to my thighs in water. The boat had sunk stern first. There was nothing more to be done in the boat so I plunged into the water. I was able to swim but a wave caught me and knocked me almost insensible. It was very rough. I tried to swim to where the boat had been. I saw Miss Crossley and Miss Smith; they were scarcely struggling. I tried to swim towards them but I was beaten back. An oar was near and I pushed it to Miss Crossley and cried to her to catch hold. But the oar was beaten back to me. So I pushed it over again and cried to her. But I didn't see her grasp it. I think she was insensible. Miss Smith's head was clearly out of the water then. I was dashed under the water again but when I came to the surface everything was right away. I could see nobody in the water.

I got some funny looks at Nelson library when I asked for some books on ladies' fashions of the period. The girls had posed for a picture earlier on in the week along with a group of other happy holidaymakers. There they were, a bit fuzzy and smudgy, in straw boaters, wearing white, high-necked blouses with puffed sleeves and long dark skirts. From the fashion books I found out what they were probably wearing underneath. The skirts in the 1890s were often so heavy they were hooked to the inside of the bodice above. Then there'd be a petticoat, just as full as the skirt, and drawers, great baggy things that reached down almost to the ankles. The bodice of the period was very deceptive. I read, 'Outwardly appearing loose and simply gathered, but under the flimsy surface is a well-cut and stiffly bonded garment, pinching in the waist and keeping the figure well under control.' Hmm. Rather like a straightjacket does. And from the photograph you could see that their boots were tightly laced-up over the ankles. They weren't so much wearing clothes as ledgers.

And another thought. Even without their heavy clothing, it's doubtful whether the girls would have been able to swim. Nelson didn't have a proper public baths until 1931. There is a record of some public baths in the town a generation earlier, but one bather recalled that they weren't often cleaned out. 'By Friday neet they were reight nurishin', he said. Not the sort of place you'd expect young Sunday school teachers to relish visiting.

Mr Lane, the other oarsman, gave his account of the events: 'The ladies were very quiet indeed and did not seem at all afraid until the water actually came over the side.' As he sank, someone grabbed his left arm and put their other hand on his right shoulder. He found the weight was dragging him under and so got his left arm loose and struck out and came to the surface with the person still clinging to his right shoulder. He was about five yards from the boat. The girl let loose and he seized the keel of the boat and tried to get up it. But it heaved over and he fell back into the water. He swam to the boat again and got his right hand on the keel and just as he did so, one of the girls rose from the water with the back of her head towards the boat. He got his left hand under her chin and held her head against the boat for some considerable time. Then the boat keeled over again and he was driven off. While he had hold of the girl a rescue boat pulled round to his side and someone made a grab at the girl but missed her. When he got back to the boat the girl was gone.

All five of the girls' bodies were recovered within a fifty-yard radius. The three men all survived.

After the four-and-a-half hour inquest the next day, the bodies were put on a train and brought back to Nelson. They arrived at Nelson station at 11.30 on Saturday night. A great crowd had assembled. A *Colne and Nelson Times* reporter wrote, 'Deep sighs and sobs and whisperings were the only sounds beyond the rumblings of the wheels of the hearse and the ringing of the horses' feet.' People lined the streets at midnight as the bodies were taken to their different homes while the church bells tolled.

But the crowds were nothing to those which lined the streets on the following Tuesday to witness the funeral procession. Over 30,000 people came. They came from Manchester, Oldham, Rochdale and all over Lancashire. All the shops closed as people queued for four hours in the intense heat waiting for the procession. One spectator summed it up: 'I'll never in Nelson see such a spectacle again; it's the biggest sight there's been since Charter Day.'

The writer from the *Colne and Nelson Times* wrote: 'It was a touching sight to see the mourners with arms around women tottering with grief and age and bending low to help little children whose feet had only just learned to walk. These scenes and the thought of what had happened to the cold and lifeless forms made all breasts heave with deep sighs and sobs, and eyes grow red with weeping.'

At the cemetery only those from the procession were allowed in. A witness reporter wrote: 'As a result, three parts of the cemetery was literally surrounded by a sea of faces, and out of this great crowd came not one single sound of anything but what was appropriate to so solemn an occasion.'

At the memorial service the following Sunday, the Rev. G.H. Pickering took as his text the stilling of the tempest on the Sea of Galilee. He contrived to turn the tragedy into a message of hope. Jesus Christ, he said, had come to them just as he had walked across the waves to the stricken disciples. Their spirits had been saved. And this would lead others to Jesus. The girls had died for the other young people of Nelson. If they didn't come, they would be letting the five girls die in vain.

There was a surfeit of memorial publications showing pictures of the girls and the spot on Derwentwater where they drowned. One had the title *The Boating Accident* and was black-edged and priced thrupence. At the request of the town clerk an elegy was composed by a Fellow of the Royal Society of Literature from Cheshire.

I visited Nelson cemetery on a grey March day. The memorial stone to the girls is nineteen feet high and shaped like a church steeple. It's made of grey Scottish granite and cost £161 12s. to erect out of public subscription. The names of the girls, picked out in gold paint, have faded from facing over a hundred years of weather coming up the Calder valley from the south-west. The headstone shows that the girls were all laid together, with the insepa-rables, Frances Crossley and Helena Clegg, side by side.

I don't know what it is that I find so touching about standing here. It is as if the mass outpouring of grief all those years ago had left its imprint on the place. But what touched the nerve of sympathy of so many people in a town and at a time when young deaths were commonplace? Was it because they seemed such exemplary young women? Or was it some mute sense of outrage at the inexplicable injustice of it all which brought them here in silent protest? All I do know is that as I stand here I can see them, Mary Jane Smith, Nancy Pickles, Mary Alice Reed, Frances Crossley and Helena Clegg, all in their straw boaters and white blouses and long, heavy, heavy dresses.

CHAPTER SIXTEEN

THE VICTORIANS: CIVIC PRIDE

WHETHER IT BE in graveyards, terraces and factories, or grand civic buildings, the legacy of our Victorian ancestors here in Lancashire is in stone: ornate, confident and enduring stone. It is only when you look back from the latter part of the twentieth century and our flirtation with concrete and different artificial and prefabricated building materials which have generally aged so badly – and like the high rise flats of the '60s and '70s have had to be knocked down – that you appreciate the appeal of real stone. For me, the golden age of Lancashire was a stone age. Yes, I know the great square spinning mills of Oldham and Rochdale and so on, the viaducts and other railway architecture, are red brick, but for me, it's Pennine stone, the gritstone bedrock of our county, which truly defines us and gives us our uniqueness. Without our core of stone buildings we are that shabby and anonymous urban sprawl which litters the plains to the north and east of Manchester and which so depresses the spirits. I've just made the journey to Manchester on the A roads through Littleborough to Rochdale, Royton and Oldham, skirting the town centres and passing through a post-apocalyptic landscape where all sense of order and good planning has imploded in a crazy scramble of 'out-of-town' retail development linked only by deserts of derelict landscape, the dispiriting modern world in which so many Lancastrians whose ancestors worked so hard to gift us our modern legacy of wealth and affluence must grow up and live their lives confined by ugliness.

From the ancient Egyptians to the Incas, from the classical worlds of Greece and Rome to the great medieval cathedrals of western Europe, building in stone is the means by which mankind has asserted himself over mortality and guaranteed that the great symbols of his civilisation have survived the destructive passage of time. But it also takes confidence in your achievements and a belief in your place in history, and the Victorians had that in abundance. And so, despite the sprawling, cheerless suburbs which have been allowed to creep up since, the hearts of many of our towns are still made of stone, and it's the town halls, the libraries, the banks, the chapels, and mills which have escaped the wrecker's ball, where the true and distinctive Lancashire survives.

The heart of Manchester is Albert Square and the great town hall. It was formally opened in 1877 after taking ten years to build. It's on a par with the great medieval cathedrals of England, but it was raised not to the greater glory of God or the power of the church but to the corporate spirit of the golden age of Manchester's commercial success. It was a symbol of the pride that Mancunians felt in their achievement, as well as the administrative headquarters of all the municipal functions of the dawning modern age. The architect was Alfred Waterhouse and the design is Gothic. Lean gargoyles jut awkwardly out from the central tower, the spire of which is tipped with a gilt ball which looks like a giant sea urchin. I stood for a long time among the pigeons and Japanese tourists in the square, with its fan-shaped cobbles, trying to decide whether I liked it. I was in august company. There was Prince Albert, Prince of Saxe Coburg and Gotha, coyly sporting a well-turned calf from his extraordinarily elaborate monument, erected before the building of the town hall. But no amount of flattery could persuade Queen Victoria to attend the town hall's opening ceremony and she even ignored the appeals of Disraeli. I think she took a rather dim view of some of the radical politicians the city had sheltered. One such, John Bright, of anti-Corn Law fame, looks ruminatively out towards the town hall. And a bronze Gladstone, right hand raised in oratorical pose, is denied the dignity he would have expected by the presence of a pigeon perched on the top of his head and copious quantities of bird lime anointing his brow.

The square has a very European feel, which I'm sure will please the city fathers of today with their beady eyes upon the tourist markets. But it lacks the humanity that a clutter of outdoor cafes around its perimeter would confer in warmer climates. In fact, there's something coldly formal about the building, with the monotonous march of so many symmetrical arched windows, the mass of beige stonework and the cold grey slates pressing downwards from the pitched roof. It's probably rather too pompous and self-important for most modern tastes and I found myself craving a touch of the anarchy and sense of fun which in the past has appeared at Christmas in the form of a huge inflatable Santa Claus clambering up the tower.

But any hint of pomposity is soon shed once you step inside the building. All right, the Gothic architecture continues, with long vaulted corridors and stone staircases with marble pillars like organ pipes, and you'd have every

Manchester's august town hall.

PHOTOGRAPH: AUTHOR

right to expect a chilling Kafkaesque bureaucracy at work inside here. Not a bit of it. It is all thoroughly democratic, bustling with ordinary people about their ordinary lives, unintimidated by the grandeur of their surroundings. There might be a sculpture hall stuffed with busts of the great and the good of Manchester's past – Richard Cobden, who was an alderman here between 1838 and 1844, Sir Joseph Heron, the town clerk, whiskered like a woolly ram, Gladstone again, looking distinctly down at t' mouth, Sir Charles Hallé and a three-headed bust of John Barbirolli, resembling nothing so much as a hydra-like monster from *Dr Who*, and dozens more – but people breeze in and out undaunted by such a collection of luminaries. When we went in and were told that there were no official tours that day, no one objected when we tagged along with a group who were attending a jobs fair in the Great Hall. The hall is 100 feet long, with a gilt roof showing the coats of arms of all of Manchester's important global trading partners. Down the centre are chandeliers crammed with huge light bulbs like glowing ostrich eggs. At the far end is a grand organ. But the hall's most celebrated features are its murals depicting famous events from the city's history painted by Ford Maddox Brown. Unfortunately today they're all masked by the green baize stalls of the jobs fair, full of smiling recruitment maidens from retail, fashion, finance and telecommunications handing out lollipops and barley sugars. This is rather interesting and shows that Manchester's appetite for commerce hasn't diminished over the last 100 years or more. When the Ford Maddox Brown paintings were completed there was a resolution put forward by some of the leading Conservatives on the council for them to be whitewashed over and replaced by adverts for locally manufactured products, which sounds to me like a bad case of the resurgence of Manchester Man, that much-satirised figure from earlier in the century based on the stereotype of the successful cotton manufacturer as a bone-headed, blunt-speaking, totally business-orientated philistine.

Happily the murals still remain, though we did have to sneak behind the trade stalls to get a look at them. They begin with the Romans building a fort in Manchester using forced labour from the Britons, and progress chronologically around the hall as far as a grim and bespectacled John Dalton, the atomic chemist, dipping a stick in a stagnant pond in order to collect specimens of marsh gas. I particularly like the one of William Crabtree of Broughton, a pal of Jeremiah Horrocks from Hoole near Preston, the amateur astronomer. Crabtree is helping out Horrocks and is watching the transit of Venus across the sun in 1639. He's in his attic and the sunlight is streaming through a hole in the shutters onto a screen where Crabtree, dressed in what looks to be his wife's floral dressing gown and wearing some white flip-

'There was a stereotype of the Manchester cotton manufacturer as a bone-headed, blunt-speaking, totally business orientated philistine'

flops, is gazing transfixed at this celestial phenomenon. In the background, festooned with toddlers, is Mrs Crabtree. She seems to be saying, 'Oh, for Goodness' sake, Crabbie, why can't you stop messing about and get a proper job?' Like, perhaps, 'a rewarding career for inspirational leaders' with Asda (on offer at stall 14 here today). Or how about something with Group Four Securicor, where he could develop his pecs like the man in charge who's built like a Sherman tank? Meanwhile, at the other end of the hall near the door, Albert again, and a flatteringly youthful Victoria, turn away from these scenes of vulgar Mancunian commercialism, clearly thoroughly unamused.

I like the relaxed and informal way they seem to treat their august town hall in Manchester. We wandered unmolested down corridors covered with diamond lattices of red and gold tiles and windows sagging with lead, along marble floors inlaid with busy bees and cotton flowers past statues of stern Victorian patriarchs wagging fingers, expecting at any moment to be shooed away by some liveried lackey eager to protect the dignity of the surroundings from riff-raff like us. I looked out of a window and down onto some offices overlooking a shadowy cobbled basement area, hoping to catch sight of some dusty scrivener busy amending the fine print of the latest Weights and Measures regulations. But all I could see were scenes of unallayed merriment as a children's party was in full swing in a flurry of bright balloons and sticky buns. At the end of one corridor was parked a portable bar with beer pumps, awaiting the next civic shindig. And in Committee Room 23, where a notice led me to expect a meeting of the Finance and Grave Municipal Matters Committee earnestly at work, all I could see was a long table groaning with sausage rolls and glistening vol-au-vents awaiting the members' hungry attention. I must remember to remove any criticism of Manchester from these pages in the hope that I'll be offered a job working at the town hall. It looks as though it could be a right lark.

An undoubted boost to Manchester's commercial success came with the arrival of the Ship Canal in the last decade of the Victorian period. Prior to that, Liverpool had been the gateway to her trading markets, and dock charges and railway rates had been a serious drain upon the profits and competitiveness of the great Cottonopolis. And it wasn't just Manchester which suffered, but every manufacturing town in the surrounding district. No wonder the council officials in Bacup forked out to dress their wives in such finery at the opening ceremony. Because of the opposition from the Liverpool Dock Board and the railway companies, the bill for the Ship Canal's construction took 175 days of parliamentary business before it was passed. Another vested interest opposed to the canal was Sir Humphrey Francis de Trafford, whose 1,200-acre estate would be cut in two by the waterway. But after over six years' work, at a cost of £15 million, using as many as 17,000 labourers, 173 railway locomotives and over 6,000 wagons, the 35½ mile canal was opened, on New Year's Day 1894. On this occasion her Majesty deigned to turn up, staying the barest minimum amount of time in a city she clearly didn't love, despite its huge contribution to the prosperity of her reign.

The Ship Canal today. Empty.

PHOTOGRAPH: AUTHOR

Cotton might have been the inspiration for the building of the Ship Canal but ultimately it was to be other industries which benefited most. Sir Humphrey de Trafford, having been persuaded to part with his ancestral acres at a bargain basement price of £300,000, the world's first industrial estate was developed alongside the canal at Trafford Park. Engineering and the new technological industries usurped the once-green parkland and created the great hinterland of factories and warehouses that still survive today, albeit in a modern form and on a much reduced scale. During the First World War munitions, aircraft and chemicals were produced here. There was even a Ford car plant. The largest engineering works in Britain, Westinghouse Electric, later Metropolitan Vickers, built steam turbines. I recall Titus Thornber telling me of how he worked there before the last war in a vast drawing office of over a thousand men. As a country man he hated it. I too needed to overcome my fondness for wandering amongst the remote and lonely places of our county and brace myself for a visit to the site of this powerhouse of industrial Lancashire, beginning with the old Manchester docks at the end of the Ship Canal in Salford Quays.

CHAPTER SEVENTEEN

THE INDUSTRIAL HEARTLAND TRANSFORMED

YOU CAN CATCH the tram to Salford Quays from round the back of the town hall near where, on 21 October 1803, John Dalton propounded his theory of the atomic structure of matter to the Manchester Literary and Philosophical Society and changed the way we look at the material universe for ever. The journey takes you through the building site of red oxide cranes and grey concrete which is the south-west Manchester of today. As you hurry along the flanks of the Irwell that are cluttered with warehouses, a tantalising glimpse of the Pennine hills rises beyond the flats of the city to the north: another kingdom, another world. The tramway snakes around a switchback of curves through car stacks and office blocks where the sky is trapped in giant sea-green screens of glass. And then you hit the Quays, watery enclosures surrounded by Mexican grills and American burger bars and the huge monoliths of concrete and glass which are the new developments, some so new they're still in their plastic wrappers. Adverts blaze, offering new apartments, duplexes and penthouses. (Duplexes? We've never heard of those in Burnley.) 'A new way of living. An oasis of tranquillity just 10 minutes from the pace and excitement of Manchester city centre.' Could a company calling itself 'Countryside Properties' really be selling these? Inviting us to their 'Marketing Suite' to sign along the dotted line? Here, where 100 years ago the transatlantic cargo boats nudged their mighty bows into the docks amidst the creak and groan of cranes and the clamour of armies of lightermen? Now, as you step on to the Quays at a place called Anchorage – aptly named for the perishing wind that strikes off the cold waters of the docks – the first

Monoliths of concrete and glass. Salford Quays.
PHOTOGRAPH: AUTHOR

thing you notice is the silence and how empty it seems of human activity. A trio of fresh-faced joggers in lycra pad past along the esplanades in front of the quiet waterside apartments. Overhead a gull loiters self-consciously, a dim race-memory, lurking in his tiny birdbrain, of a place once vitally connected with the sea. The wind cuffs the turbid waters of the quays into life, creating wraith-like shadows which swirl across the surface before disappearing as quickly as they appeared.

Ghosts. You can't get the idea of ghosts out of your head. Ghost ships bearing raw cotton from across the Atlantic and then returning with the daytime labours of Nos 1 and 2 sheds at Jimmy Nelson's to America, West Africa, the Far East. Britain's bread by Lancashire thread. Then the sugar and timber boats, the grain, the steel and chemicals, to return with the tanks and armaments and engines of the First World War. All the history, the creative and destructive history of Lancashire in the last hundred years written upon

The boulevards of Salford.

PHOTOGRAPH: AUTHOR

these slate-grey waters for the wind to wipe clean and leave behind this brave new modern world of sweeping high-rise apartments and discount shopping stores, restaurants, an art gallery and theatre, all, as I say, so eerily silent. You wonder where the wealth has come from to create all this. In the past you could see wealth being made in the clouds of smoke and steam issuing from every mill and engine house, hear it in the clatter of looms and the hiss of pistons. But today's wealth sneaks in and out of bank accounts; fortunes are made by invisible deals, by the press of a key on a computer and the scatter of figures across a screen. It's John Dalton's atoms, his invisible electrons, doing all the work, and building these glass castles in the sky.

The Lowry: love it or hate it.
PHOTOGRAPH: AUTHOR

I walk along one of the boulevards where the trees are rooted in cast-iron gratings and have been grotesquely polled into some subtopian parody of a tree, because in this world of glass and steel and plastic credit cards even Countryside Properties don't want to remind us of what real nature looks like in case it stirs uneasy memories of a lost innocence where happiness was not dependent upon such lavish consumption. And then at last I can see the Ship Canal with the sunlight splintering on the water and the western horizon beckoning as it must have done to those Manchester businessmen who financed it, promising dazzling wealth and fortune in the markets of the world. But today the skyline is cluttered with cranes and warehouses and oil storage tanks, and the only ships you are likely to see are the canal cruise boats in summer and the odd battered boat bringing scrap to the metal works at Eccles. Next to the War Museum, with its roof rising to the sky like a cleaver, is a new bridge that takes you across the canal to a building which shines like a palace of burnished copper. The bridge is as sleek as a scimitar in steel and blue glass, with towers that lift it wholesale above the waters of the canal to allow the ships to pass. And then there's the Lowry. What can you say about the Lowry, the flagship of this whole fantastic development, with its cheese grater tower and chaos of fractured forms and competing materials? You either hate it or love it, see it as a modern mish-mash of disorderly shapes or else an exciting departure from the staid formality of the past.

I enter the building uncertainly, to be met by a sudden torrent of people. So this is where everyone has been, to the theatre to watch, believe it or not, *Sleeping Beauty on Ice*. There are bossy grandmas ('Now does anyone want to go to the toilet before we get into the car?), grandchildren in knitted pink ponchos skating across the polished floor waving Cinderellas on a stick. There are coach loads of pensioners from Prestwich who explode with mirth at my suggestion that they may want to take up ice skating themselves after this. And all this in the new home of Lancashire's most famous artist, Lawrence Stephen Lowry, the queer, old Salford recluse and inventor of hairpin folk and dogs like scraps on a string. What on earth would the old curmudgeon have made of all this? I fear that the answer might have been: not a lot. I hurry up the posh escalator to his gallery, determined to reassess, to try to say something good about this patron saint of Lancashire art with his hooked and bent figures in sepia brown spilling out of factory gates under smoke-clogged clouds dwarfed by black skyscraper mills in pictures painted out of soot and smoke and terminal misery.

The lady next to me, who had clearly had an education which none of the people in the picture could ever have dreamed of, is talking to her mother about the 'dynamism of the figures' in the crowd. This to me is pure tosh. They are somnambulists, stupefied by work, shrunken by their surroundings of chimneys and towering mills and black, unforgiving church steeples; men and women reduced to the bare bones of humanity by the factory system, by the big, black thumbprint of God and the factory owner, who were one and the same thing. The pictures are dismally depressing. One shows a doctor's waiting room full of the hollow-eyed already-dead; glum shades brow-beaten by misery. A man in a trilby looks out from a canvas like a startled cadaver. A father and his two sons stop you in their tracks with their haunted eyes. 'Share our misery,' they shout. 'Don't ever dare to be happy.' Lowry's paintings are a chronicle of despair. They are a denial of any of the joys of creation, just as they are colourless in tone and stark in execution. A painting called *A Man Lying on a Wall* is just that and shows a man lying flat on his back with a fag in his mouth. This is clearly one of Lowry's bleak attempts at humour because his cigarette points straight upwards just like the factory chimney behind him. People mingle with cripples in a schoolyard, not because people were tolerant of deformity – I remember that much from my schooldays – but because Lowry is saying we are all cripples of one kind or another and the source of our deformity is there in the industrial environment.

> 'Lowry's figures are men and women reduced to the bare bones of humanity by the factory system'

Now we in Lancashire don't really need an artist to tell us that the ugly urban environment of black mills and mean terraces can warp and crush the human spirit. To the artistic establishment of the south of England Lowry may well be seen as a genius for pointing this out. But to me he was a rather humourless misogynist who painted what he saw and, as you can find out from one of the rare TV interviews he gave towards the end of his life, displayed admirable Lancashire honesty by not making any claims to greatness himself. Now, in death, he's probably having the laugh of his life looking down and seeing what a fuss has been made about him.

As a contrast with the raw and unbearable honesty of Lowry's bleak vision of working life here in Lancashire, I couldn't help but be reminded of the famous painting by Ford Maddox Brown which I'd been looking at a few hours earlier in the city Art Gallery in Mosley Street. Ford Maddox Brown's *Work*, painted 100 years earlier, shows how the Victorian establishment preferred to see work as something ennobling and dignified, endorsed with no less than biblical approval. Under the text, 'In the sweat of thy face shall thou eat bread', it shows a street scene with navvies busy digging a hole. There is, however, remarkably little sweat in evidence. The men are sturdy and muscular, more like the sculptured gods which adorn the friezes of Victorian civic buildings than mere men. The scene is a blaze of colour and the workmen are dressed in bright turbans. One wears a bow tie and a richly brocaded waistcoat with a blossom pinned to it. He even has a copy of *The Times* tucked under his brawny arm as he stands with his toolbox waiting to do his bit. Set beside the matchstick-thin shadows of Lowry of the next century, it is an absurd piece of Romantic propaganda and it illustrates the Victorians' huge capacity for self-delusion. For me, they were the inventors of the 'have a nice day' optimism which today we seem to have borrowed from the Americans to paper over the cracks in our own dog-eat-dog consumer

A sickly smell of bran mash. Trafford Park.
PHOTOGRAPH: AUTHOR

society. At the same time as Ford Maddox Brown was splashing on the rich oils and bathing the bulging muscles and noble brows of his workmen in dazzling sunlight, Charles Dickens was offering a somewhat different version of Victorian working life in his grim depiction of Coketown in *Hard Times*, based upon a contemporary visit to Preston.

And if you should need further persuasion of how at home the Victorians were with self-delusion, with hypocrisy, continue past the Ford Maddox Brown painting in the Art Gallery to the collection of erotic paintings purchased by the straight-laced gentlemen of the corporation of Manchester in the late nineteenth century. Observe the naked sensuality of J.W. Waterhouse's *Hylas and the Nymphs*, the smouldering sexuality of the bare-breasted Sappho, or Syrinx turning herself into a reed to escape rape by the god Pan while in the process exposing herself 'for the viewer's pleasure', as the frank modern caption explains. Were the *hoi polloi* of Manchester encouraged to come and gaze upon these pictures, I wondered? The womenfolk? Or were they kept under lock and key and reserved for the 'pleasure' of the male town hall dignitaries? It's the kind of consideration you might like to bear in mind when you next visit the town hall sculpture hall and study the marble busts of Manchester's Victorian glitterati.

> 'I'd rather have my teeth drawn with coal tongs than go shopping'

The following day I spent in Trafford Park to see what had become of this industrial heartland of early twentieth-century Lancashire. I stood on the Centenary Bridge over the Ship Canal, built in 1994 to commemorate 100 years of the canal. The air is full of a warm, cloying smell which at first I can't place. I call down to a workman in a yard full of huge storage tanks and gantries of steel pipes. 'What do they make here?' I shout. 'Not a lot,' he replies unhelpfully. So I had to guess. The yard is full of stainless steel road tankers with 'Foodstuffs Only' written on them. And then I recalled where I'd met the smell before. From my boyhood, when my aunt kept hens. It was the smell of the bran mash she boiled up to feed them. So they were making animal food. Or was it human food? Is there any difference in these days of bulk-produced factory fodder that comes in tankers like petrol? The bank of the Ship Canal is lined with huge storage cylinders 150 feet high. Next to the canal you can feel a cold wind creeping along the murky waters. It's welcome if only because it disperses the sickly smell of the bran mash. Overhead a heron plods westwards, adding a welcome touch of the primeval to this landscape of steel pipes and regimented silos.

At the other side of the bridge is a retail park of vast, prefabricated hangars. A ship is docked next to a line of grey concrete-clad silos. It is called the *Arklow Brook*. The factory opposite says Akzo Nobel and Akcros Chemicals and it's on a road called Lankro Way. Modern industry has spawned its own argot of unpleasant-sounding names. There's no hint of a previous rustic existence in these names as there is in the street-names of Nelson, nothing to anchor us in the historic process that has brought us from the fields and villages of pre-industrial England. It is as if all memory of Eden has been expunged in the furnaces of industry, by the hammers of the steel mills, the concrete mixers and asphalt rollers. The machine is our master now and not Nature. So anyone like me strolling along the pavements of Trafford Park is an aberration. A car passes and some youths throw a bottle at me. I am a deviant. No one walks on Lankro Way. In fact, I don't now why there is a pavement, unless it's for the lorry drivers who park up there to throw out their dinners. The hedge between the road and the canal, where the hawthorn and redcurrent bushes are starting to green up, is knee-deep in discarded takeaways. Any opportunity to make a path along the banks of the ship canal for people to walk along has been ignored. There's no heritage trail along this once vital artery of industrial Lancashire. Why not? Does it all have to be willow weaving and corn dollies? Here only industry and its obligatory attendant mess reign.

At the end of Lankro Way is a scrapyard with mountains of rusted swarf and twisted metal. There's a special radiation detection system at the weighbridge, which I find sinister. A security man at a nearby reception office tells me that boats bring scrap from Ireland. Once it was people we imported. He tells me that his own factory makes hazardous chemicals, and I can see containers of caustic soda and hear insistent and unsettling bleeping sounds coming from the tanks and cylinders half-hidden by a screen of broom and laurel and mahonia just coming into yellow flower. He tells me how this area of Trafford Park used to be really busy but that nowadays it's mostly quiet like it is today. Today is Good Friday.

Phoney exoticism. The Trafford Centre.
PHOTOGRAPH: AUTHOR

But it's far from quiet at the Trafford Centre. I'd observed the Centre's exotic mosque-like dome rising in the distance above the bridge of the Arklow Brook. I knew I'd have to pay it a visit, even though I'd rather have my teeth drawn with coal tongs than go shopping. But the Trafford Centre is the next phase in the area's history, the next strange twist in the road of human progress. From the feudal parklands and Sir Humphrey Francis de Trafford via the world's first industrial estate to a giant retail park. A paradigm for the rest of Lancashire? Of Britain?

People are arriving like pilgrims to Mecca. The car park I drive into is almost full and it's still not noon. Nothing could have prepared me for this wonder of the consumer age, this temple to the credit card. I cross a drawbridge over a sunken concrete moat of waste skips and wheelie bins into a sweeping glass-roofed mall. You enter through pink rag-dabbed plastic columns with fancy capitals picked out in gold paint. There are palm trees splaying roofwards, lifting the eye from the marble floors beyond the gleaming brass rails of the balconies with their fake brass incense burners and plastic topiary to murals of naked muscular Caesars and Botticelli maidens. But who are the figures above? Modern portraits of blokes in golf sweaters. I guess that they may be the real gods of this place, the directors of the Trafford Company, the visionary businessmen who dreamed up all this. But no one I ask knows. Nor do they care. Theirs is the happy buzz of expectation, the sweet sigh of contentment as they search and acquire the very latest fashions and electronic gimcracks. But for me, alas, under this sweeping arc of skylight and burnished balconies, I am imprisoned in a circle of Dante's inferno. I don't want a pair of shoes from a shop that can't even spell the word – Schuh? I am happily reconciled to ending my days never having tasted one of Gourmet Joe's New York pretzels. And it needs to be explained to me that the Bodyshop is not some sort of morgue. But, I'll give them their due: they've thought of everything. Everything that might smoothe the progress of money from your pocket into their tills. There are even crèches and cinemas, and something which intrigues me beyond all else: a prayer room. It's there on a sign and I follow it, wondering who will be there and whether I shall meet the real god of this place.

> 'They've thought of everything that might smooth the progress of your money from your pocket into their tills'

I tentatively enter a tiny, airless room by the side of Debenham's. Bibles and prayer books line a wall in strip-lit cases. There's the Torah and the Koran as well as a Gideon's Bible. And next to them there's Jesus looking sad. And at one end are showers for those who want to wash their feet. And, most remarkable of all, out of one wall, next to a six-foot high wooden cross, protrude a pair of giant hands. Giant hands, cupped in supplication. For me, this is the one true god of the Trafford Centre, a pair of disembodied hands, outstretched to take your dosh. I'm sorry if I offend those for whom this symbol means something sacred, but the Prayer Room really did make me sick. Put it down to the heat, to air-conditioning on top of bran mash, but that right-on, modern approach that sees no irony in lumping together our material and spiritual needs in one marketable package, that has God and Mammon cosying up to one another, is hypocrisy on a scale that even the Victorians would have balked at.

It's mostly young people who crowd the Trafford Centre today, to judge from all the bare stomachs and pierced bits on show, the jeans stretched to splitting point. But I really do feel sorry for the children, the gangs of eight-, nine- and ten-year-olds that cruise the malls, the young teenagers who are all over the latest mobile phones, the fancy trainers and fashion tops, and who seem to be growing up to think that this is a treat, a real day out. Kids that should be climbing trees and making dens and revelling in all the freedom and adventure of the natural world about them are already hooked on consumerism with all its gadgetry and gimmickry and ephemeral trendiness. All too soon they will grow up to become the wage slaves of the must-have society and this time of innocent and exhilarating exploration will be lost for ever.

I'd heard that the food halls at the Centre were wonderful, but I looked in vain for anything local. A black pudding, maybe? Some parkin or some home-cured ham? Meat from lambs fed on the hills of Bowland or pigs fattened in the Ribble valley? If they were there at all, they were lost in the welter of foreign imports: concoctions in mayonnaise, Mexican tortillas, Hungarian meatballs, Chinese spring rolls and Indian curries, American popcorn and prawns from Thailand. And so with the shops: all multinational with global branding. There's nothing to tell you that you're in Lancashire. There's nothing about the Centre's meretricious decor or the phoney exoticism of the architecture that tells you you're in the county that was the crucible of the Industrial Revolution, that clothed the world; nothing at all to link us with the history and traditions which brought us this far. Nothing like the Crompton Centre in Bolton, say, which at least makes you feel you're in Lancashire with its old-fashioned market

> Mexican tortillas, Hungarian meatballs, Chinese spring rolls and Indian curries, American popcorn and prawns from Thailand.

stalls in the foyer before it hits you with its anonymous chain stores beyond. I think they should dismantle the Trafford Centre and float it away piecemeal down the Ship Canal to the open sea where it could sink or else disappear off to be re-united with the hotchpotch bastard world of global marketing it represents.

Nearby, at Barton-on-Irwell, I went to look at a church just by the Ship Canal that is recommended by Simon Jenkins in his *Thousand Best English Churches*. It's All Saints, converted in Victorian times by Sir Humphrey de Trafford whose family were in Lancashire back in the time of King Canute.

According to Jenkins, the interior is a masterpiece, full of floral capitals and a chancel reredos 'like a wedding cake, adorned with so many angels it looks on the point of take-off'. Good Friday or not, the gates of the church were locked. As I rattled them, the priest, Father Blundell, came out and told me it was closed. Dry rot everywhere. Unless someone came up with a million pounds it would stay shut until it fell down. A million pounds. I looked back at the domes of the Trafford Centre and its bulging car parks. I wonder how long it takes them to make a million pounds?

CHAPTER EIGHTEEN

LIVERPOOL

IN MY SEARCH for some of the glories of the Victorian age it remained for me to journey west along the Ship Canal as far as Liverpool. It would have been nice to take one of the cruises which run throughout the summer months, but it was still only Easter and at a cost of almost £30 I'd have expected a discount on a trip across the Atlantic on the *Queen Mary II* to be thrown in as well. So I journeyed to Liverpool by the more conventional route of the M62, a trip of about as much historical resonance as a meal in a Little Chef. However, once in Liverpool and on the docks road, I was back on the trail of Victorian architectural grandiloquence. And how!

The Tobacco Warehouse at the Stanley Dock on Waterloo Road is frighteningly colossal. When it was built in 1901 it was the largest warehouse in the world. Today it is a mouldering dinosaur, a monument to the seemingly limitless commercial ambition of Victorian Lancashire and a mausoleum to the millions whose premature death can be accounted for by the weed. I don't know whether this was the reason I found the building so frightening. The sheer scale of our addiction to tobacco can be measured by its 12 storeys and 300-yard length. But these were the days when everyone smoked. Witness the black and white films of Mitchell and Kenyon found in Blackburn recently, or those sepia prints in the family album showing dad and his mates on the works outing to Blackpool, standing there by the charabanc, gabardine macs flapping around their knees in the wind off the prom, from every mouth a Woodbine or Senior Service or Players Navy Cut lolling nonchalantly, all blissfully ignorant of the harm it was doing them. But it's more than just the purpose of the Tobacco Warehouse that awes and terrifies; it is its ugliness, a combination of raw, red-brick utilitarianism and its current wretched state of decay. And it is the Stanley Dock itself, built in 1848, which seems to set the standard of grotesqueness. On the riverside, marking the entrance to the dock,

Liverpool's Tobacco Warehouse: overwhelmingly awful.

is a hideous turreted clock tower, signalling perhaps to those who arrive that they are entering a world where all sense of beauty and refinement has been sacrificed for grosser ambitions. (Is it the knowledge that the early tobacco trade was founded on the evils of slavery that is skewing my judgement and making me so uncharitable? But then you could say the same of cotton, although I've never felt so overwhelmed by a cotton mill.) The turreted theme continues as you enter the dock, with stone towers set above the blackened red brickwork. They're like something out of *Gormenghast*. The water of the dock is like motor oil, with a dark green, septic tinge. Just above the water level the dock sides are encrusted with black barnacles clinging together like colonies of alien life forms and disappearing into the murky depths in their thousands. Grey, torn skins of polythene hang off the razor wire of the swing bridge which is a rickety structure topped by a bleak wooden shed which shakes every time a lorry passes over it along the busy docks road, threatening to cast me into the dank dock amongst all the loathsome bivalves. I watch the occasional jogger run past, men in hoods who look like boxers with puffed and scarred faces. Perhaps the only way to get out of an area like the Liverpool docks is to fight your way out. I'd like to go inside one of the warehouses, but am too afraid. A discouraging notice warns 'Dangerous Property. Keep Out.' The blackened, broken windows are access to an interior of shadows, of dead, lost souls.

And then a miracle, one of the startling incongruities that stay in your mind for as long as you live. A swan floats past me into the dock. A calm, white, stately sailing vessel on the dark waters in the shadows of the crumbling warehouses. I am filled with fear for the beautiful creature. But she swims gently around the dock as if surveying this ruin of human enterprise, this monument to folly, a curious, intelligent look upon her black brow as she gazes around. Then, slowly, sadly, she turns and paddles silently away, back under the bridge to where she rejoins her mate, a dazzling white male, his feathers raised in a ruff of courtship. Together they sail out into the daylight of the river, their wakes gently melting away into the dark waters of the dock, like time itself.

If the Albert Dock was in half as bad a condition as the Stanley Dock before it was restored, it must have taken great vision to create the tourist

The Stanley Dock. Or Gormenghast?
PHOTOGRAPH: AUTHOR

attraction which it is today. The Albert Dock was first opened in 1846 with the surrounding warehouse used as secure storage for goods of high value. It has the elegance which goes with wealth, and even today the floors above the shops are all converted into luxury apartments. But a grey sky presses on the dock this afternoon which the water absorbs with a glum opaqueness. I might be wrong, but storm clouds could be brewing over the Albert Dock. When I visited it, too many of the shops that surround the dock had 'To Let' signs up. And many of the shops in business seemed too pretentious. I don't know who they're aimed at. I can imagine the gift shops appealing to the tourists, but who's going to buy a reproduction deep sea diver's helmet in brass and copper for £650? Hardly the sort of thing you buy on impulse while on a day trip from Pontefract. And I had no trouble resisting the white leather settee, described as a 'Grand Confort Petit Modèle 3-seater sofa designed by le Courbusier. Another shop announced smugly that it sold 'furniture that creates desire not interest'. We went into a café called Ha! Ha! Where the food was, well, laughable. They served ice tea and incinerated Mediterranean vegetables in shrivelled ciabattas. But I liked the gift shop selling minerals and semi-precious stones. There were geodes clustered with deep mauve quartz crystals that blazed in the light, sea-blue turkurenite (never heard of that before), yellow citrine and beautiful lapis lazuli pendants – just the sort of thing you associate with a trading port and some of its more exotic destinations. In front of the Tate Gallery, someone called Dave is restoring a Baltic trader which they dug out of the silt at the bottom of the Mersey six years ago. From the bowels of the boat come the noise of hammering to the sounds of a sea shanty, followed closely and bafflingly at heel by a recording of Frank Sinatra.

'It must have taken great vision to create the tourist attraction that the Albert Dock is today'

The works of modern art on display at the Tate are a bad advert for the twentieth century, many of them representing destruction, pain, anxiety and confusion, not everyone's cup of iced tea on a day out at the seaside. I can't imagine anyone who has come to see the Beatles' Story exhibition under the entrance near the car park then stepping into the Tate to study the sculpture of the Storm Man, a riven, mutilated bronze figure with a face like crushed cinders said to 'speak eloquently of human suffering'. But Liverpool is clearly a catholic city in more ways than one.

But I have no reservations about the success of the Maritime Museum. As you step inside, a sequence of paintings graphically illustrates the history of the development of the Liverpool waterfront. They step back in time from a picture showing the last regular liner to sail from Liverpool, the Elder Dempster's *Aureol*, built in 1951. Against the background of the famous 'Three Graces' – the Liver Building (1908–10), the Cunard Building (1913–17) and the Mersey Docks and Harbour Board building (1907) – the white *Aureol* sets sail upon a blue Mersey against an intensely blue sky. A sugar lump floating in blue Bols. But step to the next painting and the scene in 1873. The Three Graces are but an architect's dream and while there are steam ships, the canvas is dominated by sailing ships. Men plough out towards their ships in rowing boats on an angry Mersey, while overhead the sky is a drama of sunlight smashing through mountainous clouds. Then in the next painting it's back to the Liverpool of 1836. Again the Mersey is storm-tossed, as though, even in harbour, the artist is keen to show the primal power of the sea and the bravery of all those who set sail into such a hostile environment. The warehouses look more elegant and a forest of masts and rigging continue the clean vertical lines of the buildings. You see the tower of a church. The scene is almost pre-industrial, pre-lapsarian. A picture of the waterfront in 1817 is dominated by windmills, and distant fields show the area is still rural with even more church towers and spires. (Does economic prosperity lead to godlessness? Discuss.) A prospect of Liverpool painted by an unknown artist in 1725 shows a positively barren waterfront with just one dock, Liverpool's first, which had been opened in 1715. Galleons are firing a salute in the foreground. And the final picture shows Liverpool in 1680 when the town was still dominated by its medieval castle. The whole collection preserves in paint 250 years of the most prodigious expansion, when fortunes were made and lost. I was reminded of a story told to me by Sir Bernard de Hoghton, whose family owned Liverpool in the very early days, and who, through the profligacy of one of its members, lost it all at the gaming table. Talk about kick yourself.

Next is a room devoted to the heyday of Liverpool as a passenger port and gateway to America, the destination of the Cunard Queens. It is full of the sort of facts beloved of the Trivial Pursuitist. For example, did you know that Cunard used 356,764 tons of coal a year at the turn of the twentieth century? And that in 1920, Cary Grant sailed to America after a stint touring the North West as a stilt-walker? But on a more personal if less bizarre note, I know that a number of my grandfather's brothers – he came from a family of 13 – sailed from Liverpool to California in 1904. TB ran in the family and they thought the climate would be better for them. As a consequence, I share the DNA of the offspring of a family of walnut growers in Sacramento, whom I don't suppose I shall ever meet. And talking of walnuts, a bizarre inventory of goods taken on board the *Titanic* when it left Southampton in 1912 included 100 cases of shelled walnuts – a tidy number of Waldorf salads there – 75 cases of anchovies, 63 cases of champagne, 856

'Slavery was the foundation on which much of Liverpool's early industrial wealth was formed'

rolls of lino, three cases of rabbit skins, a case of feathers and one barrel of earth. What this last item was for, I can't imagine, unless one of the luckless passengers hoped one day to be buried in it instead of being swamped by the deluge.

In the basement of the Maritime Museum lies an exhibition which acknowledges an unpalatable truth about the foundation of much of Liverpool's wealth in the early years of the industrial era. In 1752, the port had a slaving fleet of 88 boats capable of carrying over 25,000 slaves. Probably unbeknown to the handloom weavers and spinners of Lancashire, the cloth they were weaving which was going to the markets of West Africa was being sold to buy slaves who were then shipped over to work in the cotton plantations of America and the West Indies. The boats then returned home with the raw cotton for the further manufacture of cloth. The conditions aboard the slave ships are dramatically recreated in the museum. You have to pass through the bowels of a ship which is black and claustrophobic, with narrow wooden shelves where the slaves crouched. You can hear the wail of the wind, the creak of the spars and the sudden thud of the waves against the hull. A description captures the appalling inhumanity of the business:

> Men packed together below deck and secured by leg irons, so cramped they were forced to crouch. Air in the hold was foul and putrid. The lack of sanitation and suffocating conditions meant a constant threat of disease: fever, dysentery and smallpox.

It goes on to describe how the slaves were force-fed if they wouldn't eat during the two-month journey and how one in five of them died. It's thought that as many as 20 million Africans were transported across the Atlantic in this way, though some sources put the figure as a lot higher. In 1781, the slave ship *Zong* from Liverpool was gripped by fever and the captain ordered the crew to throw 133 of the captives overboard. When a prosecution was brought against the slavers, the case was quashed when it was successfully argued that slaves were in fact property and could, legally, be disposed of in such a manner.

One small boy at the exhibition was looking at the collection of shackles and iron punishment collars used to restrain the slaves. His dad was explaining what the exhibition was all about. 'They used to steal people from other countries and put them in here,' he said. 'Why?' asked his little boy. 'Because they were mean,' replied the father. Much of the social life of eighteenth-century England was dependent upon the products of slave labour. Not only cotton for their clothes and finery, but sugar, coffee, tea and chocolate and, of course, tobacco. In 1788 Liverpool sent a petition to Parliament arguing that the abolition of the slave trade would damage the interests of the town.

It's a relief to get out of the basement and leave behind this sorry chapter in Lancashire's history. Looking across the river to Birkenhead, rain, river and sky merge in a grey mist. Against the backdrops of the silent cranes and the warehouses of the old shipyards, the Liverpool to Dublin ferry rests between journeys. At the Pier Head the Three Graces look out to sea from whence, once, came their wealth. It may be dull weather, but the famous trio are looking rather grimy, like wedding cakes from a wedding that long ago ended in divorce. They're fine and solid buildings but seem built more on

Liverpool river front.

PHOTOGRAPH: MALCOLM GREENHALGH

wealth than inspiration. The liver birds are tethered to their perches and were never meant to soar. But perhaps that is only to be expected of an edifice built on something as prosaic as insurance. To me, the Liver Building is the least satisfying of the three. It possesses something of the monotony of an exotic warehouse, with its identical windows, and it didn't surprise me to learn later that it was one of the first buildings to use reinforced concrete. The confidence of the Victorians has started to ebb and we're entering the modern age of doubt and uncertainty. The Liver Building is something of a final flourish, a last act of architectural bravura. The Cunard Building in the middle is much more restrained. The architects boasted the improbable names of Willink & Thicknesse. Their work is more subtle and elegant than that of the others, especially the Docks Building with its clutter of domes and cupolas. But thank goodness recent plans for a Fourth Grace to mark Liverpool's status as Capital of Culture in 2008 have been shelved. Had it gone ahead it must surely have become known as the Three Graces' Ugly Sister.

But while mentioning ugliness, surely there can be nothing to rival Liverpool's Anglican Cathedral. It casts its lumpen shadow over the whole city. It is twentieth-century brutalism masquerading as medieval majesty, another Liverpool building where size seems to have dominated all other considerations. It is grandeur without warmth, a bullying sort of grandeur. We are back to west Lancashire red sandstone again, but in this case the colour is murky pink. The main south doorway with its fine sea-serpent iron gates is impressive but unwelcoming and I'm not surprised that it's kept closed. It is mass without detail. God is not so much in here but imprisoned. Even the entrance to what is described as the Western Rooms has the look of a Her Majesty's prison with its portcullis-like oak door. From this side the cathedral sits on slabs of rock, barren save for a few shrubs, birches and hardy willows. Perhaps the church takes the name of St Peter too literally. Built on a rock, it is a bare, lithic thing itself. The bronze giant in the loin cloth above the west door is by the sculptor Elisabeth Frinck (Scousers have dubbed it 'Frinkenstein'). If he is supposed to represent Christ, he looks more dismayed than compassionate. But inside, all is forgiven. The bleak exterior contains a noble heart.

The glass above the west door is an intense cerulean dotted with fiery embers of red and gold. The windows in the north and south transept gleam with a polished, pearly luminescence with Christ in glory above suspended in the silvery light. Only the east window disappoints in comparison, sombre and cluttered with shadows. But it is the shadows which are the cathedral's glory. It is as if the stonework, which looks so dull outside, gives off a shadowy mist which lifts the eye ever higher up the soaring pillars into the mysterious stillness of the stone vaulting. Standing at the junction of the nave and transept there is a sense of huge emptiness, of shadowy stillness, which invites you to fill it yourself with your own sense of the great mystery of Creation.

> 'the bleak exterior of Liverpool Cathedral contains a noble heart'

Standing outside, the city's other cathedral beckons. You must walk half a mile or so down Rodney Street to see it. Central Liverpool is full of fine terraces built by the city's successful merchants and traders and Rodney Street is one of the finest. It is broad and elegant, three-storey houses in red brick, a welcome change after the ponderous stone of the outside of the cathedral, with pillared entrances of Ionic and Doric columns and slender wrought-iron balconies. Gladstone, I'm told, was born, in 1809, in Number 62. Today it must be the Harley Street of Liverpool because it blinds you with its polished brass nameplates listing legions of doctors and specialists. But realism soon replaces refinement in Liverpool. Young men in hoodies swagger down Hardman Street, living up to the street name. Police sirens screech. A pub in South Hunter Street called the Hope and Anchor has replaced its traditional sign with Edvard Munch's contorted screamer. What on earth are they trying to say about pub life in Liverpool? And then we're at the Roman Catholic Cathedral, known with a typical Scouse humour variously as Paddy's Wigwam or the Mersey Funnel. It is an architectural wonder of the 1960s, and yet I can't get the notion of the cold war and concrete missile silos out of my head.

We go into the cafeteria to sustain us on our pilgrimage and a girl with a degree in looking bored serves us tea and something called a cookie. (I'm still looking for some honest parkin or an Eccles cake.) The teabag lies in

Liverpool's Anglican Cathedral. A bullying grandeur.
PHOTOGRAPH: AUTHOR

the cup, stubbornly refusing to cloud the water until it had to be mugged to release its infusion. The cookie contains enough sugar to soak up the Gladstone Dock and we rush up the 50 steps to the cathedral on a sudden surge of insulin. At the door you are confronted by a modern bronze relief, a human face with horror-stricken eyes starting out from the feathered recess of a terrifying bird. This is in the medieval tradition of gargoyles and green men, but the difference is that the creature of fear and despair is man himself.

At the other side is another bird. A liver bird turned nasty? I look in vain for any explanation of the symbolism in the display in the cathedral foyer, Instead, I learn that the cathedral, after being completed in 1967, had to be restored in the 1990s at a cost of £8 million, which must be some sort of judgement on modern building. The designer was Sir Frederick Gibberd, whose other claim to fame, mentioned without any hint of irony, was the design of Terminal Three at Heathrow Airport. The quality of light inside, created by the stained-glass walls and tower is praised by the writer in the foyer, and he's not wrong. The spectrum colours from the tower flood down towards the central altar and there are great steams of blue and aquamarine running down the walls. One ruby red panel above the Reconciliation Chapel is coruscating, a burning bush, if ever I saw one. But God can't be in two places at once, can he? I mean, is he here or across the way at the Anglican Cathedral? Perhaps we should view the two together. God in his glory is here

Liverpool Catholic Cathedral. Architectural wonder of the sixties.

PHOTOGRAPH: AUTHOR

in the brilliance and light of the new. But in the traditional cathedral we confront his shadow. Your choice will depend on which you prefer. Mystery or revelation.

At least you know to whose greater glory cathedrals are built. With a great civic monument like St George's Hall it sometimes doesn't seem quite so clear. The hall is a colossal classical structure completed in 1854 befitting the commercial greatness of Victorian Liverpool. Four lions, their manes flecked with mildew, guard the approaches. Steps rise towards the giant Corinthian columns topped with floral capitals and pigeon nets. High above, lion heads range across the corbels. It is generally regarded as one of the finest neo-Grecian buildings in the world. But when I see a human figure sitting at the top of the steps, dwarfed by the giant columns, I wonder about the ordinary people who made our great northern cities possible. It wasn't the ubiquitous Prince Albert sitting on his horse to one side of the hall or Victoria at the other. (Was she as sniffy about Liverpool as she was about Manchester?) It wasn't General William Earle whose statue shows him brandishing his sabre and leading his men to glory in the Sudan in 1885. But the oblong war memorial that stands right in front of the hall comes closest to what made Liverpool and Lancashire great. In bronze relief it shows the common citizens of Liverpool laying their flowers at the grave of a fallen soldier. These were the people upon whose work-bent shoulders such edifices were built. The sailors, the weavers, the dockers, the slaves. I wonder what they thought of these great public buildings to which they were expected to contribute, after the first swelling of pride subsided; when they saw yet another royal monument going up as the city fathers cosied up to the Establishment and looked eagerly for their knighthoods? It's no coincidence that the turn of the century began to see the rise of the labour movement, as working men and women began to seek a fairer share of power that acknowledged their own role in making the country prosperous. And there can be no city in England where that transfer of power from a civic elite to the ordinary citizens has been more complete throughout the twentieth century than in Liverpool.

> 'I wonder about the ordinary people who made our great northern cities possible'

I would have liked to have seen inside the St George's Hall but the entrance was barred by two burly workmen. 'Sorry, you can't come in,' I was told. 'It's closed for alterations.'

'When will it be open?' I asked. 'How long is a piece of string?' was the reply.

There's a lot of work to be done before the city takes on the mantle of European Capital of Culture. At the time of writing this the city centre is distinctly down at heel. I didn't see any of those assiduous street cleaners who ship the litter into their bins before it hits the ground which I saw in Bolton. There's none of the spruce image-consciousness of the born-again Manchester.

We took a subway from St George's Hall towards the shops and on the walls was painted 'Liverpool. A Cultured City'. Was it Scouse irony? Because the subway was filthy. We had to pick our way through pools of rainwater and sodden litter. Next to a dismembered grit container which vandals had dragged down into the subway, sand was strewn everywhere. It was a mugger's paradise. Church Street was more like a proud city centre shopping street should be, wide, with buildings with handsome embellished frontages. But into Lord Street and things began to degenerate again. I was hoping to find a bookshop in this would-be city of culture and discover what Pevsner could tell me about the interior of St George's Hall. But I'm surrounded by ugly ersatz discount stores and get-away-from-it-all travel shops. The herringbone pattern of the brickwork underfoot is interrupted by careless patches of tarmac. Two fire engines arrive in a pandemonium of sirens to a department store and I find myself thinking of how the great fire of London provided the impetus for the rebuilding of the city, for Wren and Hawksmoor. We bump into Victoria again in Derby Square (built on the site of the long-demolished castle), a massive 20 foot bronze statue looking majestically from a domed baldachin (a canopy supported by columns). But the historic transition from respect to anarchy, from royal sycophant to yob, is complete. Today the monarch of Liverpool's glory years is plastered with graffiti as far as spray can and felt pen will reach. And all this right outside the Law Courts. The steps of the monument look as though they haven't been swept since the *Titanic* set sail. Liverpool will have to be quickly disabused if it thinks the Europeans are going to put up with this sort of thing.

An interesting comparison is to be made between the Victorian legacy of dour terraced streets in the mill towns of Lancashire and what is to be found at Port Sunlight across the river from Liverpool. Mill bosses like Jimmy and Amos Nelson built houses for their workers out of self-interest. They were the barracks blocks for their armies of weavers. But William Hesketh Lever, the Bolton-born soap baron, built houses for his workers out of sheer idealism. After the monotony of the grey mill town terraces, it's astonishing to find that not a single row of the 30-odd acres of housing in Port Sunlight is identical. He used 30 different architects to design the garden village, and to the workers who worked in his factory and their families, who were entitled to live in one of the 800 cottages built between 1889 and 1914, it must have seemed like paradise on earth.

Each house is either a three- or four-bedroomed old English cottage with kitchen and parlour and an allotment outside for the tenants to grow their own vegetables. Eden returned to the town. You can spend a pleasant hour wandering around this utopia. There are Tudor gables with red herringbone brickwork between the timbers or white plaster between quartrefoils reminiscent of Speke or Rufford Old Hall. There are gables so ornamental that they wouldn't look out of place at Hampton Court. There are stone-clad roofs and roofs of red tiles, twisted chimneys, and chimneys that rise from the ground on elegant columns. Every assortment of ornamental brickwork and leaded windows you could imagine is to be found. What a contrast with the drab conformity of mill town terraces. And everywhere there are lawns, gardens and flowers. The lawns are swathed in shimmering narcissi. There are beds of purple hyacinths, yellow primula and blue pansies, and roundabouts crammed with pink tulips. And behind the tree-lined avenues are sunken rose gardens and ornamental ponds graced with bronze sculptures. Lever provided social centres, a hospital, libraries, a theatre, schools, churches, everything a body or soul could need, including the splendid Lady Lever Art Gallery. Out of Sunlight soap and the boiling and rendering of vegetable oils, animal fats and caustic soda, arose the elixir of high culture. Reynolds, Millais, Epstein, Turner, Dante Gabriel Rossetti and Frederick Leighton, all and many more are in the gallery. It is as if, once the working man had learned to wash the grime of his labours away, he could discover his own shining white soul underneath waiting to be nourished. And Lever saw that they still had the energy for self-improvement by introducing an eight-hour day for his workers. Pure idealism, as I say (though Lever was the first to acknowledge that he did get more work out of his employees this way), but wonderful. And here in the grimy old Lancashire of the early 1900s, with its tales of towns so soot-encrusted and skies so choked with smoke you could only see the hills once a year when the mills shut down for the wakes week holiday. Manchester Man must have look westwards and thought Lever was off his head.

But where was the factory where these lucky people worked? Just across Wood Street, as quiet and genteel a setting as anything St Annes has to offer, is Lever House. It is elegant, balconied and crowned by the royal crest in honour of the warrant awarded by Queen Victoria in 1892. And stretching to either side is the wide, but always gracefully proportioned brick frontage of the soap works. Today it is noiseless, smokeless and smell-free. For even though behind the façade stretch long avenues of modern chemical plant with gleaming metal cylinders and silver pipework, this is the modern home of Unilever, makers of Persil, Surf, Dove, Comfort and more. (Lever was the first master of the soft sell, the use of seductive images through word association – Sunlight soap with its suggestion of dazzling purity for a product which up until then had been a pretty gross concoction of boiled-up animal remains.) I stopped a very clean young man as he stepped out of the factory and asked him why everything was so quiet and clean. After all, it's still a chemical plant. He told me that all the chimneys have moved to Warrington where all the dirty work, so to speak, goes on. Today they simply import the various powders to make liquid soaps.

And soap has spread its shining, clean, iridescent film over Port Sunlight. Today, 75 per cent of Lord Leverhulme's houses are privately owned. The immaculate gardens are maintained by a trust. It is as near as you'll get to Utopia if what you want is order, cleanliness, space and domestic and horticultural harmony. A visit leaves you feeling like you do after a bath, clean and relaxed. Only one nagging doubt (you've been waiting for this) occurred

Port Sunlight. What a contrast with Milltown.

PHOTOGRAPH: AUTHOR

to me, and this was long after I'd left and dived back under the Mersey into Liverpool. I never saw anyone in any of the houses. There were plenty of visitors like me, admiring the gardens, pottering around the Visitor Centre, studying the exhibits in the Art Gallery. But where were the occupants of Port Sunlight? At work? In bed? Or were they quietly wrapped up in scented cellophane and put away until all the visitors had gone home, just in case they made the place look untidy?

CHAPTER NINETEEN

STICKING TOGETHER

WHEN THE FIVE NELSON WEAVERS DROWNED in Derwentwater on 12 August 1898 there were outpourings of sympathy from throughout Lancashire. People were touched by the tragedy because the girls who lost their lives were just like themselves. They did similar jobs in the all-encompassing textile industry, lived in crowded terraced houses built on the same utilitarian principles, worked in mills under a similar Gradgrind regime, attended chapels of common denominations and suffered from the same hardships through slumps in trade and the chance visitation of disease. People were alike, and if not, they soon grew alike. They were citizens of a new era in social evolution, forcibly divorced from their rural ancestry by relentless economic imperatives and transplanted into a harsh new urban environment dominated by the factory and the machine. This social cohesion might have brought tears to the thousands of eyes that watched the funeral procession of the Nelson weavers, but it was to become the defining strength of the Lancashire community. And one of the earliest manifestations of this solidarity was in the Co-operative movement.

Ah, the Co-op, that all-providing mother to generations of pre- and post-war Lancastrians. You will remember them with affection if, like me, you were a child of the '40s and '50s. They were the umbilical that kept us nourished during those sepia, unfussy days after the hardships of the war, before we grew soft and pampered by consumerism, magnolia paint and motor cars. A grocer and butcher in every community (as many as 30 in my own small town of Colne and district), tall gabled buildings with solid stone corbels, mosaic thresholds and coloured tiles in bas-relief from floor to ceiling, our co-ops were handsome and solid, the outward flourishes of great wealth. But they were no vain edifices to a remote and proud capitalist master; they were our own, our bit of back-street socialism, owned by us, the customers, who shopped there every day at the mahogany counters with their cool marble slabs, bought the pounds of sugar weighed out in the dark blue sugar bags, the collops of ham from the big, red, hand-wound bacon slicers and slabs of fat yellow butter straight from the wooden butter tubs. And by the simple recitation of a divi number – a number indelibly written onto the memory of every Co-op child as if it had been written in the blue indelible pencil the assistant kept behind his ear and licked before he wrote it down on the pink remembered divi slips – we shared the profits through a twice yearly dividend. It was once as much as 2s. 11d. in the pound, or 15 per cent, refunds in cash for mum to spend on school shoes or uniforms or grey woollies and gabardine macs, yes, at the Co-op. Because it wasn't just grocers and butchers on every street corner, but the Co-op outfitters in the town centre, the furniture shop and the bakery with the Co-op café above where they did wedding receptions and ham teas for a funeral. For they weren't just our everyday needs in this life which the Co-op catered for, it also saw us decently off into the next. It was genuine cradle to the grave socialism. As kids, before television began to mesmerise the nation and sap the social life of our communities we used to play out at night under the yellow islands of light beneath the gas lamps in front of the Co-op grocers at the end of our street, only dimly aware of what the long board in a cupboard up against the wall was for. We knew you could bounce a ball off it and it made a nice hollow sound that brought the neighbours out. And we knew it was called a night board. But the knowledge that people came to collect it to lay out their dead until the Co-op funeral service could come in the morning, never troubled our carefree heads; why should it when you're young and know you're going to live for ever? There wasn't an aspect of life that in those years the Co-op didn't cater for, and it drew us all together around its benign and all-embracing apron.

> 'The Co-op was the umbilical that kept us nourished during those sepia, unfussy days after the hardships of war'

The roots of the Co-operative movement grew from a common hardship, a shared exploitation. When the 28 Rochdale 'Pioneers' opened their first shop in Toad Lane in 1844, it was the hungry forties. In a debate in the House of Commons in 1841, the MP for Rochdale drew attention to the plight of the townspeople. Some 3,000 people were living on less than 1s. 10d. a week. Eighty-five families had no blankets, and 45 had no beds. Children were walking around without shoes. The adulteration of foodstuffs by shopkeepers and some of the mill owners who ran shops under the pernicious truck system (workers paid in lieu, obliged to shop in the owners' shops), put sand in the oatmeal, plaster of Paris and chalk in the flour, earth in the cocoa and dead leaves from the trees in the tea. When the Rochdale Pioneers opened their premises in Toad Lane it was as an 'honest' shop, selling pure food in correct weights at reasonable prices, with, of course, the magnificent divi. The local

shopkeepers hated them. They urged all the wholesalers to boycott them. But on the opening night they only laughed. In a small, dark room with a plank on two barrels as a counter, the only things for sale were flour, sugar and oatmeal contained in sacks on the floor, and a piece of butter on the counter. To buy the stock, one of the founders, David Brooks, had taken a wheelbarrow and walked to Manchester and back, a trip of 24 miles. But the Rochdale Pioneers were idealists. They weren't just catering for the needs of the body. They knew that education was the key to the improvement of the cotton workers' lot. So upstairs in Toad Lane they started a library. Beginning with just half a dozen books, by 1862 they had 5,000 and took 14 daily papers and 44 weekly or monthly periodicals. Working men came to the library as a sanctuary, to sit in front of its open fire and help themselves to knowledge which until then had been the preserve of only the rich and privileged. The Co-op was a pioneer of social egalitarianism.

The notion of working-class self-improvement lasted into the 1940s at the Co-op. At Colne library they showed me a syllabus of educational activities they laid on. There were debating classes, a women's guild, literature classes, lectures on foreign travel, fellowship choirs, brass bands and Saturday social nights with a dance and a supper. The Co-op kept its idealistic shine into the 1950s, and I remember some of its ardent supporters in our neighbourhood. But middle-class aspirants, and I'd include my parents among these, were already showing their disapproval at the taint of socialism that attached itself to the Co-op. Help yourself, not one another, was becoming the watchword. The Co-op grew slow and cumbersome. It was slow to change and heavy with local management committees. It quietly fell asleep, trading on its past

A new use for the old Colne Co-op.
PHOTOGRAPH: AUTHOR

reputation as the multiple grocers began to take over. In the 1960s thousands of branches closed down, furnishing premises for undertakers, joinery shops, carpet warehouses and launderettes, all the many uses you can find today when you come across one of their unmistakable, proud stone buildings, usually on prominent street corner sites. Ours, where we played at night, is now a house. I wonder if it's haunted by old Mr Crook, the paternalistic, brown-overalled manager who knew us all by name, and Pat the butcher who always saved mum a special cut of meat for the weekend. Only the memories remain as the Co-op has slipped into the history books along with its glorious ideals, its place usurped by today's giant supermarkets where, if you asked for some divi, they'd send for one of their security guards.

Religion was another force which bound people together. Initially a source of succour to those ground down by the evils of early industrialisation and promising rest and reward in the life to come, the churches soon became social magnets providing feast day suppers and outings as well as, through their Sunday schools, furnishing rudimentary lessons in reading and literacy which the secular authorities failed to provide. I recently obtained a list of the churches in Burnley drawn up by the Lancashire Family History and Heraldry Society and was astonished to count over 70 non-conformist churches and chapels in the borough, the vast majority dating from the Victorian period. To this can be added another 25 Church of England and Roman Catholic churches. By far the greatest number of chapels belonged to the Methodists. Like the Co-op buildings many of them still stand, put to dozens of different secular uses, from night-clubs to plumbers' merchants. They are a distinctive feature of the architectural landscape of our Lancashire towns, with their gaunt outlines and neo-classical frontages, and they are a lasting footprint in the unique progress of our people.

After the restoration of the monarchy in 1661, the Church of England was determined to avenge itself upon the Puritans and non-conformists of the Commonwealth period. The 1662 Act of Uniformity outlawed any kind of dissent and non-conformist ministers were banished from the communities and churches they served. But what better way than persecution to reinforce the community bonds they were determined to destroy? If you are looking for some of the roots of Lancashire cussedness and individuality, our somewhat cynical regard for authority and determination to do things our own way, you could do worse than to start here. With the accession of William and Mary and the Toleration Act of 1689, dissent prospered. Quakerism, with its emphasis upon mutual assistance, became widespread, and when John Wesley arrived to protests and riots from the established order, Lancashire soon took him to their hearts. Hence the 20 Wesleyan Methodists chapels in my list of Burnley churches, a record in stone of our enthusiasm for the unorthodox to be added to all the Primitive Methodists and Methodists, the nature of whose differences I won't pretend to understand. But each schism etc. had its adherents, their chapels becoming focal points for all their social activities as well as worship, which in some cases continue to this day but flourished in the early years of the twentieth century and are recorded by people like Emma Edge, Florrie Birtwell and Muriel Blenkinsop in my published collection of Lancashire memories, *The Century Speaks*. Whitsuntide walks and processions with each church marching under its own wonderfully embroidered banner, brass bands, sports days, bazaars, concerts and meat and potato pie suppers, all provided the ingredients for a rich social adhesive. And when you consider that the working week lasted for 5½ days and there were few rival forms of entertainment to fill the precious hours left for recreation, the importance of church and chapel to our forebears can hardly be over-emphasised.

Some of the uses to which their non-conformist chapels have been put today would have the pious elders of yesterday somersaulting in their graves. I remember a boy at school called Lesley Langdon who was a Methodist of precocious religious fervour. One day he stood up in assembly and to the great discomfort of the staff and the secret delight of the pupils, denounced the wickedness of the age. These were the dangerous and incendiary '50s when crepe soles crept in, together with ties as thin as shoelaces, and to the Devil's music known as rock and roll Elvis the Pelvis began rotating his hips in a scandalously suggestive manner. What would poor Lesley have made of things today where, in godless Burnley, they've turned some of their chapels into night clubs with names like XS, lit with lurid-coloured spotlights and pounding with disco music like some Dantean vision of hell? Never one to shirk my research, I determined to visit one such, a former Baptist chapel known as Jireh in Boot Way in Burnley, reincarnated as a music bar called Bootleggers.

Under the shallow classical pediment of this small but rather handsome building is the date 1853. But to judge from the sounds and flashing lights coming from inside it has been transformed by the twenty-first century into what the Victorians would undoubtedly have regarded as a latter-day Gomorrah. My son, a student of local low life, had told me to expect drunken girls dancing in cages, but apparently the place has undergone some sort of conversion recently and more seemly practices now prevail. I chose a Sunday evening for my visit, naturally, and my mind was rooted in the past as I imagined dark-clad mutton-chopped elders with moral disapproval writ upon their brows like the Ten Commandments, clutching their Bibles and hurrying inside. A girl going past wearing little more than her sun-bed tan and a smile, seeing me hesitating at the door, shouted encouragement. 'It's all right, love, you don't have to pay to go in.' The doorman gave me a rather quizzical look and I thought he was going to bar me on the grounds of being too old for this sort of thing, but the place was rather empty and I think they must have been desperate for customers. Inside I was met by swirling spider webs of psychedelic light and decibels, hundreds of them. A more than life-size model of Captain Hook leers down from a rowing boat suspended from the roof.

'We don't really have any choice in the way history takes us'

The Road to Hell. Baptist chapel to disco bar.
PHOTOGRAPH: AUTHOR

TV videos display a love-lorn maiden staggering around with a vast, red inflatable heart. I buy a drink and sit down in the corner before I'm floored by the sound waves. I'm actually sitting on a pew and it anchors me back into the 1850s. Are the stone walls still soaked with the prayers of the pious, or have the swirling lights erased the tape? I ask one of the lads in charge what he thinks the Baptists would have thought of their church being turned into this. 'It's the way things are going,' he replies with a hint of ruefulness. And I think, yes, we don't really have any choice in the way history takes us. We're just carried along like the lights on the wall, until someone comes and switches them off.

It wasn't long before the powers that be found a new way to exploit the close-knit communities of Lancashire. That when they did so it turned out to be the greatest betrayal of the men of Lancashire, with a loss of life unparalleled in the history of warfare up until that time, is one of the great tragedies of the twentieth century. And how ironical that the idea of using men who lived and worked side by side to enlist in the Pals' battalions of the First World War belonged to Lord Derby, the historical feudal overlord of Lancashire who in medieval times was charged with the protection of his subjects but who, on the battlefield of the Somme, unleashed our Lancashire lads in their hundreds upon the machine guns of the German army. For it was Lord Derby who suggested to Kitchener that men with close personal ties, who lived in the same streets and towns and worked in the same mills, would be keener to enlist and make for a better fighting force if they were allowed to fight alongside their neighbours. Manchester alone recruited 15 battalions and in Accrington over 1,100 men from Burnley and Chorley, Blackburn and other East Lancashire towns, volunteered in just ten days. It would be a mistake to think that they were all working-class men. The officers, too, were recruited from the community, coming from the ranks of mill owners and the landed gentry. On 1 July 1916, the first day of the Somme, Lancashire suffered over 6,000 casualties. Despite a week's bombardment of the enemy positions, the military authorities had fatally underestimated the strength of the German dugouts. When our men went over the top, at a slow walk (they were carrying about 66lbs of equipment each) through narrow gaps in the barbed wire, the German machine guns mowed them down, as one Accrington Pals signaller reported, 'like meadow grass'. In less than 20 minutes, 235 Pals were killed and 350 wounded. The town of Accrington went into mourning.

One incident in the war stands out because it illustrates to me the callous indifference of the military machine to human life and its treatment of soldiers as cannon fodder. I know that, pro rata, more junior officers died than ordinary soldiers in the conflict; nevertheless, the military strategists, the generals and politicians, insisted upon treating the conflict, as in the musical satire *Oh What a Lovely War*, like a game of cricket. If our lot killed only one man more than theirs, we were winning and the slaughter was justified. In Lyn Macdonald's *They Called it Passchendaele*, the author interviewed hundreds of survivors of the war, including Lieutenant P. King of the East Lancashire Regiment, who describes being lost in no man's land, trapped in a mud-filled shell hole for over 24 hours with a group of the 'Burnley Mashers'. The Mashers were named after their song, which takes on a particular, almost pathetic, resonance in the context not of a night out in Burnley but in the mud, blood and carnage of the trenches.

> We are the Burnley Mashers,
> When we go out at neet
> The lasses al admire us
> And think we look a treat.

Bullets and shells whistled over their heads and exploded around them all day and night and the cries of the dying and mutilated rang in their ears. Finally they were relieved and Lt King was able to lead what remained of

Cut down like meadow grass. The Accrington Pals.

his men back to battalion headquarters. The commanding officer, a Colonel Whitehead, from Burnley, was sitting in a hut with several other officers drinking whisky. When King and his men appeared, the colonel curled his lip and said, 'At last! The bloody cotton-wool soldiers!' and dismissed them without even offering them a drink. When I first read this, the behaviour of Colonel Whitehead so incensed me that I determined to look him up in the files of the *Burnley Express*. I learned that he'd lived on until his eighties, only to be killed in a car accident sometime during the 1960s.

You can begin to see how the shrapnel of the war must have entered the souls of so many survivors and observers, slowly sounding the last post on a class system that had survived for centuries and had set members of society so far apart. But it was a slow process. The war heroes, so many traumatised in a way that no one ever recognised, never mind spoke about, returned to the Victorian terraces of the mill towns and the old way of life. I never once heard my own grandfather refer to the war, even though after his death he left behind an inch-long piece of shell casing taken out of a wound to his head after he'd lain in a bomb crater for three days with his companions dead around him.

It was undoubtedly hardship which brought about the sense of togetherness which was the strength and glory of Lancashire during the Depression years in the 1920s and '30s. Here, we are at last moving into times of living memory. My own work of chronicling the lives of local people for the radio in the 1970s and '80s involved drawing upon the recollections of people who had lived through these difficult years between the wars. By and large, these people are, alas, all gone now, and it might be just nostalgia on my part, but to me they were vintage characters the likes of which I never expect to see again. Lugging around a heavy reel-to-reel tape recorder, I used to corner them in pubs and clubs, shopping centres and old folks' homes, men and women in their seventies and eighties who told me stories of a Lancashire which few today would ever recognise.

> 'It was hardship which brought about the togetherness which was the strength and glory of Lancashire during the Depression'

During the 1920s and '30s the old staple Lancashire industries of cotton weaving and coal mining slid from crisis to crisis, with unemployment running to over one in four of the working population. In textiles, competition from the Far East was the bugbear. From producing over 8,000 million square yards of cloth in 1912, Lancashire output had slumped to just over 3,000 million by the eve of the Second World War. Competition between cotton manufacturers was suicidal. Tales abound of hard-hatted and hard-headed bosses travelling by train to Manchester and cutting each other's throats on the Cotton Exchange by splitting farthings over the sale price of their cloth. To improve competitiveness, bosses wanted to increase the number of looms each weaver ran, from four to six, as well as cut their wages. Conflict inevitably ensued. In 1929, almost 400,000 textile workers were locked out, and in 1932 the whole of the Burnley district was brought to a standstill over wage reductions and the dispute spread to other parts of the county. In just over two decades the number of mills halved. Coal mining, the other big Lancashire industry, inevitably suffered from the silencing of so many hungry steam engines. And coal mining had another problem. During the previous centuries when demand was high, the coal seams which were more easily worked were used up. Mines got deeper and deeper, some reaching almost a mile below ground, with dreadful working conditions of heat and poor ventilation and a consequential slump in productivity. These are the times George Orwell records so famously in *The Road to Wigan Pier*. Lancashire people, so well used to living under the clouds of rain and factory smoke, could now add to this the shadow of unemployment.

I remember interviewing Mary, from Burnley, who as a child recalled taking poppies round the mill after the First World War. She was only taken on at the mill by being a scab or a 'knobstick' during one of the strikes when workers were being forced to take extra looms for no more pay. She recalled standing at the door of the shed and seeing six looms that weren't working.

The boss, Tertius Spencer, came up to her and she said to him, 'I wish I were on them looms.' And he replied, 'Well, can you weave?'

'Aye,' she said, 'I'm a good 'un.'

So he set her on and she was on the same looms for forty years. 'They were frightening days,' said Mary. 'They weren't worth having. They were all right if you could get through, but a lot of them couldn't. They were poor things. I remember one that drowned herself. She left her beret on a nail in t' factory and no one would touch it. It were there for a long while.' She told me, 'If God appeared to me and said, "You can live your life all over again it t' same way," I'd say to Him, no, I'm not bothered.'

Another old weaver I spoke to couldn't disguise the bitterness in her voice as she described the humiliation of queuing for work in the warehouse. 'We stood like a row of cattle, 20, 30 or 40 of us. The men didn't stand a chance. You'd only get work if you were a flighty bit that the tackler fancied and he could get a bit of a tickle.' She recalled standing for six months before she got work. On short time they were reduced to working just two looms all week and taking home less money then they would off the dole. 'You didn't say anything. You'd just to accept it. If you weren't the same religion as the boss you were out on your heels the first job you got; even if you didn't go to the same chapel as the manager, never mind the boss.' She remembered bosses that put up a list of every weaver's earnings to shame those who they thought weren't pulling their weight.

The incomparable Jack Webster, the archetype for me of everything that was resilient yet warm-hearted about the old Lancashire folk, lost two brothers in the First World War. He recalled the village mill at Walmer Bridge on the edge of the marshes in west Lancashire between Much Hoole and Longton. Squire Crewdson owned the mill and all the houses in the village, Jack told me. 'They rang the bell at a quarter to six every morning and the tempo quickened as the time approached six o'clock. The workers passed through the watchhouse where the manager stood with his watch. If you were late you were fined, the later the greater the fine. Everybody was under the thumb.' All Jack's sisters and brothers worked at the mill and if there was anything wrong with their weaving they used to have to take their cloth home to repair the flaws or 'floats'. He remembered that the cloth went to India and the weavers had to buy their own bobbins of gold thread to weave into the pieces.

> 'You'd only get work if the tackler fancied and he could get a bit of a tickle'

Jack, who was born in 1903, was too young to work in the mill when the family was at Walmer Bridge, but he remembers being able to recognise everyone by the sound of their clogs. No two pairs of clogs were the same. He bewailed the passing of the clog, warm in winter and cool in summer, and indispensable to a weaver standing at his or her looms on cold, damp flags all day. When Jack's family moved to Colne, it was like a big city. He missed the peat mosses alongside the river Douglas near to the mouth of the Ribble. His dad used to say, 'It's a wonderful country to live in. You can steal as much as you like and no one will miss it.' As boys, they helped themselves to peas and beans from the fields because 'it was a hungry country in those days'. His dad had a Neptune's trident, ten feet long, and he used to walk up the estuary and when the sand beneath his feet bubbled he'd plunge his trident in and come out with a 'snig' or eel. Mum cooked them while they wriggled. At harvest time when the wood pigeons came in droves onto the land, his dad would shoot them and bring them home. By the light of the oil lamps, his mother would slit their crops and out would come the peas and beans, and she'd drop them onto a hot shovel on the fire when they would parch and they'd eat them with salt. There was usually a rabbit or a hare and the occasional grouse or pheasant for the pot.

But things were different in Colne, Arcadia left behind for the mills of Satan. Jack remembered working part-time at 12 years old, sometimes going to school in the morning, sometimes in the afternoon. Afternoons in school were worst. After being up before six and working in the mill until 12.30,

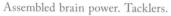

Assembled brain power. Tacklers.

the classroom was hot and his eyes soon grew heavy. The teachers never bothered trying to teach the part-timers. They were already lost to the mill. Jack recalled working 56 hours a week, just before his thirteenth birthday. Living in Earl Street in Colne, and working down the hill in Greenfield Road, his mother calculated that if he took seven minutes to run the mile back home and five more to return to work, he had 18 minutes of his breakfast half-hour to eat a decent porridge breakfast at home. I can see him glowing like the lad in the Readybrek advert, but more from his exertions than the oatmeal breakfast. Jack was never one to be downed by circumstances, and he epitomised for me the true backbone of Lancashire folk that has seen them through so many hardships. 'If you get where people are hard-pressed,' he once told me, 'If anyone gets a chance to enjoy themselves, they will do. And it's a hundred percent enjoyment. We could laugh at owt.' Jack's motto, 'If tha doesn't expect owt, tha'll not often be disappointed', should be written on Lancashire's coat of arms, if they ever get round to making one.

My favourite story of Jack's is the one about a mill worker pal of his who wasn't very good at his job. He was always being hauled up before the management for poor workmanship. One day he was ordered to report to the boss. When Jack saw him afterwards, he asked, 'Have you been sacked, Tommy?'

'Oh no,' said Tommy. 'I went up and t' boss said, "You're finished. We've had enough of you. I'm sacking you." But Tommy replied, "You can't sack me." The boss said, "I can. I'm doing it now." "No," insisted Tommy, "you can't. I gave ower when I were coming up t' steps to see you.' And he just laughed. Next time Jack met Tommy, he'd got another job. He said, 'How are you doing? Is it any better?' 'Naw,' said Tommy. 'They're all alike.'

Generally, the men had a better time in the mill than the women because often they were tacklers, or overlookers, who enjoyed some status in the mill hierarchy. Textiles employed four times as many women as men, and a bad tackler could make their lives a misery. The tackler could bring his weaver bad warps or make them wait while a loom was broken down. The women were united in the indignities and dangers of the mill. There was the constant noise and dust, and the risk of shuttles flying out at 60 mph and hitting them in the face and even blinding them. They used to have to clean their own looms, carry their own heavy pieces up to the warehouse, and any waste was inspected and they could be in trouble if it was deemed excessive. As a result, waste was often smuggled home or else put down the toilet, with disastrous consequences for the mill's sanitation. Often, the toilets were flushed with water from the mill dam which had come from the steam engines and was still hot. You could almost hear the bacteria chuckling in some mill toilets. But crouched in their alleys at break times or exchanging sympathies at close quarters over the noise of the looms and away from the eyes of management, an intimacy was born. It's the one thing that old weavers lamented about the passing of the mills, the loss of that close fellowship, or sisterhood, that is born of duress. Long hours in the alleys under the barrage of decibels and the threats of a hostile management, could almost compare to troops in the trenches. No wonder they let their hair down when they could. I heard stories of Christmas Eves when the more tight-fisted mill owners grudgingly let them switch off their looms at three o'clock to celebrate Christmas. But there would be no pay and no one could leave until 5.30. For weeks before they'd saved a penny a week for a party, and someone would be sent out for cream cakes, mince pies and a trifle; maybe even a bottle of sherry, though woe betide if the boss was a strict Methodist, for if he found out, there'd be instant dismissal as a Christmas present. Then they'd sing carols, perhaps dress up and have a mock wedding, anything to lift the dreary year-long servitude of the mill and allow a chink of happiness into their working lives.

Like Tim Bobbin's satirical jibes at the establishment of bosses and magistrates more than a hundred years earlier, in the mills of our grandparents they got their own back on the tyrannical tacklers by inventing that unique institution of the 'tacklers' tales', anecdotes designed to make the men seem stupid. My favourite is the one about the tackler who came home with a grandfather clock he'd bought only to find that it was too tall to fit into his small cottage living room. So he cut a hole in the ceiling and whenever they wanted to know the time someone had to go upstairs and look under the bed.

It must have seemed sweet revenge for the girls to huddle in their alleys at breakfast time and enjoy a laugh at their male masters. But the degree of male chauvinism encountered in our communities of only a generation or so ago was enough to make a modern feminist reach for her castration shears. I've sat with men in working men's clubs who have argued for male-only membership on the grounds that, 'There's only trouble in a club when women are let in'. The reason? 'There's certain women will 'tice [entice] a feller on and it causes trouble. Keep 'em out and there's no danger of any trouble.' If this sounds pathetic to a modern ear, it no doubt is. But maybe we should remember that the Church has taken a lead in the demonisation of women ever since the book of Genesis was written. I prefer to see the men-only club members hiding away from their partners behind their pints of beer and dominoes as men hiding from their own weaknesses, their own susceptibility to temptation. One of the male chauvinist brigade who himself had been a tackler, looked scornful when I met him in Colne library. He'd spotted a poster advertising keep-fit classes for women. 'Keep fit for women?' he sneered. 'They had them 70 years ago when I were a little lad, keep fit classes for women. They lasted all week. Washing on a Monday: them wringing machines, great big things wi' wooden rollers. Possers. You should have seen t' arms they had on 'em. And they were doing that when they'd been working all day in t' mill. Keep fit classes? Work kept 'em fit.'

But it was the fear of children which drove the greatest wedge between men and women. Ignorance of birth control and its lack of availability could have startling consequences. One lady I met in Colne recalled a family called Eccles who had 21 children. 'She were a little, thin, anaemic woman and he

A keep fit mangle made by Worswicks of Wigan.

PHOTOGRAPH: AUTHOR, TAKEN BY KIND PERMISSION OF WIGAN PIER

was a big, fat feller. They all stood at a big wooden table at meal times.' In a social centre in Colne back in the mid-'70s I was astonished by the frankness of some of the revelations. One woman told me:

'We were frightened of having children. If you missed your period ... kind of thing,' she apologised, '... you were up and down asking all t' old women how to get right again. You had to do. They said, "Get a packet of pennyroyal or get in a hot bath." They had all sorts of ways.'

'Did you not understand how to prevent having children?' I asked.

'No, we didn't in them days. You daren't sleep with your husband hardly, you were that frightened of having children.'

Her sister told me, 'I didn't know, when I had my baby, where it were coming from. And my mother-in-law said, "It'll come from where it went in". And I nearly died when I heard that. There were no sex lessons or anything. We were four girls at home and my mother never spoke about it. They thought it were rude to talk about sex in those days.'

I asked them, 'How understanding were your husbands?'

'Well, you were frightened of letting 'em have owt. You were terrified. You never enjoyed sex because you were frightened of having more children. Doctors were no help. You had to go round to these old women and they'd tell you what to do. You know like, when you'd had a bit of a do with your husband, they'd say, "Get out of bed and have a wee straight away". And there were these backstreet abortionists. You paid £5. I've been many a time. You had to in those days because there was no money. It was secret. You daren't tell anybody, because she got put in prison because someone told the doctor about her. He said, "If you don't tell me where you've been, I'll have you put in gaol just as you are now," and she had to tell where she'd been. And the woman got two years.'

Poor living conditions for the workers was the lot of men and women alike. As one man told me, 'We were used to unpleasantness in the mills because that's all you knew at home.' They had no carpets in their house, and he described to me how he used to have to 'bray' sandstone and scatter it over the floor – the 'Irish lino' we heard about in Bacup. When it got dirty they'd sweep it up and put fresh sand down. There were no plumbed-in baths, only a tin bath. Readers of *The Century Speaks* will recall David Palmer's hilarious tale of the 'walking bath', a tin tub that was shared by a number of neighbours and did the rounds on a Friday night, carried from house to house on somebody's head. People without baths could go to the slipper baths at the corporation swimming pool, something I remember doing when I bought my first house in Foulridge in 1969 and had to make do without bathing until a bathroom was installed. I went to Nelson and paid a shilling for the deepest, hottest bath you could ever wish for outside the Savoy Hotel. There was even an attendant to fill it for you and clean it out afterwards. And all for a bob!

'You never enjoyed sex because you were frightened of having children'

Spartan domestic conditions were common among the workers in the 1920s and '30s. A man who got married during the 1926 miners' strike wouldn't go into debt and he and his wife started out with just a bed, a table and a long form to sit on. He wouldn't buy coal until the miners returned to work. People not only shared attitudes, like in this common suspicion of hire purchase, but they showed solidarity with other workers in trouble. Hostility towards the bosses who lived in conspicuously grand circumstances (Amos Nelson was building Gledstone Hall at this time, you will remember) might have been expected. But I observed remarkably little resentment from the men I spoke to in Colne. I've long been intrigued by the town's flirtation with Conservatism. For many years the arch-Tory David Waddington was MP for Nelson and Colne, uncomfortably sandwiched between the tenancy of capital punishment abolitionist Sydney Silverman and today's rather radical Labour member Gordon Prentice. It was a question I posed and failed to answer earlier after writing about the massacre of Peterloo. Was there any legacy of radicalism born of the disparities in wealth that were so apparent in Lancashire textile communities? While working men were braying sand or queuing for the dole, the cotton manufacturers were ensconced in their genteel and carpeted enclaves up on the hills well away from the smoke of the factories. In Colne, the retreat for the wealthy was Red Lane, grand late Victorian and Edwardian houses generously spread out over Colne Edge and looking out over Craven to the wild heights of the Three Peaks. Other were leaving their mills in the valleys early to jump aboard the 4.30 afternoon train to Blackpool where they'd taken up residence in St Annes – or St 'Arnes', as one old Colner sarcastically pronounced it. It may be that many of the men I spoke to had been tacklers and, as I say, had enjoyed some status in the mill, but the lack of resentment among them was conspicuous. In fact, they expressed a respect for their taskmasters and the values they stood for. As one man who worked at Haslam's in Waterside, which closed down in 1932, told me, 'They were stern and unbending but fair. With a shed full of 1,000 people the bosses had to be tough.' He recalled one boss who was

Haslam's Mill, Colne, today.
PHOTOGRAPH: AUTHOR

putting his own son through the mill, locking him out for being late in the morning. Another man who worked 36 years in the mill was finished in 1950 without any redundancy. Instead of turning his resentment upon the system he reserved his contempt for those who did get redundancy money later on. 'They were drinking and gambling it all away and spending it all out on the town,' he told me. I got more than a clear impression from these men that, had the clog been on the other foot and they had been in the boss's shoes, they would have behaved in the same way themselves. 'A good boss was paying for t' stuff that I was weaving. He was keeping my childer with the wages he paid. It was his money, his building, and I should have bin t' same myself. If I employ you to do a job and you can't do it right and it takes you too long, well it's out of my pocket and not yours.'

So I wonder whether conservatism, with a small 'c', was a key to the character of many Lancastrians, especially those with their roots in the smaller mill towns. When, for the first time in 200 years cotton imports

Victorian pragmatism, Slater Terrace, Burnley, today.
PHOTOGRAPH: AUTHOR

outstripped exports and the massive mill closures of the late 1950s occurred, people turned to other things with little fuss, with an adaptability which was a credit to them. In fact, many of us seemed happy to stand by and see our links with the past severed. In the 1960s mill chimneys began to topple like trees in a Brazilian rain forest. Cosy, familiar town centres with their smoke-blackened Victorian shops and market halls were replaced by bare concrete shopping precincts backed by out-of-town developers who apparently cared nothing about our history. The people in charge wanted to be seen as making a new start, wiping the slate clean of the archaic image of cloth caps and shawls and encouraging investment and jobs in new technology. In 1997 I interviewed people about the Trafalgar Flats in Burnley which were built in 1968 and which epitomised this vision of a fresh start. Seventeen tower blocks and almost 400 new flats. Even the naming of the blocks was symbolic. They were named after the ships and admirals of the famous victory at Trafalgar and rang with the confidence and success of the old Empire: *Triumph*, *Vanguard*, *Victory*, *Monarch*, names from an era before the mills began to cast their dark shadow. It's as if the developers were saying, 'We'll cut out that dark loop from time, pretend it never was, and start again.' It was an extraordinary public rejection of the role played by those millions of cotton workers who'd made Lancashire great. But it did seem to be like a new beginning. The flats were surrounded by gardens with roses, trees and fountains. Inside, there was an embarrassment of luxuries for those brought from the Victorian back streets of Burnley: central heating, not one but two toilets, janitors and gardeners to polish the stair wells and lifts and groom the gardens. Even the building materials of concrete and fascia boards were a break with the traditional stone of the past. And new blood was injected into the town by bringing key workers in from Scotland, Ireland and Wales to work in the newly established electronics industries like Mullards.

But the dream soon curdled. The seventies saw to that. Vandalism, drugs, a policy, as the estate grew more and more run down, of the council to put all its rotten eggs in one basket and house all the problem families there. Add to this the inherent design flaws of dark stairwells and remote balconies, so difficult to police, and the experiment in high-rise living, repeated as it was throughout urban Lancashire and Britain at large, is now seen as one of the great social failures of the twentieth century. Within 25 years of opening, Trafalgar Gardens was boarded up and waiting for the bulldozers.

'The experiment of high-rise living was one of the great social failures of the twentieth century'

And what had gone before, what the flats had replaced, suddenly didn't seem so bad after all. Whatever its failings, the old Trafalgar of row upon row of congested, often insanitary terraces had one thing going for it which the high rise architects of 'the latest ideas in progressive designs for living' according to the *Burnley Express*'s fulsome billing of the flats in 1968, didn't have: a vibrant sense of community. Visit Slater Terrace on the side of the Leeds and Liverpool canal just off Trafalgar today, and you get some impression of the physical intimacy, the singleness of purpose, which drew all those people together who first worked in the mills.

The houses are built tight up against the wall of the mill, deep in the long shadow of its chimney, back to back with single-storey basement dwellings below an iron balcony and two-storey dwellings above and all inches from the canal. For the canal was the artery that fed the mill. The mill windows now are empty casements looking out from a shadowy, abandoned interior. But in the mill wall, beneath a gaping black doorway like a gormless mouth, are the cast-iron foundations of a hoist, a crane that once lifted the raw materials out of the canal boats before returning the finished cloth back along the canal to Liverpool where the canal ends near the Stanley Dock. And from thence, the world. It is a remarkable piece of industrial economy: men and machinery virtually living under one roof and the marketplace tied to your doorstep by the long ribbon of the canal. If you ignore the inhumanity of housing people so close to their dirty, noisy workplace and the stinking canal, it is a typical piece of Victorian pragmatism. I can hear Mr Gradgrind applauding.

Across the canal stands another of the few remaining Burnley mill chimneys. I think of the twin pylons of the war memorial at Vimy Ridge, for war and work – of the old kind that killed the spirit – are both a form of death, and I think of the chimneys as a monument to all those unsung heroes of the cotton industry who have passed so quietly into the night. In the late '80s they had a plan for conserving Slater Terrace and its surroundings and they sandblasted all the stonework, fitted new chimney pots, put on new doors and new window frames. But all for nothing. The bubble of optimism burst and now they are back to slum status, boarded up, with the pigeons picking amongst the weeds in the stone guttering, nettles, brambles and ferns creeping up the walls from the canalside to meet the black stains running down the stonework left by rainwater from the roof which can no longer find a drainpipe to run down. A notice on Sandygate reminds you of the hope that people had for the area then. Now it is buckled with age and scrawled with graffiti. It was all to have been part of the Weavers' Triangle Conservation Area. Slater Terrace was to have been a 'canalside hotel'; there was to have been a 'public events square'; and the Old Clock Tower Mill was to have provided a conference centre. (Ah, the ubiquitous conference centre. What on earth do they find to confer about in all these wretched conference centres these days? Or are they something the planners put down when they can't think of anything else to do with a building?) But today, the Clock Tower Mill has gone. It was pulled down recently. For the first time in a hundred and fifty years it has let in the light down by the canal at Sandygate bridge

> 'It was just one big community because everyone was in the same boat'

Whit Walks.

and you can look out across the Long Causeway high on to Boulsworth. I remember snooping around inside the mill just before they knocked it down. You had to duck through a gap in the fence at the canal side, and it was like entering some dark cathedral to a dead god. Inside, the air hung heavy with the smell of burnt wood and sour old plaster. You could stand inside the hollow centre of the mill on piles of rotten cloth and matted weft and gawp upwards through the tower, through broken laths to where the sky sailed high above. It scared me. I felt I was in the presence of vindictive old ghosts, bitter that such a great empire had been left to pass. I remember hurrying out back onto the canal side and seeing a kingfisher fly past in an electric blue flash.

They should have kept the Clock Tower Mill as a monument to the workforce of Burnley's cotton mills. As you drove through the centre of the town it was there on the skyline, a totem to a lost tribe, a poignant but potent symbol of what we were and what became of our textile industry. A proud chimney and the skeletal outline of the roof timbers like the carcass of some great beast. Why pay someone like Anthony Gormley when we had our own ready-made sculpture? Instead, it is now just a razed rubble bed for docks and dandelions to grow, with a hopeful sign inviting redevelopment.

The people of old Trafalgar remembered the mills in their sooty heyday. There was Clock Tower, Sandygate, Caledonia, Trafalgar, Mount Pleasant, Waterloo, Woodfield and Bellevue. The houses were packed into an area not much more than a quarter of a mile square. There was Hardy Street, Keppel Street, Lydia Street, Mile Street, Lomas Street, Moss Street, Lord Street and more.

Mary Lord who I spoke to in 1997 remembered living in Lisbon Street. 'Everyone knew everyone else. They were the salt of the earth. If you were ill, there were always people who would come in and look after you. People would bring you meals, give you help, and they didn't expect any payment or anything. It was just one big community. Because everyone was in the same boat. Nobody had any money.' She remembered bread and jam as a staple food, with stewing beef made into a big potato pie at the weekend which you often shared with other families.

Lyn Millard, who was a bobby on the beat in the old Trafalgar, remembers how the people were mainly honest working folk. He compared it to a village, with its own shops and a social centre in the Unitarian church. But he recalled how depressing it could be because of the pollution and congestion. He told me that many young men in the 1930s escaped by joining the army.

Tom Hamer was brought up on Trafalgar in the hungry thirties. 'People clung together. We were rough but didn't steal. We had our own code of conduct. People didn't break into gas meters. As a kid, if you had a penny you didn't buy sweets but went to Pea Bob's, Bob Thornton's, and got a penn'oth of peas. You were always hungry.'

As a policeman, Lyn Millard had to deal with a lot of suicides. 'Burnley was said to have the highest suicide rate in the United Kingdom for many years. A lot put their heads in the gas oven with a blanket over. Often they drowned themselves in the canal. They usually left a note saying their life wasn't worth living'. He recalled a suicide in Mitre Place where a man left a payment book for a credit drapers. 'He'd owed money on two blankets. There was nothing else in the house.'

Eileen Wilkinson was a staunch defender of the values of the old Trafalgar and resented Tom Hamer's talk of bugs in the walls and how, if you left a house empty, they all moved next door like mice. She told me how proud people were, even in death. She spoke of a suicide who tied a scarf around her head so that her jaw wouldn't drop and the people who found her wouldn't find her revolting. Mrs Wilkinson's memories of old Trafalgar were like precious heirlooms tucked away to protect them from damage by others or from the condemnation of history. She recalled how feast days like Whit Walks lit up the whole community, all the more brightly for being set against the shadow of poverty. 'They were an explosion of colour, all the banners and brass bands, the gaiety and sense of fun.' At times like this she saw a clear link with the pre-industrial age of rural innocence, with what she described as 'a past of Merry England and what Shakespeare called "this happy breed of men"'.

Mill town scenes of merrymaking were at their height when the mills closed down for the local wakes weeks. There are many stories of skylines obscured by smog for the rest of the year making a short but miraculous appearance as the boilers were shut down. That must have been a welcome delight. But the old habit of sticking together didn't stop with the silencing of the looms. Mass migration to the seaside meant that work mates and neighbours often met up together to enjoy a game of cricket on the sands at Blackpool or dance together in the Tower Ballroom. What had begun as a middle-class health fad of taking the seaside waters became an annual working-class ritual of fresh air and fun. Scenes of railway station platforms dangerously crowded with holidaymakers waiting for the seaside specials filled the local newspapers, which must have been particularly galling for those left behind.

I remember in my childhood that if you couldn't afford to go away the stock answer to the question, 'Where are you going for your holidays?' was always, 'Well, we're just going off for days.' This usually constituted a ramble in the country to places like the Watermeetings, half way to Pendle Hill, armed with a bottle of pop and some sandwiches. (OK, liquorice water and jam butties, if you want me to lay on the poverty thing.) Textiles enjoyed a short-lived boom after the Second World War before our Japanese competitors got back on their feet again, and the 1950s were the heyday for special excursions on the railways. All week at Colne the railway sidings were filled to bursting point with carriages and on the eve of the holidays train after train pulled out of the station packed to the luggage racks with passengers making for the coast. When I look at these pictures today and see the number of tightly belted gabardine raincoats, it gives the lie to the saying, 'The sun always seemed to shine in those days'. What I think the people who say this are expressing is the sense of unalloyed happiness which nothing could dampen at a time when pleasures were strictly rationed and were all the more intense and satisfying because of it. And when you look at the pictures of chapel, Sunday school and youth club excursions to the seaside, there's a wide-eyed smiling innocence which you could never hope to capture in a photograph today.

I journeyed to Blackpool to find out what the resort has to offer the more fun-jaded holidaymakers and day-trippers of today. I park in a car park underneath the great red bodkin of the Tower. A plaque on a toilet wall informs me that this is the site of the old Blackpool Central Railway Station, closed down after the last train left on 1 November 1964. Mill towners must have arrived here from all over Lancashire, so it was a good place to begin.

The sky is a clear blue and makes the Tower look all the more antiquated in its cladding of red oxide paint. It's Saturday and the season hasn't really begun – if there is such a thing as a season here any more – but all the same I'm met with a bevy of can-can dancers. In hot pursuit is a group of lads looking rather worse for wear from the night before and making the kind of noises we've come to associate with certain sections of an Old Trafford cricket crowd after the lager has been flowing freely all afternoon. It's still only 12.30 p.m.

'I'll take you to see the sharks,' says a passing mum to her child, making it sound more like a threat than a promise. Gypsy Petulengro is still going strong. Nowadays she has press cuttings posted up outside her door. After a soap star's alleged visit, a shock prediction from one of the tabloids shouts, 'You'll have a baby of your own!' The popularity of fortune tellers at Blackpool seems undiminished, and I wonder if it's a legacy from the old days when life in the mill seemed inescapable unless fate came to the rescue. Music from the Country Hall of Fame spreads syrup over the streets in front of the Palace Disco. Under the concrete staircase a family dines out off the floor which is stained with puke and pigeon droppings. Here's a sight that would have given Engels an apoplexy. For this is not the Manchester slums of the 1840s, but Blackpool today. A generation ago it was an illicit delight to come here and purchase a pork pie from the pie shop in Talbot Road and, abandoning all decorum, eat it there and then in the street. But eating in the street was an activity punishable by death at my secondary school. Your name was read out in assembly in a roll of shame. But in those days that was what Blackpool was all about: being able to break the rules, let your hair down for a bit. A kiss under the pier, getting a bit squiffy at Yates's Wine Lodge, all out of the way of the nosy neighbours who would report back to your mum, though, as I say, it wasn't always so easy to escape them even at the seaside. It was all fairly innocent then.

But today's excesses are hard-core. The youths are everywhere, young men in squads of up to twenty, hogging the pavement, intimidating to the older end. There's something threatening about the way they hold their arms out from their sides as if they were trying to point out that their biceps were too big or were drawing attention to the fists swinging from the ends. There's a truculent roll to the shoulders which is a tough guy parody. The clue to their presence I discovered is written on the backs of their T-shirts. Among the sprinkling of obscenities which passes for humour these days, one says 'Groom', another 'Best Man'. Blackpool has marketed itself as the Mecca of the stag and hen weekend. It looked to me like all they were after was getting drunk and getting laid. I witnessed it at work outside one of the clubs on the prom where the bouncers, with faces like crumpled leather boxing gloves, stand blinking in the sunlight. Round the corner sashay seven young men dressed identically in spotless white suits with black open-neck shirts. They're just about to step into the bar when a pony and trap arrives to a cacophony of hen calls. A gaggle of girls dressed in loincloths and leopard skin bras tumble out. Without the slightest formalities apart from the odd jungle greeting, they meet up and are off together into the crowd. It's a sort of mass dating or collective coupling. Blackpool offers the casual observer of humanity endless entertainment. I'm surprised they haven't got round to marketing it as The Human Zoo.

> 'I'm surprised they haven't got round to marketing Blackpool as The Human Zoo'

Blackpool. Lost innocence.
PHOTOGRAPH: AUTHOR

Through a street off the prom I spot the Winter Gardens. This was always a hotbed of human eccentricities, annual get-togethers of groups of people united by mutual passions. In the past I've mingled with pigeon-fancier miners with coal dust forever ingrained into their necks, bending to coo over their favourite show bird; hairdressers fluttering over the latest styles; bodybuilders anointing their pectorals with shining unguents before standing on the stage and making their stomachs ripple like washboards; and morticians letting their faces slip for just once a year. Even the politicians came here, if you really were looking for someone to have a laugh at. But today the Winter Gardens are all shut up and the exhibition hall has a no entry sign on the door. Only the shadowy annexes show any signs of life, with the mesmerising flicker of fruit machines luring youth inside to try its luck among the meretricious tat. This is the ominous shape of things to come if Blackpool gets its way and becomes the 'Las Vegas of the North'.

I wonder nostalgically about the Tower Ballroom and whether it is still luring in the dancers to swirl and samba their way through the afternoon under its stuccoed balconies and gilt ceiling. But I haven't the appetite to return past the bouncers outside the Tower Lounge, who when I first came past were goating about swearing like troopers, their heads shaven so closely they resembled nothing so much as animated silverskin onions. I pass a stall selling rock and, yes, they've got some shaped like male genitals.

I knew I wouldn't like modern Blackpool, and I'm sorry to say so for the sake of all the decent souls stuck trying to make a living there. It always was a big, brash money machine, especially after the hard-up weavers all left, the ones who took their own food for the landlady to cook in stalag-style boarding houses and paid for the use of the cruet. As I walk away from the Winter Gardens down Victoria Street, a huge herring gull swoops down at my feet and starts to shovel up the remnants of a flattened chip. Its eye is a hard bead of greed and the Arctic wastes of its own soul are locked inside there.

Blackpool is a perfect barometer of the morals and mores of the times. It is no longer part of the innocent Lancashire psyche of a couple of generations ago. Now it has taken on the persona of everything that is crude and loud-mouthed and shamelessly yobbish about the lowest examples of our youth culture. It is 18 to 30 holidays, Zoo TV and tabloid tits and bums all rolled into one. It is a mirror held up to the ever-expanding ranks of low life human nature. If I hate it it is because I am old and stuck in a Bamforth picture postcard world of innocent, saucy fun, and for me Blackpool has gone too far. You can keep your marauding mobs of drunken yobs and sexually predatory females dressed as cave women; I'm still looking for the lost innocence of a seat in the sun to bring some colour back to the pallor of the mill, or a paddle in the sea with clothes raised no further than the knees. But today the beach is virtually empty. The tide is coming in in great skipping rope loops of white wavelets, sweeping away the past where there wasn't enough room to swing a towel for all the holiday deckchairs and kids in one-piece bathing costumes with buckets and spades. The sea stretches away into a slate-blue line where sea meets sky and the earth curves away into the ocean's vastness. This must have been the big attraction of Blackpool to the mill workers. The sense of freedom, of unrestricted horizons, after the confines of valley, mills and terraces. And the sparkling clarity of the air and light must have seemed magical, and the pristine sweep of the shore, forever washed clean by the sea.

At last I reach the North Pier. Where the boards start, the old folk sit out of the cool breeze swapping memories. There's a George Formby exhibition on somewhere nearby, according to a poster. But no, that was last year and no one's bothered to take it down. 'But how time flies, Mabel! It only seems like yesterday that we used to stay at Mrs Dawsons and she'd never let us have a key and we'd have to be in by 10.30 prompt or else the door was locked.' Overhead the gulls laugh at the way we humans bother about mortality. Why not live for the day like the kids on the prom, they say. That's Blackpool's message.

The pier used to be a real magnet, drawing everyone to sit and talk or walk as far as you could along the boards out to sea without getting wet; far enough to look north to Blackpool's sister, Morecambe, where all the Tykes from Bradford used to go, the ones who wove that funny fluffy stuff that grows on sheep. Today it's clear enough to see the Lakes, the blue mountains melting into the blue sea. But you can't get the smell of chip fat out of your nostrils, probably not even if you could walk as far as the Isle of Man. It's still lunchtime and oceans of fish and chips are being fried and the breeze is blowing the smell out to sea. The smell overwhelms everything else and takes away my appetite.

'New opportunities for upward mobility that came with mill closures and improved education drove mill town communities apart'

You probably think from all this that I'm being sniffy about Blackpool, and you could be right. Something happened to us during the '50s. Up until then we were one homogenous group. Where I lived in Colne, our terrace contained office workers, someone fairly high up in the town hall, a teacher and even a small-time manufacturer, as well as the mill workers. And we all shopped at the Co-op. I can't remember any 'I'm better than him' talk. But as soon as I went to secondary school we had a headmaster who was shamelessly elitist. As well as punishing us for eating in the street or failing to raise our caps to teachers and ladies, he used to talk about 'the great unwashed'. We, he preached, were a new breed and we'd entered a new age, a 'meritocracy'. We were destined to rise above our fellow man by virtue of the opportunities his school provided. Now maybe Mr Safkin was a one-off, but he was respected in the community and parents wanted their children educated by him. They wanted something better for their children than they'd had. Something better than the mill. And they got it. Their children went away to college and university and became professionals. Out of the ranks of the aspiring working class arose the new middle. And today, the middle class wouldn't be seen dead in Blackpool.

But this new opportunity for upward mobility that came with the closure of the mills and the improvements in education drove the mill town communities apart. There was a brain drain of all the sons and daughters of mill workers bright enough to benefit from higher education. When they'd finished at university or teacher training college, they rarely returned. High-skill industries were slow to come to old mill towns. Instead, employers preferred to take advantage of the renowned dexterity of the mill workers by offering only low-skill jobs in assembly work. Flimsy new factories on industrial estates replaced the once distinctive outline of the mills with their saw-toothed weaving sheds and totemic chimneys. The familiar neighbourhood Co-ops closed down and the American-style supermarkets muscled in. Town centres became unrecognisable as cosy Victorian intimacy gave way to windy concrete precincts. Churches, chapels, youth clubs all closed their doors as we closed ours and sat in front of the flickering TV screen, learning how the rest of the world lived and growing restless for change. And the advertisers saw our discontent and moved in with their promises of happiness through consumption. Cars, holidays in Majorca and a new house on a posh estate away from all those cramped terraces. And the old sense of community and sticking together was lost in the mad scramble of getting on. And before we knew it, we had changed and Lancashire began to look like anywhere else in modern Britain.

CHAPTER TWENTY

THE LASTING LEGACY

I SET OUT on this journey in search of the real Lancashire, those features that have resisted the encroaching tide of modern uniformity and which make the place and its people distinctive. I've dwelt upon our history because it is our past which shapes us, and the bulk of that history has been the nineteenth and early twentieth century when the Industrial Revolution gave us our unique image. Today, many people have been happy to cast off that image of shawls and clogs and trouble down at t' mill. I don't deny that we need to move on, and only the most ardent sentimentalist would ignore the squalor and hardships of those times and turn the clock back for the sake of the fellowship and sense of community that we enjoyed. But there has been a denial of our industrial past by many who have shaped the modern Lancashire which borders on the pathological. If a person continually hid their past and where they came from, we would at the least view them with suspicion, at the worst, we would call for the psychiatrist.

A healthy community is proud of its past, providing it has nothing to be ashamed of, and happily co-exists with it. The very first Lancastrians knew this, and the Bleasdale circle whose outer stockade provided shelter for the Bronze Age farmers of Bowland had at its centre the urn burials of their ancestors. But the remains of our more recent ancestors have too often been bulldozed away. We have knocked down thousands of mills or else hidden them under some new commercial guise. Where is the genuine article, its machinery and whitewashed sheds, its unique mix of smells of cotton weft and oil, something to remind the next generation of the debt they owe their ancestors in making this county great and the country rich, a tribute to the hardships the people endured and the skills and patience they possessed? I can only think of the Queen Street Mill in Burnley, preserved in working order but which for many years held on to life by the slenderest of threads.

Or the Ellenroad mill in Rochdale with its magnificent steam engine. Or the quaint, shadowy mill at Helmshore, going back to the very dawn of textiles and now a museum.

I mention there a museum. The heritage business of the 1980s and '90s has spawned a plethora of museums. Take your touring map anywhere in Britain today and there they are vying for your attention. The Museum of the Fustian Smock, The National Collection of Historic Privies, The Museum of Ancient Sagger Makers. All well and good for a Bank Holiday afternoon where you can escape from the drizzle, but is it history? Does it inspire a warm sense of recognition that we ourselves belong to the same continuing historical process, the same rich weft of humanity? That we are not simply some isolated blip on the radar of time? In a word, is it real? Or is it some fossilised, sanitised view of the past, some dressed-up version of history dreamt up by the PR guys in the tourist trade to get people into the gift shops and the cafes?

It was with these misgivings that I went to Wigan Pier. Less than 20 years ago everyone was singing the praises of this heritage venture. The brochures still refer to it as 'the experience of a lifetime'. Unfortunately the experience must have palled on most people and it's looking rather down at heel. An

Heritage cobblers.
Wigan Pier.

PHOTOGRAPH:
AUTHOR, TAKEN BY
KIND PERMISSION
OF WIGAN PIER

indication of its waning popularity is that when I visited, it was is no longer open on a Friday or Saturday and it seems to rely heavily upon a captive audience of children on school trips. It was late May, just the time when people's thoughts start to turn to a day out after being holed up for so long by a Lancashire winter. But the Orwell pub looked as if prohibition had struck, dark and dingy enough to deter all but the most desperate thirsts. Nevertheless, we bought our tickets in the ticket office which doubles as a gift shop and browsed the paraphernalia of a pre-electronic age of childhood, when Barbie was but a tinselly glint in the marketing men's eyes. There were whips and tops, skipping ropes and boxes of glittering marbles. There were shelves of Uncle Joe's Mint Balls that 'keep you all aglow' and black jars of edible coal dust. I should have observed there and then that this was to be the beginning of the saccharining of history.

We were soon out and on to the canal side and making for the 'Way We Were' Heritage Centre. The date is 1900 and the first steps of your journey take you through a coal mine. Life-sized models of men with blackened hands lurk in dark stalls to the recorded sounds of coal being shovelled and picks struck. The first man sits there clutching his chest and gasping as if in the last stages of pulmonary collapse. Beyond him a man in a flat cap wearing a rather yonderly smile is leading, on a piece of sisal string, a donkey which is pulling coal wagons. Further in and two half-naked men are lying on the ground working at a mocked-up coal seam. Of course, there's no heat or dust, no sense of claustrophobia or darkness, only the rather muffled sound of the recording coming from the other stall. It is a curiously flat experience, as lifeless as the models themselves, however good they may be. An urchin crouches, opening and closing a ventilation door, but I find myself only glancing at him dispassionately before moving on. It is only when I've passed through the mine and am walking past the pit office that I'm suddenly aware that there's someone standing there at the window with their back to me. For a brief moment I think it's a real person, a visitor like myself, and I'm about to say something, a muttered excuse as I try to lean round her to peer through the window at the dead-eyed pay clerk. But then I realise that it's only another model, a pit lass complaining that she's been short-changed in her wage packet. But the incident makes me aware that in order to bring our history alive we need to get as close to it as possible in order to bridge that imaginative gap in time. The tableaux of working miners are just a spectacle; you look and move on, still in your cocoon of modern comfort. For the appalling conditions of Wigan miners in 1900 really to hit home, you need to live it. Now this sounds impossible, although I understand that the Big Pit Museum at Blaenafon in South Wales is grabbing all the headlines because it does just that, sending visitors down in the cage to the coal face in helmets with safety lamps and frisking them for their mobile phones or anything which could trigger an explosion of methane gas. And at Wigan Pier they succeed in achieving this kind of authenticity not in the mine but in the schoolroom.

In the schoolroom the visitor is subjected to the bullying and ritual humiliation which seems to have been the basis of Victorian education. There were only eight of us but we were ordered to line up outside the classroom, boys in one line, girls in another, and then, at the sound of a bell, the door was flung open and the schoolmaster, Mr McKendrick, flexing his cane threateningly, began haranguing and abusing us. First we were wedged behind the tiny schoolroom desks, an experience, I should imagine, not unlike being put in the stocks. Then we were ordered to look straight in front of us and by no means dare to look the teacher in the eye, this being deemed the height of disrespect. I began now to understand the expressions on the faces of the schoolgirls in the authentic enlarged photograph outside the schoolroom. Dressed in their smocks and aprons, their hair in ribbons, there was not a single pair of eyes in the whole classroom that didn't look worried, haunted or plain scared. It said so much about the regime of repression and fear which underpinned the social system of our great grandparents and kept the working classes in their place. And during the next 15 minutes we were to sample dramatically the kind of inhuman authoritarianism that kept Wigan miners belly-down at the pit face.

Mr McKendrick exuded such an air of menace that when we were ordered to our feet for prayers I found myself singing a hymn for the first time in almost 50 years. Not just singing but bellowing, in fear of my life. We had to have our heads inspected for lice and our hands scrutinised for any vainglorious adornments such as rings. The poor woman in front of me was hauled to her feet and denounced as a Jezebel for wearing her wedding ring. We were made to take out our slates from the desk and spell out the three Cs that made Lancashire great. Coal, cotton and the canal. We had to stand to attention and repeat the spelling of these words and scratch them on our slates. Of course, Mr McKendrick was an actor, but he wasn't going to let his mask slip for anyone. When I facetiously attempted to misspell cotton, his wrath descended and I was made to feel like a bumbling imbecile. After a prayer invoking the glories of the Empire, Mr McKendrick brought an end to the most uncomfortable 15 minutes and left the room. There was no coming back afterwards like I'd expected, saying, 'OK, folks, it was all just a bit of a lark. I'm really a nice guy who enjoys stroking kittens.' We had been given a lesson in Victorian schoolroom terror tactics and we were shell-shocked. Outside, we stood around feeling rather foolish and belittled. But the experience was real, and I shall remember it long after I've forgotten the model pit brow lasses pushing their coal tubs. We'd all been fairly middle-class people with a well-conditioned respect for authority, but I for one, fancying myself as a bit of a rebel, was shocked to find how easily Mr McKendrick had been able to find and press the right button to reduce me to fearful obedience. I'd love to have been with a party of today's youngsters to see how they would have reacted. How easy would it have been to cow and control them?

The well-maintained realism of the Wigan schoolroom is the perfect antidote to any inclination to sentimentalise the past. The carefully arranged

No bugs in these walls. Wigan Pier.

PHOTOGRAPH: AUTHOR, TAKEN BY KIND PERMISSION OF WIGAN PIER

interiors of a worker's family house were rather less successful in avoiding the cosy heritage business fantasy of history. No bugs in the walls or suicide notes on the gas oven, but a wholesome picture of working-class thrift, diligence and piety. Biblical sayings on the mantelpiece and baskets full of needlework, home-made peg rugs and crocheted antimacassars. The backyard and wash house is a model of orderliness, even though the huge cast-iron mangle with rollers like tree trunks confirms the cynical Colne tackler's view that there was no need for keep fit classes for women in those days. David Palmer's tin bath is nailed to the toilet wall, while inside a model householder is enjoying a few moments of quiet contemplation on the toilet without as much as a fly or single obnoxious odour, even though he was sitting on one of the notorious earth toilets. (As its name suggests, no drain, just earth below.) Only the presence of a stuffed rat on the toilet roof offers an unsettling hint that what we are witnessing may not be the whole, or anything like the truth. In the recreated pub, the landlady diligently polishes the glasses beneath an ode to her calling with the rousing chorus, 'Hurrah to the pump, hurrah! Her blessings are pure and free.' A view that the Temperance Movement of the times, inspired by the wholesale miseries and domestic tumult of drunkenness as an escape from the abject realities of life, might find hard to swallow.

Our entrance ticket entitles us to take the 'Amsterdam' waterbus the short journey along the canal to the Trencherfield spinning mill. The pilot grumbles that he's only taken six passengers all day and this is the last trip. A sense of its own history hangs over this part of the Wigan Pier experience. It's had its time. People are no longer interested. Despite our being promised a view of the giant steam engine, the mill is locked. The café opposite is boarded up. Opie's Museum of Memories is closed and forgotten. The mill looks abandoned: the red oxide fire escape zig-zagging past the gloomy blackened windows, some broken, some boarded up, others with ragged grey curtains hanging from them like dead skin. Oh dear! So much for our heritage. We

New hope for Wigan Pier?
PHOTOGRAPH: AUTHOR

return by foot, dejected, along the canal where the ragwort and dandelions grow from the lock gates and the brickwork is black and crumbling and breaking with ferns. Our sense of depression is complete when we have to pick our way over two young winos slumped under a canal bridge. Recording this I feel like some latter-day Orwell chronicling yet again the miseries of Wigan Pier.

But not everyone has given up hope for Wigan Pier. At the gift shop we pick up a glossy brochure which proclaims that it has 'a very exciting future'. The site, it appears, is to be redeveloped with a new, unspecified, 'heritage themed attraction', a purpose-built theatre, shops, pubs, a restaurant and an hotel. All in all, it gushes, 'a fantastic new attraction for the twenty-first century'. Forgive my cynicism, but are they saying if we make out heritage sites a bit more like the Trafford Centre or Salford Quays or the Albert Dock, with lots of shops and things, people will come back? In other words, that we won't accept our heritage unless it comes gift-wrapped with all the cellophane of modern commercialism? I'm not suggesting that a day out exploring our history should be a misery of sack cloth caps and ash toilets, but for the sake of our children learning about it for the first time, it should be as close as possible to the truth, with some of the uncomfortable emotional experiences that might involve, and not just another day out at the shops.

I returned to Manchester to see how the past doesn't need to be destroyed to make room for the present. Years ago I'd listened to tales of bosses dressed in their bowlers and pinstripes taking the train twice a week to the Royal Exchange and haggling over the price of cloth to keep their weavers in work. Standing outside the Exchange today in Cross Street you can't fail to be impressed by this bold, square monument to cotton. Except for the dripping scrolls of the capitals, it has a rather plain but solid presence which symbolises the confidence that the builders must have felt about the permanence of cotton as the foundation of Lancashire's prosperity. How could they have dreamed that such a thing would ever pass away in 1886, which is the year carved on the first datestone, or even in 1914, carved on the wing next to it? But it did, and I'm here to witness the extraordinarily successful use to which the building has been put today. It is, of course, the Royal Exchange Theatre. Climb the steps and you enter a forest of pink mock-marble columns. They lift the eye to the glass domes where the blue light falls like a cloudless sky. At its final extension, built between 1913 and 1921, the Cotton Exchange measured 1.7 acres and had 10 floors with 250 offices. It was the largest traders' assembly in the world and its members controlled almost half of the globe's 130 million cotton spindles. Three of its six domes were destroyed in the bombing during the Second World War and after the small resurgence in textiles of the early 1950s, it finally closed down to cotton on 31 December 1968. High on the west wall is a noticeboard showing cotton prices in Liverpool, New York and Alexandria. But beneath this reminder of the building's commercial past are two enlarged photographs representing its modern function: Tom Courtney and Helen Mirren, two of the actors who have helped to make the theatre famous. For in the centre of the trading floor, supported by the pillars that hold the domes, is a network of yellow steel tubes and glass which holds the auditorium of the theatre in the round. When I last came here I sat inside this giant lunar module watching a performance of *The Playboy of the Western World* and was transported to a primitive alehouse in the wilds of western Ireland filled with the smell of peat smoke, a universe away from the hard-nosed world of the haggling Lancashire businessmen who once filled the building. What an imaginative renaissance for this important building which, despite the worst efforts of the IRA bombers in June 1996, survives to bring culture out of the ruins of industry.

After the Royal Exchange I went to have another look at the Free Trade Hall. Last time I'd been shocked at the way that the concrete and glass of the new Radisson Edwardian Hotel had been allowed to assert itself brutally over the old Victorian façade. Conscious that this was once the home of the Hallé orchestra, I complained about the way commercial values have been allowed to dominate our culture. This time I ventured inside the hotel and bumped into the building's engineer who was happy to show me how they'd done their best to integrate some of the old features of the hall into the new hotel. He gave me a very impressive and well-presented brochure they'd produced on the history of the Free Trade Hall. As well as naming the hotel suites after Victorian free traders and some of the principal protagonists of the nearby Peterloo Massacre – Cobden, Bright, Hunt and Bamford – some of the artefacts from the old hall have been skilfully absorbed into the new hotel. Eight stone statues originally from the back of the hall and depicting the cultural activities of the hall have been set into the wall of what the hotel calls its Atrium Lightwell. The modern corridors are so narrow it's difficult to get a proper look at the sculptures, but I was told that they were visible from the hotel suites above. A large painting of the Peterloo Massacre by Arthur Sherwood Edwards up on a narrow first-level corridor can be seen, with a degree of neck-craning, from the entrance lobby off Southmill Street. It is a bloodless looking affair executed in thin, pastelly colours with no reds at all. It's rather like looking at the event through water or perhaps the forgetful haze of history. Soldiers on horseback are approaching the crowd but without menace. The odd fist is raised but the expression that predominates in the crowd is that of bewilderment. All in all it is a curiously passionless piece and hardly worth seeking out. It gives no offence and is a travesty of the actual historical event. But then the visitor curious enough to seek it out wouldn't want to stay in an hotel whose walls were dripping in blood. History sanitised again to suit the modern consumer.

Some of the names associated with the cultural history of the last 50 years have been preserved in the Radisson Edwardian Hotel in sections of the plaster of the old Free Trade Hall autographed by visiting musicians and actors. There's Arthur Rubinstein, Yehudi Menuhin, Thomas Beecham, Louis Armstrong, Anna Neagle and Sybil Thorndyke. But today's cultural concerns are distinctly more populist. Manchester is a footballing city. In fact, at the time of writing this, Lancashire (old Lancashire) boasts no fewer than seven teams in the Premiership. According to one 'factoid' in the Urbis Centre (one feels obliged to experiment with such neologisms in this world of the ultra modern) Manchester has more football teams per head of population than any other city in the world. This fanaticism for football is evident today in Exchange Square where they're promoting the UEFA Women's Football Championship taking place in the region. I don't know what the pit brow lasses of Wigan or the cotton weavers of north-east Lancashire would have made of all the fuss. But I bet they'd have given the modern girls a good run for their money, and to judge from the size of the coal-tub pushers at Wigan Pier ('robust and well-developed in physique') there'd be a few yellow cards handed out.

With Manchester's typical modern gusto for commercial self-promotion, people are being encouraged to play table football, kick a ball faster and harder than Beckham, have a go in front of the TV cameras at being a football commentator, or being urged to buy a four-wheel drive à la Footballers' Wives. And all to the frenetic pulse of disco music and the demented wavings of two 30-foot tall, inflated female football dolls. Presiding over the whole scene, a giant TV screen set incongruously upon a Victorian façade repeats goal action *ad infinitum*. You'd have to be a sour-faced Mr McKendrick not to be excited by it all and it certainly brings in the crowds. Later on we passed steel bands, jugglers, a model in a fashion shoot leading a horde of children down the street like a latter-day Pied Piper, while happy shoppers moved in phalanxes down the pavements and pedestrianised precincts. The vitality of the city street life is astonishing to a country bumpkin like me, and one can't fail to feel exhilarated. Manchester really does buzz.

The apotheosis of Manchester's modernity is the Urbis. To call it a museum would be a misnomer. It is a futuristic celebration of the whole concept of the city, an essay in glass and steel on the life of not just Manchester but cities throughout the world. Standing at the foot of Corporation Street its glass prow rises, all its thrust and power focused towards the heart of the city. From Victoria Station it resembles nothing so much as a glass ski slope, rising, concentrating its soaring potential energy into that huge, narrow prow, a strange spike like an aerofoil on top, angled to lead the forward thrust, nothing to impede its smooth, glassy progress into a future of greater and greater prosperity. For it can be no accident that Urbis points towards the shopping heart of Manchester, to the rebuilt Arndale, the new Marks and Spencers, Selfridges, Harvey Nichols *et al.* Urbis is a perfect symbol for the revived commercial ambition of the old Cottonopolis with its new mantra: salvation through shopping. What a contrast between the smooth flow of Urbis and the old cathedral which it dwarfs at the other side of the square; the church with its ragged castellations and knobbly crocketed pinnacles, the modern building all ocean green glass, the old, soot-stained sandstone; the brash new gods of materialism soaring above the old and driving them into their shadows.

Urbis, Manchester. A vast, glass ship.
PHOTOGRAPH: AUTHOR

Entering Urbis you take a long, open lift that follows the angle of the ski slope to the top. As you rise above the skies of Manchester you start to experience the frustration of not being able to see out of the windows properly. Bands of opaque glass act like Venetian blinds inhibiting your view of the cityscape. At the top of the lift you enter an anteroom to condition you to what lies in store. For five minutes – though to me it seemed like much longer – you are assailed by video images of different cities of the world. They are on every wall and even the ceiling, and therefore irritatingly impossible to absorb unless you can swivel your head like an owl, but even if you could, they don't last long enough to take in. Images of crowds and cars, shops and skyscrapers, all aimed at you in a barrage of flashing lights and restless techno music. It is a pretentious but pointless video, arty but without substance. Like so much of life in the consumer age it is flashy but shallow, short-circuiting thought for the sake of empty sensation. It turns out to be an admirable preparation for what is to come.

You step out of the video room and return from the world of showy images to the old-fashioned written word, walls full of facts and figures about the world's cities. I learn that 50 per cent of all humans are now city dwellers and that in 25 years' time this will rise to 75 per cent. We are told that in 1950 only New York and London had populations exceeding 8 million. Now this number has risen to 22. And so, the question is posed, What brings people to cities today? In the case of Manchester it would appear to be learning. The city awards 20,000 university degrees every year. There are sound interviews with people who have come to the city, and push-button interactive videos which provide a potted history of Manchester's different communities. There are giant pictures of homeless people living in cardboard boxes in the city, a control room showing how our activities are constantly monitored by surveillance cameras. Apparently we are the most watched-over country in the world and on average in a city such as Manchester you can expect to be filmed 300 times in a day. But why? Why do we allow this? In the welter of facts which assail you in Urbis you get very few answers. As you wander up and down the bolted steel staircases, trapped inside the ground-glass windows like a fly in a bottle, you feel a mounting sense of frustration at all the unanswered questions. So what do we do about the homeless? The snoopers? The yobs and troublemakers who spoil our cities for the rest of us? Only the irrepressible cheekiness of the people who come here lifts the mood of pointless resignation. There are notice boards where visitors are invited to post their own comments on questions such as, What would you like Manchester's next big event to be? One wag wants a nudist day, another a better climate (the two must be connected), a third wants a 'putting ferrets down the trousers competition'. With more than a nod to the city's not inconsiderable gay community, someone has written, 'Something big and camp'. To the question, 'Is local neighbourhood identity a thing of the past?' One response is a gloomy, 'It never existed.' Another has scrawled zanily, 'I think old people are ace. My grandad used to be one.'

You come away from Urbis as from a vast glass ship, dazzled by its architectural daring but questioning its whole purpose. Facts and glossy colour supplement images rattle around inside your head only to drop out onto the pavement as soon as you step outside. 'Well, what was all that about?' we ask; all that undoubted technical brilliance that has gone into the building but for an idea so vague, so diffuse, as to have little or no impact. After all, cities are as varied as the human beings and their nations and creeds who inhabit them. It's like suggesting a museum of human nature. I think Urbis has arisen out of an urge to do something because we can do it but with no clear idea of what we are going to do with it afterwards. In that respect it's like the Millennium Dome or the Iraq War. In fact, it is the Dome with which it best bears comparison. Urbis was funded by the Millennium Lottery Project, and I forecast that before the end of the decade the museum will be shut down because of lack of interest and will make way for more office blocks or luxury apartments, which was probably the purpose of Urbis in the first place.

Urbis symbolises Manchester's determination to turn its back on the past and look towards the future. In that respect it is no different from the ill-fated Trafalgar Gardens tower blocks in Burnley in the late 1960s. You could argue that Urbis could have become a flagship for Lancashire, embodying everything that was great about its past achievements and setting an agenda for the future through regional diversity in an age of depressing modern conformity. But no doubt panicked by the unsavoury images of the past (in 1934, J. B. Priestley described Manchester as 'an Amazonian jungle of blackened bricks') and terrified of any accusation of parochialism in an era where the trendy and the cosmopolitan are the driving forces of international marketing and investment, the city chose the cosmopolitan path. So what could be more absurd or offensive to the innate Lancashire notions of good sense and level-headed value for money, than some of Manchester's latest fashionable imports. For example, a store that charges over £1,000 for a designer-label handbag, and encourages people to go strutting down the street splashed with eau de toilette at £56 a bottle sporting a pair of £120 sunglasses? I like to think that there's still a proud legacy in us all that would scorn such pretentious nonsense and turn round and say, 'Well, she may be rich enough for that sort of thing, but when did you last see her donkeystone her step?'

Blackburn Market Hall has resisted change like a stubborn old lady resists being shepherded across the road. All right, they've now got something they call Customer Reception at the entrance where you can pick up a mobile trolley to do your shopping on if you're not so good on your feet. And there's a man behind the counter in front of a CCTV screen, though in all the time I was there I never saw it shift beyond camera 1. There's a photographic display of the market of old showing outdoor stalls with ragged canopies looking like the bivouacked Boer army. Another picture shows men in trilbies and old Ford Cortinas. Apparently the market used to close down for four days to allow an Easter fair to set up camp, with a helter-skelter and a big wheel with roundabouts and things. You get a real sense here that the past is not so much another country as an old neighbour living next door. Some stalls don't look to have changed over the 30 years I've been coming here. Walsh's sarsaparilla stall has more modern herbal quackery than ever in this age of alternative medicines (the Lancashire Witches would have had a field day today and would be driving around in 4×4s and living at 'St Arnes'), but they still sell their good old-fashioned blood drinks. ('Noted throughout the world. Good for old and young.') At 38p a glass there were plenty of takers. 'I've bin suppin' it for 50 years and I ail nowt!' one old chap told me before dipping his snout in his half-pint barrel glass. Walsh's is proof that the past can happily co-exist with the present. Witness the head lice repellent next to the flight socks.

Next door at Mercer's cheese stall you can buy Grandma Singleton's strong Lancashire as well as parmigiano reggiano. Above the Jarlserg and the Italian garlic mushrooms, big yellow moons of creamy Lancashire smile benignly down on this happy scene of European integration. There are pies galore, ham shanks, beef stew and slices of heart and tongue on the cooked meat stalls. No one mentions the word offal. It's cheap but tasty and a link with an age when

The elixir. Sarsapirilla on Blackburn market.

PHOTOGRAPH: AUTHOR

we were all hard-up and thrift dictated that 'you ate everything from a pig bar its grunt', and they'd have eaten that if you could stick a knife in it. There's a host of fent stalls, a traditional feature of the Lancashire market where the resourceful housewife could take advantage of the waste from the mills and make her own clothes or table cloths or patchwork quilts. I know because my old mum was at it until her fingers became too twisted with arthritis. How could a generation like that pay out a week's wages for a designer frock? And wouldn't you think that in their offspring today there'd still be an independent gene that would screech, 'Stop!' and put a padlock on their purses? Today's heirs to the thrifty Lancashire mum are the Asian girls. They crowd round a fent stall in their black niqabs, chatting like excited starlings. 'Everything only 50p!' is the attraction. Good-looking material, too. Enough to make the ghosts of the Cotton Exchange gnash their teeth in despair.

There aren't as many butchers these days on Blackburn Market – the supermarkets have seen to that – but the ones there are here always generate some keen competition between one another. Again there are the traditional favourites. Individual Lancashire hotpots in foil containers, butter pies (and hang the cholesterol!), steak and kidney. Grey-haired men who have measured out their lives in ham slices, meticulously cutting potted meats and selling them in 115 gram portions which, you soon realise, is a precise metric equivalent of the good old-fashioned quarter. There are concessions to modernity on the market. I watched one elderly lady sitting happily having her nails done at the Heavenly Nails stall, which specialises in 'quality extensions' and 'nail art'. And someone has set up a stall for computer repairs, where young men stand around earnestly discussing gigabytes and broadband. But by and large Blackburn Market is good old-fashioned no-nonsense stuff. No trendy bunkum about lifestyles and 'must have' designer labels. It's at its most heart-warming when you listen to the back chat that goes on between the customers and the stall holders, warm and lively human contact that makes the elderly look forward to market day and hurry down from their lonely flats to brush shoulders with old friends and workmates and have a good Lancashire natter. And, realising this, the organisers always leave the open café at the hub of the market where people can flop down at a table and rest their weary legs and, over a good cup of tea and maybe an Eccles cake, catch up on the news and latest scandal, or else reminisce until the voice thickens and you need to wipe away a tear or two. How I envy them. And what a contrast with a modern store I passed on the way, with aisles of sterile refrigerators under harsh strip lights, soulless and empty. Shopping reduced to the bare white bones of an economic transaction at an automated till.

On the fish market it's sad to see how the rows of different fishmongers I remember have shrunk to just two stalls. You can buy the trendy varieties of TV fish such as monkfish and sea bass if you're well off enough to pay £16 a kilo. And today, halibut is for the super-rich at £20. But haddock and cod are still the old favourites ('Thick end or tail end?'). Salmon, which used to be a tinned treat for Sunday tea, is back on the menu because it's farmed and so cheap these days. The fishmongers work, half a dozen of them to a stall, backs to the customers as they chop off the fish heads which seem to gawp in surprise as they're slung into a bucket. The conversation flows and twists like a shoal of herrings. I lament the hike in fish prices these days and am told: 'It's scarcity. Those big foreign factory ships just hoover up the fish these days.' I mention Fleetwood and am told that quotas mean that they can only fish from the old Lancashire port for 14 days every month, and if it's stormy that's even fewer. 'They have to drive the fish down from Scotland to sell at Fleetwood! That's madness isn't it?'

The madness of modern food distribution, where supermarkets are shipping food up and down the country hundreds of miles from where it's produced and could be sold immediately, is beginning to dawn on our retailers. On Blackburn Market I picked up a leaflet describing a welcome initiative. It's a local produce guide called *A Taste of Lancashire* and it lists the different stalls where you can buy home-grown produce. Only a few days earlier I'd observed the same careful sourcing of local foodstuffs at The Three Fishes pub at Mitton near Whalley. It's the brainchild of Nigel Haworth of Northcote Manor. The menu lists all the names of the local producers, which amounts to over thirty, with a map on the back showing where they farm. There's Worthington Farm at Tarleton where Peter Ascroft grows, amongst many other things, his purple carrots. There's Barry and Gillian Pugh of Pugh's Piglets and Suckling Pigs at Garstang, or Jim Curwen of Marshaw Farm at Abbeystead, a local rearer of lamb and beef whose meat goes into the

> 'The madness of moving modern food hundreds or even thousands of miles from producer to seller is beginning to dawn on the supermarkets'

Bowland Forest cottage pie on the pub menu. Or Reg Johnson's corn-fed chicken breast bred in Goosnargh along with his ducks and geese. And, of course, there are the farmhouse cheeses: Chris Sandham's, who from the map looks to be somewhat just off the M6 north of Preston, and Mrs Kirkham's who is at Goosnargh and whose Lancashire cheese goes on top of the fish pie. And there are many more. They read like a roll of honour, of Lancashire celebrating its own 'local heroes', valiantly fighting a rearguard action against the absurdities of the giant supermarkets racking up the air miles by flying in tired-looking petit pois from Kenya or tasteless out-of-season strawberries from Spain. And, as befits heroes, on the walls of the pub are hung their pictures. There's Andrew Holt of Ireland's at Waterfoot proudly holding up a plate of his black puddings, shiny and black as polished ebony. And Andrew Lanigan of Lytham positively gloating over the sparkling freshness of his fish. How ironical that it's taken so long to rediscover what we took for granted when I was a child: that your milk came from the farm down the lane every day, along with the eggs or the chickens, or that the small market garden nearby grew your fresh vegetables.

And to one like me who, to the despair of his moral guardians, discovered the delights of the hop at a very early age, it would be out of character not to mention some of the local breweries, including Thwaites of Blackburn or Lees', Holt's and Robinson's of Manchester, all busy brewing their real ales to the distinctive recipes which they know through long practice appeal to the local palate, and valiantly resisting the mighty global brewing conglomerates with their tasteless, fizzy, chilled-to-extinction chemical concoctions.

As we learned from the old Co-op, shopping locally reinforces a sense of community. A vast supermarket stuck out on a windy trading estate accessible only to those with a motorcar does as much for your chances of meeting and chatting to people as eating too much garlic. Built and stocked to a national or even international formula, they take no account of local habits and tastes. There's an honourable exception in Booth's, who try to source as much as possible of their food locally, to the benefit of both producer and consumer. But shopping in most modern supermarkets is a dreary and soulless experience. Ploughing your lonely furrow with your trolley along the aisles amidst shelves stuffed with produce decreed by marketing teams who can't tell their Bury puddings from their Chorley cakes, is a disheartening experience. But fortunately, Lancashire folk of a certain age won't be discouraged from having a good natter, however hostile the circumstances. So I relish the anarchy of the pair who block the aisle with their trolleys, to the fury of the scowling go-getters, while they discuss our Cynthia's gallstones or the latest stupid directive from the council to park your wheelie bin fourteen inches from the kerb otherwise your rubbish won't be collected. Scorn not the little old Lancashire lady in the plastic rain hood, you pushy youngsters and pompous planners; she has fought and won more battles than Napoleon. She

Asian gents, Nelson centre.
PHOTOGRAPH: AUTHOR

may look frail and brittle, but she is made of a metal forged in the furnace of struggle and hardship that was Lancashire's past. And you'll never see her likes again.

Some of our shopping centres, despite their hospital sterility, still recognise the need for folk to stop and natter. At the Arndale Centre in Nelson, which has recently been commendably renamed Pendle Rise, with reference to something at least of local significance, people congregate as they always have done, thank the Lord. Beneath down-lighters which skewer you with all the intensity of laser beams and hanging baskets brimming with plastic poinsettia, the old Nelsonians sit reminiscing and putting to right a world spinning rapidly out of their, and our, control. My ears start to twitch and I hear them discussing an armed raid at the Asda store (another frustrated customer?), and how the story had missed the local evening paper because nowadays it comes out at 1.30 p.m. 'What about the Sporting Pink that used to have the football results almost before the last kick of the ball at Turf Moor on a Saturday?' recalls one. 'Another backward step,' is the universal verdict to a chorus of clattering teacups. For today they sit and chat at tables outside a café, perhaps one of the advantages of having twinned the town with a place in France called Creil during the 1970s. This is Nelson's version of café society, and it's as warm, lively and welcoming as anywhere on earth, though expect to be asked your name, where you come from and whether you know so-and-so, all within the first five minutes. And there's a democracy afoot in some of these old mill towns which knows no barriers of creed or race. For next to them are three elderly Pakistani gents, still wearing their topis, having come straight from the mosque. I don't know what they are saying, but I'll bet it doesn't alter much in translation from what is being said next door amongst the teacups. The same human concerns. The same nostalgia for the past. The same puzzlement at the ingratitude of a world that chooses to ignore them now that they've got old. I said it about the girls buying fents on the market in Blackburn: I believe the Asians, with their close family ties and sense of community and their canny ways, are the natural heirs to the old mill towners. And that's why the older end in Nelson often treat them with so much tolerance. What a pity that the ugly stain of racism is being allowed to attach itself to some of our Lancashire towns and taint our traditional reputation for warmth and friendliness.

> 'I believe the Asians are the natural heirs to the old mill towners'

Outside, what used to be known as the Place de Creil brought a welcome touch of exoticism to the old mill town. As in so many redeveloped Lancashire town centres there was even a fountain, until the planners realised that they don't tend to work as well filled with cans and discarded takeaway trays, so they switched them off. What do we want with any more water tippling down from the skies anyway? Now the square has been nibbled away by development to make way for another cheap discount store. What is left is just an area of bare flags where the pigeons chuckle gutterally and importune those local people hardy enough to brave the cold iron seats. Workmen never seem to leave the centre of Nelson, fussing with the brick cobbles that are arranged in patterns of different colours, but all drab beiges and greys and blotting paper pinks, as if to match the anoraks and Danimacs of the predominantly elderly population who potter past, no doubt wondering, like me, what was wrong with the old stone setts and flags of the past. The planners can't make their minds up about Nelson. They're endlessly trying to revamp it and make it more attractive. First they stopped the main road coming through, which was good. But now they've brought the cars back, allowing people to park in front of the shops and behind all the wrought-iron railings they've inexplicably erected. This is plain silly when there's a half-empty car park over the bus station. They've left an empty space in the heart of the town for the wind to swirl and the rain to lash when they know from the social success of the old Arndale that to shop in Lancashire people need a roof over their heads. The old clock tower, like a deep-sea diver's helmet, looks sceptically down, no doubt wondering what will happen next. It remembers when Nelson thrived; its weavers got the best wages around and could spend their money in the town at places like the super-chic Hollywood Hat Shop where, I was told, before the war all the latest hats appeared as soon as they'd been on the screens of Nelson's seven cinemas, an extraordinary number for a town of 40,000 people. And what a magnet those cinemas still were in my youth. More romances began on the back seats of the circle at the Grand Cinema than any modern computer dating agency could ever dream of. And at the Imperial Ballroom, every pop group worth its number 1 spot appeared before crowds from all over Lancashire packed together under its hangar-like roof. Now, all today's poor, once-proud Nelsonians have, apart from their messed-about shopping centre, is their monstrous concrete bus station, which is a cross between a Ukrainian grain silo and the cargo hold of a supertanker. Ten minutes inside this dismal, fume-clogged hell-hole waiting for a bus is enough to remove the will to live from the fiercest optimist. I watch the school kids tumbling off the buses and abusing one another like apprentice fishwives. Whatever happened to Joe Safkin's dream of elitism? Of Nelson training the new technocrats of the future?

But Nelson's deplorable bus station has a hidden secret. Climb the dingy stone staircase to the car park above. Go up one, two, three, four levels and open the stubbornly resistant door. You are on the roof and can step out into the open skies. No one parks there because not enough people come to shop in Nelson these days, so you can have the place to yourself. A stunning panorama of the whole district. High above the grey rooftops and the monotonous roar of the traffic, you can suddenly reach out and touch the countryside, run your fingers round the hills. It's a wonderful symbol of the new Lancashire. We've taken the lid off our towns, opened up our narrow streets and oppressive mills to the sky and let in the light and the fresh air. And we have let our captive spirits free. Everywhere you look these days the hills are visible. The

Reach out and touch the hills around Nelson.
PHOTOGRAPH: AUTHOR

countryside around us beckons. And it whispers, 'Come away. Come away. You don't need to be trapped any more.' In the old days it was something people always used to say when they were extolling the virtues of our region: 'It's so easy to get out, to get away into the countryside.' Well, it's never been so true as it is today. In London you are trapped, set in concrete, and to lift the spirits there isn't a hill to be seen. You'd walk for two days and still not be rid of all those buildings, the clamour of the traffic, the burden of all that humanity around you. But here in Lancashire we are free, free to follow the call of the house martins as they skim over your head above the rooftops here in Nelson. 'Come away. Come away,' they cry. 'Escape and be free.' And there to the north lies Pendle Hill, a great, grey whale basking in a sea of green fields and woods, welcoming benignly. Tomorrow I shall accept the invitation.

I climb up the stone steps towards the big end of the hill. Higher and higher. Past the house martins that fall and twist about the sky like blown leaves. High into the early summer air which is full of the baby bleating of

Sunset from the top of Pendle Hill.
PHOTOGRAPH: AUTHOR

the new season's lambs, the deeper sounds of the anxious ewes. Higher still to where the swallows thread the air, their flight more direct and purposeful than the martins'. A party of elderly ramblers is already coming down, chattering away. The talk is of old knees, the bane of the elderly walker. 'They can do microsurgery these days to remove the bits,' I hear. We stop and chat. You can't get on up Pendle Hill on a day like this for stopping and chatting. There is a camaraderie. It is the antithesis of the town, with motorists snarling at one another, mouthing insults, knuckles white against the steering wheel. For here, time slows down and no one is in a hurry. There is time for the decent, civilised business of fellowship. We have left all our suspicions behind, all our resentment of our fellow men, because here there's room for everyone, room galore. We are no longer rats trapped in a crowded box, exhibiting all the signs of stress. And we're united in the hardship of the hill, too, the struggle of the climb. Perhaps it's like the war and people need hardship to unite, the fight against a common enemy, just like in the old days of poverty and the mills. Today, for us, the enemy is just age and weak knees. But everyone is so relaxed. It is because we belong here and can be ourselves. This is where we came from so many generations ago, before the forced imprisonment in town and factories, before the subversion of our true natures by the Industrial Revolution.

I stop and look back at the valley towns. From here on the high hill everything is in its proper perspective. The workaday valley with the grey roof slates shading towards purple, the sun on the Bradstone brickwork of the new estates, no longer seems to dominate. Instead, it's the landscape, the hills and moors dappled by the moving imprint of the clouds, that has taken over again. You get a sense of the primal contours of the landscape re-emerging. And something deep and long-obscured within our natures is responding with a feeling of excitement and joy.

At last I reach the top of the hill and it seems like the edge of the world and I'm ready to step off into the billowing white clouds, the blue ocean of the sky. Swifts, the dare-devils of the sky, skim past my head, one minute hugging the flanks of the hill, the next out into the ether switching and swivelling in their aerial ecstasy. The first butterflies of the year sun themselves on the warm stones, bands of brilliant orange igniting their wings. You've finally cast off the chains of the town now and are part of the natural world again, your spirits soaring with the invisible, trilling skylarks out across the green valley of the Ribble to where the dark presence of the northern mountains smoulders in the cloud haze. You see the Three Peaks and the slumbering folds of the timeless Forest of Bowland. And moving westwards across the summit of the hill towards the descending sun ('Look, dad, there's Blackpool Tower!') there's the flash of a hot house in the sun in the fertile flatlands of the Fylde, and the Ribble estuary shining and spilling into the sea. Then, south over the Rossendale hills lies the grey shadow of Manchester, the city which, like all cities, for all their tower blocks and glass, are inward-looking, self-absorbed, oblivious to perspectives such as this.

For here, at the top of Pendle Hill, you are at the real centre of the Lancashire world. This is the axis where the ever-varied nature of our county is laid out. From empty moors to cluttered mill town valleys. From sprawling built-up plains to lush farmland and wide estuaries. From re-invented cities to unspoilt villages. For this variety is the essence of Lancashire, its uniqueness. And sewn into the rich fabric of this landscape is the county's long history. There is Bleasdale with its Neolithic circle where my journey began. And arrowing north the Roman road from Cow Ark to the foot of Croasdale. Beyond that the chain of Norman castles running up the Lune valley and the Scottish border. Here below, the Ribble valley that brought the monks of Whalley to their quiet retreat, but later brought Cromwell and his armies to the Battle of Preston. That defile in the Bowland hills is the road northwards through the Trough that took the Lancashire witches to their shameful ends on the gibbet at Lancaster.